AMAZON
STRANGER

Also by Mike Tidwell

In the Mountains of Heaven: True Tales of Adventure on Six Continents

*In the Shadow of the White House: Drugs, Death,
and Redemption on the Streets of the Nation's Capital*

The Ponds of Kalambayi: An African Sojourn

AMAZON STRANGER

MIKE TIDWELL

THE LYONS PRESS

Guilford, Connecticut

An imprint of The Globe Pequot Press

The Lyons Press is an imprint of The Globe Pequot Press.

Printed in Canada

Text design and composition by Rohani Design, Edmonds, Washington

Map of Ecuador by Oliver Williams

10 9 8 7 6 5 4 3 2 1

The Library of Congress Cataloging-in-Publication Data is available on file.

ACKNOWLEDGMENTS

My thanks, first of all, to Catherine, my wife and dear friend. No mason ever put together a stronger foundation than the one she offers this writer every day. I'm a better person because of her. This is a better book because of her.

Special thanks also to the National Endowment for the Arts for its backing during the long process of writing, and to all the Cofan Indians of Zábalo who showed blue-ribbon hospitality to an odd, untutored jungle visitor who asked too many questions.

For help large and small, thanks also to: Tom Brewer, Nick Varchaver, Mary Varchaver, Dan Prior, Jack and Susan Amick, Kitty Thuermer, Frank Reiss, Russell Kaye, Marnie and Fritz Mueller, Phil Simmons, Kit Angell, Charlie Moseley, Maureen Gough, Myron Bretholz, John Coyne, Kate and Craig Redmond, Randy Borman, Ron Borman, Andy Drumm, Roberto Cedeño, Pedro Proaño, Dorys Becerra and family, Cecilia Puertas, my editor Peter Burford, and Judith Kimerling, author of *Amazon Crude*.

In the pages that follow, I have altered the chronology of a few conversations and events in order to augment narrative flow. I have done so without distorting the basic story, which is every bit true.

FOR BARRY ARTHUR TIDWELL,

TRAVELER, GIVER, FRIEND,

1946–1992

———————

AND FOR CATHERINE

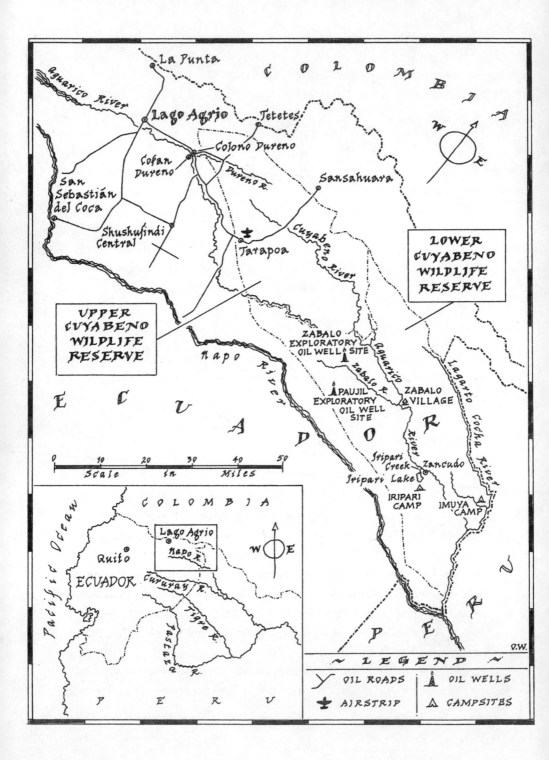

1

It's not a good feeling to be lost over the Amazon jungle. Inside an airplane. During a storm. With the navigation equipment down and visibility virtually zip. Looking for a landing strip the size of a butter knife.

It's not a good feeling especially when, already, you hate to fly, and the only reason you've lived to be twenty-nine is that there happens to be an island in the middle of the Mediterranean called Crete and our Cairo-to-Athens flight a few years back, engines barely functioning, just happened to reach the island before crashing into the drink.

So I had a bad feeling that morning sitting in the military C-130 Hercules, circling over the Amazon, those front propellers whirring over-time against a paint job of jungle camouflage. I didn't realize at first that we were lost, that the Ecuadorian pilots were searching frantically for an airstrip called Tarapoa somewhere down there amid all those Ecuadorian trees. The scheduled arrival time had come and gone, the landing gear had gone down, noisily, and come back up, curiously, and the plane had begun banking, backtracking, flying in circles.

The few odd civilians who hitchhike into the jungle aboard these mil-itary flights are given seats amid stacks of cargo, between bare, curving fuselage walls. For the deafening engine noise, the crew hands out bolls of pink cotton to jam into your ears.

So there I was on this particular flight, surrounded by cargo at the very rear of the fuselage, alone except for a crew member next to me in a baggy jumpsuit. His name was José, and he slept most of the way despite wearing headphones that connected him directly to the pilots in the cockpit.

It is my curse that even minor wind turbulence scares me badly when I fly. But my main rule is this: Never get totally terrified until the crew starts to look mildly concerned. Yet when José sat bolt upright from his sleeping position just then, pressing the headphones tightly to his ears, listening intently as the plane banked and turned another time, he didn't look mildly concerned. He looked totally terrified, which put me—by extension—in an emotional state beyond known psychiatric borders.

A split second later José ripped off his headphones and thrust them into my hands. I pulled the cotton out of my ears. "Here," he said in rapid Spanish, "put these on and listen to the pilots. If they call for me, you come and get me as fast as you can."

Then he was gone, off to a starboard window, scanning downward with mile-wide eyes. Glancing out the window myself, all I could see were clouds and an occasional treetop. I put on the headphones as ordered, a draftee, and listened to a conversation I would gladly pay to have surgically removed from my memory.

Pilot One: "It's no good! I don't see *anything!* Let's turn north again."

Pilot Two: "We've tried north! We've tried it! Maybe we're not even close."

Pilot One: "But where could it be? Trees! Trees! That's all I see. *Dios mió!"*

The voices were scratchy, full of that rough electronic sound that somehow makes even routine cockpit communication seem dire and foreboding. As I listened, I realized that not only were we lost, but I was hearing the only thing investigators would find after the crash. I was getting a grotesque and very unwelcome prescreening of that very terrible thing: THE BLACK BOX.

José was still glued to the window. It seemed academic to ask him the question. His face said everything: "Can't turn around. Not enough fuel to make it back to Quito. Must land. Must find airstrip."

And God, I thought, *I wasn't even supposed to be on this flight.* It was the classic plane-crash tragedy. There had been a change of plans, a last-minute decision to fly. A series of strange events during the past week had come together to put me on this plane at this moment—and now, in a rush, those events passed through my mind. Why, for heaven's sake, couldn't Russell and I have just had a nice, peaceful trip into the rain forest that first time, without all the intrigue? Why did we have to stumble onto a bizarre and complicated *news* story, one that was sending me back into the forest this second time? Russell was my companion, a crazed genius of a photographer who wore piranha teeth and a light meter on the same necklace and who carried an eight-foot-long fishing rod with him wherever he went. What in the world did Russell and I know about *news?* We hated news. We had abandoned newspapers for travel magazines years earlier, we hated news so much.

Which is how, the week before, we wound up in the Amazon in the first place, deep inside Ecuador's lower Cuyabeno Wildlife Reserve. Planning to focus on wildlife, nothing more, we traveled by plane, then by motorized boat, then by dugout canoe; then we walked part of the way; then we waded through swamps pulling boats behind us à la Humphrey Bogart. Then, when we finally reached the end of the earth, suffocating in the dense greenery and isolation of the Amazon, ready to do a light story on leaf-cutter ants and freshwater dolphin, we discovered the unexpected: Something just shy of a shooting war was stirring in the Cuyabeno. Beleaguered forest Indians were using dynamite detonation wire as clotheslines. Rogue oil explorers from whom the dynamite came—were muscling in illegally on the reserve, lurking behind every tree. Oil production would obliterate the forest; and the Indians, it turned out, were backed into a corner with nowhere left to run. They were making a last stand. A showdown was in the works.

All of which was startling enough even before the Oil Helicopter from Hell swooped down on our canoe that one afternoon, buzzing the water angrily, telling Russell and me, in effect, to split. But just when things couldn't get weirder, we heard the rumor about the small village down the river where the great white chief lived. The chief was an American, reportedly born and raised among forest Indians, a blowgun hunter since age four, a man gone totally native. With paint on his face and wild-boar eye teeth strung around his neck, this bushed-out Caucasian was leading the

Indian campaign to keep the oil intruders out. The name *Kurtz* settled over my mind like equatorial heat when I heard this. I saw a malarial dream of a man. Conrad's antihero fast-forwarded to the late twentieth century.

But Russell and I refused to track the rumor down. The whole jungle situation, in fact, had too many markings of a great news story, so we did the only appropriate thing: We ignored it completely. I went back to Quito when the nature tour ended, leaving Russell behind only to get a few more tree shots. And that's when, inside my head, the whisper started. A voice from my newspaper past. *Find Kurtz,* it kept saying. *Go back and find Kurtz.* I banged my palm against my temple a few times until word reached Quito that the white chief, back in the jungle, was taking hostages now as part of his bizarre crusade. The whisper grew louder. *"What are you waiting for, pal? Go on. This ain't no page-twenty house fire. Get the story.* Find *him.* Find *Kurtz!"*

And the next thing I knew, I was back on the Hercules, pink cotton in hand, José by my side. Despite myself, I was obeying the voice. I was on my way back. Back to the forest, back to the Indians, back to find Russell, back to find the oil explorers. Back to find Kurtz.

But first, God, the Hercules had to land. We had to find the airstrip. José was still staring, mouth open, out the window. The cockpit conversation was still crackling in my ears. *"Mierda!"* one pilot said. "Let's turn around! Turn around! Try west! Too far this direction!" I learned later that, by the end, there were six crew members and two civilians crammed cheek-to-jowl in the cockpit, all searching the ground for the butter-knife runway. I had the sudden urge to add my own voice to the black box— "Good-bye, Mom. Good-bye, Dad. I love you, Sis."—when at last the cockpit words hit my ears: "There it is! There it is! There it is!"

Never in my life have I been in a plane that maneuvered so sharply. It banked and dropped like an arrow to the earth, racing madly for the 1,500-foot-long asphalt strip before clouds swallowed it up again. José made his way back to his seat, putting on his earphones. I stuffed cotton into my ears, and the plane landed—herky jerky—on the tarmac, coming to rest, finally, dead still, in the middle of the jungle.

▼▼▼

There's a growing consensus among environmentalists that the only way to save what's left of the Amazonian rain forest—now on an express train to oblivion—is to make it pay. You have to treat the forest as a sustainable, commercial resource. Rubber tapping instead of ranching. Herb harvesting instead of homesteading. And tourism. Open the door to bird watchers and adventure freaks. Let in the people who bring binoculars, not chain saws, people who pay top dollar just to look. There's even a word for it now: Ecotourism. Or, if you prefer, ecotripping. It's a new sort of drug experience, recreational in form, more expensive than acid but easier on the cerebral cortex.

Which is how this whole convoluted jungle story first got its legs. To begin at the beginning is to begin with that idea, ecotripping. When, after months of wanting to visit South America, Russell and I learned that Transturi Touring, an Ecuadorian company, had begun offering ecotrips into a remote portion of the Amazon, we signed up, wheedling a freelance assignment from an editor in New York. The assignment was nothing too complicated. Just flora and fauna in pictures and prose. We would have fun while at the same time being part of the rain-forest solution, nature's customers. Trouble was the last thing we were looking for. We just wanted to trip a little, ecologically.

We packed our bags and said our good-byes. And off we went.

The tour began, simply enough, on the banks of the Rio Aguarico, a moderate-sized river flowing down from the Andes and snaking its way into the jungle toward Ecuador's borders with Colombia and Peru. Backpacks in tow, having flown 2,800 miles in thirty-six hours, Russell and I arrived at the Aguarico with a small group of other travelers. We hopped into aging wooden boats with outboard motors and settled in for the seven-hour journey to our initial base camp.

That first day on the river, as we moved farther and farther into the forest, was a singularly exquisite experience, replete with the sense of our being gradually and lastingly dipped into the unknown. This was before Russell and I knew fully of the oil-and-Indian pyrotechnics about to greet us up ahead, so we were able to enjoy with a touch of innocence and equanimity the wonderland unfolding before our eyes.

It's so immense, the rain forest, its tableau of life so immediately and obviously and impossibly intricate all around you, that it takes a while to realize you're really there, really in the fabled Amazon, that those mammoth kapok trees with their cottony crowns grow nowhere but in the densest tropics and that you could see a greater variety of birds every hour than you've probably seen in your entire life combined. But as the truth sinks in, it does so deeply, like a balm seeping through skin to bone. After a while, even the occasional Quichua Indian huts along the shore don't bother you. They're getting fewer and fewer the farther you travel, and eventually they disappear altogether, leaving only river and forest and sky. "I'm in the Amazon," you want to say over and over to no one in particular as howler monkeys stage vine acrobatics to your right and an eighty-pound peccary—bristle-haired and searching mauritia palm fruit— emerges on a muddy bank to your left.

Roberto, our bearded twenty-two-year-old guide with scars on his hands from a slew of scary jungle accidents, was pointing out these gems one by one from the stern as I took notes. Steve, meanwhile, was taking pictures. Steve was a nature photographer from Colorado, and each time I looked he seemed to be urgently reloading his film. This made me nervous because the photographer immediately next to me, Russell, *my* partner, was behaving the way he always did on assignments. He was doing nothing. Just hanging out. Dallying serenely.

"What about the monkeys, Russell?" I said, finally deciding to act. "Wouldn't they make a nice shot?"

In his own way, Russell was as exotic as anything on the river. He was a hulking, befreckled redhead from Brooklyn who wore shaded eyeglasses and a backward-facing baseball cap and a baggy pair of shorts that hung like knickers to his knees, resting above bulky, overworn hiking boots. My question about photographs seemed to irritate him. He squinted his eyes at the shore, then at the sun, then at the shore again.

"The light's not right," he said flatly, turning back toward me.

It was Russell's pat response to such situations, revealing his approach to photography, which was like that of a master surfer. Let others ride the duds. Only when the light was just right, when the perfect wave was cresting right before him, did he make a move. Until then his mind stayed mostly on his favorite subject: Fishing. Russell had many gods, and they all had fins. He asked Roberto if the armored catfish of this region would hit a spinner. He asked Roberto if a fly rod was of any use against piranha.

I gave up and went back to watching birds. After two hours, my list of sightings was getting quite long, ranging from a pair of boat-billed herons to a red-capped cardinal to a lesser kisskidi flycatcher. Pablo, the Mexican ornithologist next to me, had an even longer list. He bubbled with excitement behind his binoculars, mentioning out loud how Ecuador had a stunning 1,500 different species of birds—second in the world only to Colombia—and perhaps half of those species could be viewed right here along the Aguarico.

"We've made it!" Pablo enthused over and over again as we spotted another gorgeous Amazon kingfisher. "The candy store of birds! We're in the world's candy store of birds! We've made it!"

Pablo, whose eyes were very much bugging out just then, was in the throes of an exceptionally heavy ecotrip, I decided, and someone should probably keep an eye on his breathing.

Just then, up ahead, another animal came into view. This one was in the water, weighed several hundred tons, and was coming straight at us. It was a boat, actually, a floating hotel, a Fitzcaraldo mirage of jungle comfort put together piece by piece on the Napo River and then piloted all the way up the Aguarico to this spot by Transturi Touring. "Flotel" was the boat's name, in fact, and as it grew closer Roberto explained how its twenty cabins on three decks were designed for the semirugged jet-set crowd, for people who like to fly in and absorb nature's savagery from a sun deck, drink in hand.

At Roberto's suggestion, we tied up alongside the boat and climbed aboard, stretching our legs on the deck and peeing in flush toilets. Sensing this was our last brush with modernity, Russell offered to stand me a drink at the top-deck bar. Afterward, we decided to order a bottle of whiskey for the road. Without blinking, the bartender said, "One bottle, seventy-eight dollars." Supplies were very expensive this far into the jungle, he added. Russell let loose a long gasp. Forget the macaws screeching overhead. Forget the evil-eyed caimans (crocodilians) skulking along the shore. It was whiskey at $78 a bottle that let him know just how far from Brooklyn—or any place else—he really was. He told the bartender no thanks, and we returned to the river.

It took four more hours to reach Zancudo, the isolated and tumbledown Ecuadorian military outpost from which we would set off on foot. A two-hour hike through the forest lay ahead, then a canoe trip across Iripari Lake to our camp. Pablo, the ornithologist, seemed wary. "Just so you'll know," he said as we stepped ashore. "One translation of the word *zancudo* in Spanish is 'long-legged creepy crawlies.'"

I felt a shiver run up my legs, and I thanked Pablo for sharing.

A doctor was waiting for us at Zancudo. Her name was Dorys, a pretty twenty-seven-year-old Ecuadorian wearing tall rubber boots and a no-nonsense frown. Dorys was a walking first-aid station, hired to protect us from long-legged creepy crawlies and the myriad other hazards of this place so far from telephones and hospitals. Those hazards included poisonous frogs and scorpions and, of course snakes—bushmasters, anacondas, water snakes. I asked Dorys what antivenins she carried.

"I don't use antivenins," she said. "This is better."

She reached into her kit to produce an ominous black "stun gun," the sort people back in Brooklyn use against muggers, Russell pointed out. Dorys pulled the trigger and a blue jag of electricity crackled between the terminal heads—20,000 volts. Applied to the skin, this slowed the spread of venom long enough to allow a chance to get to a Quito hospital. But the blast treatment was very, very painful, Dorys admitted, and I began to wish Russell and I had coughed up the $78 for whiskey.

The hike through the forest, with Roberto up front and Dorys at the rear, was long and tiresome and sweaty and wonderful. Now that we were off the river, seeing things up close, a byzantine universe of Amazon insects came into focus. Leaf-cutter ants streamed across the trail, hurrying toward vast subterranean cities. A gigantic moth, delicate despite its size, alighted on Roberto's shoulder, its wings presenting a near-exact replica of an owl's face, a trick on would-be predators. And just as we were getting hungry, Roberto led us to a species of lemon tree covered with millions of tiny black ants. The tree and the ants were linked in a complex symbiotic relationship, but more intriguing was the ants' surprising culinary allure. With a wetted finger, Roberto withdrew a few dozen of the insects, popping them into his mouth. The rest of us followed suit, making a small snack of the ants—lemony, through and through—as the sun set and a gentle shower of snowlike cotton fell to our shoulders from a nearby kapok tree.

It was almost completely dark by the time we reached Iripari Lake, canoeing across its glassy water to the camp on the far shore. The camp was a collection of sturdy thatched-roof huts built for Transturi Touring by Quichua Indians. Each hut, Roberto explained, was constructed with a special forest tree harvested only during the days of the month when the moon was full—a Quichua superstition ensuring extra durability. Crowning this antediluvian architecture was something equally exotic: Solar panels. Sleek rectangular panels—ferried in by canoe—lay in startling juxtaposition atop each palm-thatched roof, feeding batteries that powered small lightbulbs below. This was, after all, an ecotour. No machinery, no generators, no engines allowed.

I fell asleep that night to the tranquilizing rich hum and rustle of the living forest—nothing added, nothing subtracted.

▼▼▼

Soft shafts of amber light streamed through my window, filtering through my mosquito net, reaching my eyes and waking me the next morning. I looked outside. The sun, a stunning fireball, had barely risen above the trees on the far shore. Just as stunning was the sight of Russell's tripod and camera set up outside, facing the lake. He had pulled out the 4-by-5 view camera, I noticed, a huge and cumbersome thing he'd painstakingly lugged into the jungle for greater creative range. Yet Russell himself was nowhere in evidence at that moment. He had taken a few sunrise shots, gotten irritated somehow by the quality of the light, and reached for his fly rod instead. Sighing, I fell back into bed, listening to the morning operetta of a hundred different birds and the gentle rhythms—*swoosh, swoosh, plunk, swoosh, swoosh, plunk*—of Russell's expert fly casting somewhere in the distance.

After a leisurely morning observing pygmy marmoset monkeys dangling from vines around camp, we all sat down to lunch, and Roberto, speaking perfect English gleaned from a year studying in the States, began holding environmental court. By definition, most ecotours have as their objective more than just taking travelers to see pretty things in hard-to-reach places. The point is to educate along the way, to hold forth on the sundry man-made hazards that directly imperil all that's on display.

The overriding environmental threat in Ecuador, of course, was oil. That much I already knew. The jungle oil boom around Lago Agrio, to the northwest, had spread over the years to devastate vast portions of Ecuador's forest. When, in 1975, Transturi Touring first organized nature trips along the Napo River to the south, that area was largely untouched except for a population of forest Indians living in a virtual state of nature.

But then came oil: Seismic testing, wells, a pipeline, roads, settlers. Today, sixteen years later, much of the area along the Napo was a rambling ruin of cleared squares and fenced-in rectangles, a checkerboard wasteland. For Transturi, the final straw came in 1990 when an oil crew brazenly erected a 100-foot-tall drilling derrick directly across from what used to be the outfit's most secluded base camp. In disgust and defeat, Transturi pulled up stakes and vacated.

The tragedy of this wholesale butchery is made worse, Roberto pointed out, by the fact that there is no rain forest in the world quite like Ecuador's. Indeed, for all the hymns sung to Brazil's magnificent forest, it is less well known that for sheer richness, for variety, and diversity of life in a concentrated area, the small portion of the Amazon basin in eastern Ecuador, southern Colombia, and northern Peru is the continent's true crown jewel, a Mecca of biodiversity. Some scientists believe that much of the Amazon basin dried out in periods of heavy glaciation during the Pleistocene Ice Ages over the last million years. But isolated areas, including stretches along the Aguarico and Napo rivers remained moist, providing refuge for existing rain-forest plants and animals as well as allowing a staggering rise in new species of both. Today, as a result, this dense forest within a forest, this candy store of birds, is also a candy store of tropical plants and animals and insects heaped atop one another—layer upon layer—in a way found nowhere in Brazil. If it made sense, consequently, to save any one part of the Amazon, this was it, this was the place: The fecund and diverse jungle wilds of eastern Ecuador.

Which was why, in 1990, conservation experts at Transturi pulled out a map and drew a wide circle around the lower Aguarico River, around a forest called the lower Cuyabeno. This was one of the last great stretches of wilderness still untouched by oil and settlement in Ecuador. And this time there would be protection. With lobbying pressure from Indian rights groups, international environmental organizations, and Transturi itself, the government of Ecuador in May 1991 established the nearly one-million-acre lower Cuyabeno Wildlife Reserve, a place off limits—on paper at least—to everyone except tourists, scientists, and indigenous Indians. Officially, the park was an appendage to the already existing "upper" Cuyabeno reserve, itself containing more than 750 thousand acres. But the predecessor park, stretching almost to Lago Agrio along the upper

Aguarico, had been significantly degraded by oil exploration in recent years like much of the Napo River area. Thus the lower Cuyabeno annex was in effect a new and separate entity, a fresh start, a park immediately heralded around the world as perhaps Ecuador's last and best chance to save part of its exceptional forest.

It was midafternoon by the time Roberto wrapped up his history of the reserve. Russell, who had been listening from a nearby hammock, swinging softly with his boots propped up, had just bolted off to chase Helena, the camp's burly semitame pet tapir. An odd-looking mammal native to the Amazon, the tapir, combines the vague features of a horse and a pig onto a 200-pound adult frame. Helena was a gentle plant- and insect-eater who also happened to have a sappy soft spot for human beings. Like an oversized puppy starving for attention, she kept loping into camp from the forest and stealing Russell's baseball cap, giving it a light chew each time. She had his cap again now and Russell was gone. Dorys, meanwhile, was feeding bread to the camp's other eccentric pet, an awkward, squawking trumpeter bird named Sophia. Sophia was kept around for her snake-killing skills, something Dorys—who hated to use her stun gun—called "preventive medicine."

I would have enjoyed these midday antics with something more akin to rapture had Roberto not kept talking. Pouring a glass of water, he returned to the subject of the reserve, and I asked him if he thought the park would succeed in keeping oil exploration away forever. He wasn't sure, he said. There were known oil deposits all along the park's perimeter, and no one pretended to think there was no oil *inside* the reserve. Less than a month after the reserve's inception, in fact, a seismic testing crew had been spotted near the park border at the Cuyabeno River. Two months after that, Indians in one village found dynamite detonation wire actually inside the park. The Indians confiscated the wire and were using it to make clotheslines. Petroecuador, the national oil company which from the start had privately opposed the park's establishment, was now saying publicly that it would stay clear of the lower Cuyabeno reserve. But way out here in the park itself, way out here so far from Quito, things were shaping up differently.

The situation, in fact, was worse than Roberto had admitted that first day. Much worse. If Russell and I had come seeking only flora and fauna in pictures and prose, we had chosen an exceptionally bad time to do so. A showdown—approaching for months and involving Transturi Touring and the local Indians versus crews of unscrupulous oil explorers—was about to reach the shoving and kicking stage. It would begin the very next day.

We were on Iripari Lake when it happened, paddling in canoes—me, Dr. Dorys, Roberto, Russell. It was late afternoon and we were bird watching, taking in another superlative dose of biodiversity. Below us in the lake's black water swam manatee and caimans and piranha of several varieties. But birds were still the marquee attraction. They fluttered through philodendron plants all around the lake—hoatzins, tanagers, yellow-rumped caciques. All the while, Roberto kept telling us to keep one eye on the muddy shoreline for the jaguar prints visible there from time to time. I had my eye on the canoe instead, where a giant iridescent dragonfly had just alighted, the biggest, most colorful dragonfly I'd ever seen in my life. Roberto was baffled by the specimen. He'd never seen one in three years of working as a guide, probably just one more of the thousands, perhaps hundreds of thousands, of life forms in this forest yet to be scientifically catalogued, much less studied.

It was then that we heard the sound, first a hum in the distance, then a growing rumble, then a shattering shriek as the helicopter burst over the tree line. It came out of nowhere, circling the small lake once before spotting us. Within seconds, the helicopter was hovering directly overhead, seventy-five feet up, the blades causing ripples on the water. "I can't believe these guys!" Roberto shouted above the noise, looking up. "Keep your seats everyone! Don't move!" With its bulbous windshield eyes and long mechanical tail, the helicopter had its own dragonfly look. It stared down at us, creating the effect somehow that we, vulnerable below, were its prey, tiny ants on water.

"It's an oil helicopter!" Roberto cried against the sound of blades. "I've seen it before near Tarapoa. They know they're not supposed to be here!" Roberto waved the helicopter away with his hand, but it stayed. I looked at Russell. He had brought none of his cameras, just his fly rod. I wanted suddenly to throw him to the caimans below.

For about sixty seconds the helicopter stayed fixed overhead, long enough for my goose bumps to grow taller with the realization that this *oil-versus-reserve business was no mere child's game. Not in the Amazon,* a place long known for its frontier law and violent endings. Nervously, I wondered if the pilots up there were packing guns. But then, just as suddenly, the helicopter banked and flew away, disappearing. The lake was quiet again. There had been no direct communication whatsoever. Not even a wave from the pilots.

"It's intimidation," Roberto said, angrily turning the canoe back to camp now. "They know what they're doing. They're telling us to leave, to clear out, because they're coming in. It's bad."

That night, in the camp's main pavilion, we gathered under a bare solar-powered bulb and the atmosphere was subdued. Then, with an incongruous lack of fanfare, a Transturi staff member did something no one anticipated. He pulled out a detailed map of the lower Cuyabeno reserve. The map had been secretly obtained a few weeks ago by Transturi officials with contacts at Petroecudor. Afraid it would alarm us, no one on the staff had shown the map to any of us tourists the day before. But now it lay unfurled on the table, and when I finally realized that I was looking at, I recoiled. There, running through the heart of the park, stretching out all along the banks of the Aguarico, were thousands of markings for dynamite placements. Virtually every region of the park had been turned into a grid of lines, with Xs spaced every three hundred meters for detonations that would give a seismic reading of oil deposits below. One line of explosions, according to the map, would run within thirty meters of this very camp. It explained everything, this piece of paper. It explained the helicopter visit and the detonation wire and the seismic testing crew near the Cuyabeno River. The oil people were coming. It was happening now. To hell with the reserve.

"What are you going to do?" I anxiously asked Roberto, still feeling tremors of shock as my eyes lingered over the map.

Another staff member had already radioed Transturi's Quito office about the helicopter incident, he said. Letters would go out immediately to the Minister of Energy and Mines and to Petroecuador and to environmental groups. Some sort of legal action was also possible, perhaps a last-minute injunction preventing exploration.

But Carlos, one of Roberto's assistants, was shaking his head as Roberto spoke. Carlos had been mostly silent since the helicopter incident. He lacked the look of fighting determination still remaining in Roberto's eyes. "No," Carlos said, lowering his gaze to the dusty plant floor. "It's over.

Nothing's going to stop these oil people now. What happened on the Napo River is going to happen here. I know it will."

Of all the emotions crowding Carlos' face at that moment, the most dominant was anger. He was filled with anger, and it had a focus. He turned to me, the American, and boiled over.

"I'll tell you what I think," he said. "I think it's funny how everyone in your country looks down here at rain forest destruction and they think, 'How could all those ignorant people tear up such a beautiful place and kill all those animals and make all those medically valuable plants extinct, and then have nothing but a big desert left afterward?' That's the way they think, isn't it?"

I didn't answer. Carlos didn't give me time to.

"But you see what the problem is here in Ecuador?" he went on. "It's oil. We're trying to protect this forest by using it for tours, to let it earn money without being destroyed. But oil is more valuable. Our country needs oil to pay its debt to your banks. Your country needs oil because everyone has two cars. So my question is, who's really destroying the Cuyabeno forest, Ecuadorians or Americans?"

It was a fair and obvious question, and during the long discussion that eventually followed I did nothing to challenge Carlos' conclusion of where the real problem lay. When all the bizarre plots and subplots had played themselves out in the jungle, the final story was rather straightforward: Entire ecosystems were being obliterated in northwestern South America to keep highways and shopping-mall parking lots full in Chicago. Or, put another way, broadening the view, it was an exceptionally sick form of double jeopardy: Oil that warms the planet with CO^2 was obtained by leveling a forest, which, once it dies, accelerates the same process.

But Roberto, for now, was less interested in grand analyses than in sticking to the specific subplot at hand: The growing threat of seismic testing in the lower Cuyabeno reserve. As it turned out, our knowledge of the situation was thus far incomplete. Roberto had until now failed to mention one of the last key weapons in the fight to keep oil out. "And what's funny," he said, glancing significantly around the room, "is that that weapon happens to be a gringo. He's a man from North America."

It was then that Russell and I learned for the first time about Randy Borman. For the past two days we had seen and heard a lot of unusual things, and our imaginations stretched in many directions. But the moment Roberto began describing Randy Borman, I wondered even more just what sort of true-life novel we had stumbled into.

According to Roberto, Randy was a thirty-six-year-old Caucasian living in a village down the river, presiding as chief over a band of Cofan Indians. Born in the jungle to American missionary parents, members of the Summer Institute of Linguistics evangelical group headquartered in Texas, Randy had grown up in large respect like a Cofan, speaking the language, hunting with blowguns. The Cofan were true forest people, not Andean immigrants like the Quichua. They decorated themselves with face paint and flower bracelets and wore macaw feathers pushed through their pierced noses. In 1981, when his parents ended their forest missionary work, Randy decided to stay behind. In 1984, when oil production by Texaco Oil had decimated the Cofan's homeland near Dureno to the west, Randy led a band of Cofan Indians to the isolated lower Aguarico. Now the Indians had nowhere else to go. They had migrated once to escape oil and their backs were up against the Peruvian border. As perhaps the only Indian chief in South American history with deep knowledge of both Western and Indian ways, Randy had so far proven himself adept at defending Cofan rights and he was instrumental in helping establish the lower Cuyabeno reserve. Now, with oil threatening everything again, he wasn't about to yield quietly, Roberto said.

"But what is he?" I asked Roberto, trying to get a better fix on this man. "Is Randy an Indian or an American or both or what?"

"He's an Indian," Roberto said. "He's white like you and speaks English. But he lives in a village and hunts animals and up here"—Roberto pointed to his head—"he's really Cofan, I think."

I have to admit that so taken was I by the Conradesque implications of all this, sleep came to me slowly that night, postponed by flights of imagination. It crossed my mind to visit this man myself, to see firsthand what sounded like an honest-to-god Kurtz figure alive and well on the shank end of the twentieth century, digging in at his own final station. But it also sounded, at second blush, a little too much like a news story for my taste and for that of Russell. We just weren't the investigative types. Period. No apologies. And besides, Roberto, the very next morning, was adamant in saying the tour should go on as planned, with no detours. Despite the awful seismic map and the helicopter scare and everything else, there was much, much more wildlife to see and he intended to show it to us.

Thus instructed, I strung my binoculars around my neck, pulled out my bird- and plant-life guidebooks, and, without too many regrets, let the idea of finding Kurtz pass from my mind.

▼▼▼

A long morning of travel took us to our second base camp the next day, situated near the Peruvian border. We began in canoes, leaving Iripari Lake via a swampy blackwater creek. Roberto was pointing out a series of strange trails left on the shore by bushmaster snakes when our canoes began to snag and falter in the swampy creek.

"Get out and push," Roberto ordered in frustration. "Don't worry. The piranha only bite if you're already bleeding. Jump in."

With a splash, Russell and I obeyed. Water and mud rose up to our hips. Rechristening our canoe the "Amazon Queen," I pushed and pulled and grunted until my legs quivered with exhaustion and my arms were covered with the prickly bites of dozens of tiny black spiders.

Later, paddling again, we reached the Aguarico, then took a left on the Lagarto Cocha, a blackwater river separating Ecuador from Peru. And it was there, on the Lagarto Cocha, gliding below overhanging mimosa branches, that the moment arrived. It was that single, crystallizing, most-perfect moment, the one travelers carry away from a trip saying, "This is it. This is why I came."

They were together, a male and female, sleek and gray, swimming side-by-side, coming toward us from upriver. Anyone who's ever seen the wondrous rise and dive of dolphins on the open sea knows their special grace and beauty. But to see the Amazon version, to see that friendly presence up close, almost within arm's reach on a freshwater jungle river, is to witness something truly magical.

The dolphins slowed upon spotting us, rising and spewing air to starboard, eyeing us with the same curiosity with which we eyed them. It was then that we saw the calf, just months old. It was pink in color, plump of body, tagging close behind its elders with a delicate, cresting dorsal fin half their size. Only when the family finally disappeared behind us, cresting and blowing one last time around a bend as if to say good-bye, disappearing in the murky water with the help of natural sonar, did we go on, glancing back now and then, smiling.

We smiled more as we finished the day, reaching our second base camp without seeing a single sign of further oil-crew activity. The second camp was on a lagoon called Imaya, abutting the Peruvian border. Again there were solar panels atop crude thatched roofs. And again the timber for the huts had been harvested during a full moon.

Too tired for bird-watching, Roberto and Russell and I deposited our gear and went down to the lagoon's murky water to fish for piranha. For bait, Roberto brought a bag of raw beef chunks cut into cubes, pilfered from Manuel, the tour cook. Roberto and I used his gear: Bundles of old fishing line wrapped around sticks like kite string. We loaded our hooks and slung them into the water. "You know," I said to Russell, who was using his fly rod next to me, "I don't think I've ever fished with beef chunks before."

Roberto got the first bite almost immediately, pulling in his line hand over hand. The two-pound piranha that landed on shore had beady eyes and reddish scales and teeth just as you imagine: Upper and lower rows like the pointy edges of a sharp, lethal saw. It took five crushing blows from a canoe paddle to kill it and finally end the awful reflex snapping of those jaws.

I caught the second piranha. Like Roberto's, mine arrived bleeding from fresh, gaping bite wounds on its back and sides. The wounds, Roberto explained, were inflicted by other piranha in the water who pitilessly cannibalize their struggling, vulnerable peers as they're being reeled to shore.

Meanwhile, Russell had yet to make a catch, and in a move both bonkers and highly typical of him, he decided to wade into the water for better reach with his fly rod. Roberto assured him it was okay as long as there were no cuts or sores on his legs. But I was nearly hyperventilating glancing at Russell's succulent calves and thighs submerged just feet from where I was pulling in a second and third chomping monster. When at last Russell made his own catch, he was so elated and proud he took the piranha and, before it was cleaned for cooking, had the jaws removed to wear on a string around his neck. There the jaws stayed the rest of the trip, large and awe-inspiring, a toothsome jungle trophy dangling just below his now-jungle-worn baseball cap.

The sun had set and the camp was thick with the aroma of frying fish when later I returned to the lagoon to sit by myself for a while. It was a wholly different place at night, the forest, a nocturnal wonder of grunting caimans and cooing owls and phosphorescent glowworms floating through eerie blackness. With only a small patch of starry sky above me, I felt enveloped and secure for a moment, contentedly thinking back to the day's sightings of docile river dolphins and electric-blue morpho butterflies.

But the feeling didn't last. A heavy note of melancholy stalked Russell and me as we prepared for bed that night. Try as we might, neither of us could shake off the implications of Roberto's awful map. In our minds we kept hearing dynamite explosions, thousands and thousands of them, following the seismic Xs spread all over that morose piece of paper. Was it already too late for any other outcome? we wondered. Could Roberto and Randy Borman and the river Indians really find a way to save, at the last minute, this irreplaceable land? Or was it in reality all just one big elaborate joke, the idea of forests as sustainable resources—of ecotourism and all the rest—having arrived far too late in the path of steamrolling Western cupidity to make a difference. Ghastly enough was the checklist in Ecuador. The Napo River: Gone. Dureno: Gone. The lower Cuyabeno: Hanging by a thread. And who says it can't all disappear? Every bit of it? We tend always to think after each ecological defeat that we'll save some other place farther down the river, over the next mountain, deeper in the interior. Funny how that had been the very idea with the lower Cuyabeno reserve.

That night, for the first time on the trip, I had trouble sleeping. When finally I drifted off, it was to the sound of a lonely guitar being strummed somewhere in the distance. It was a Quichua Indian, one of Roberto's assistants, singing a Spanish love ballad. The song was soft and sad and full of long, slow moans that broke my heart into a thousand pieces.

▼▼▼

My last day in the jungle was a blur of arduous travel and fast, strange developments. The plan was to go by motorboat all the way up the Aguarico, reaching the Tarapoa airstrip by afternoon. Along the way we would drop Russell off at the Fitzcaraldo riverboat near the Cuyabeno River. So much fishing had left him a little short of photographs for the magazine piece. He would stay on the big boat a few days, getting forest shots from the top deck, while I waited in Quito.

"Now remember," I said as Russell clambered onto the riverboat deck, reaching back for his tripod from Roberto. "Just pictures. No fishing. Please don't fish, Russell."

He agreed, but with a throaty chuckle refused all my offers to carry his rods to Quito for good measure.

The rest of us pushed on. We had barely traveled another mile upriver when, with great excitement, the motorboat driver began shouting across our small boat to Roberto, pointing to something on the left riverbank. The moment Roberto saw the thing in question, he pounded his fist against a gunwale.

"What?" I asked Roberto. "What is it?"

"See that clearing on the shore over there?" he said. "It's a heliport for the oil people. Indians don't make clearings like that. We know the style. We saw those on the Napo. It's for helicopters to land, and it's *inside* the park."

The clearing had not existed five days earlier during our journey in. Roberto very carefully memorized the location on the river: More information to radio back to Quito. The oil confrontation was escalating.

And more was in store. I was already airborne inside the Hercules, having said good-bye to Roberto and staff on the Tarapoa tarmac, when Pedro took a seat by my side. Pedro was a Transturi guide heading back to Quito, and the first thing he said to me was, "Can you believe what happened to Randy Borman and the Cofan?"

I sat up in my seat. "Believe what happened to them?"

"You mean you didn't hear? They took hostages last night. One of the Cofan on the river told us. They found a seismic testing crew in the forest near their village and they're holding them as hostages to keep the oil people out of the park."

Immediately, I wanted off the plane. I wanted to go back. Hostages? Really? This was something too big for even the likes of Russell and me to ignore. But the Hercules was well into the air by then. The Aguarico was getting smaller and smaller outside my window.

That night in Quito, I spent long, restless hours trying to decide what to do. Should I really go back? Was the hostage story true? Did this guy Randy, this Kurtz figure really exist, or was he, as almost seemed the case, some sort of bizarre forest myth dreamed up by the Cofan, a great white protector spirit hovering only in the upper branches of a few superstitious minds?

A Quito newspaper settled everything the next morning, however. The hostage story had filtered into the capital. A back-page article said twenty-three oil workers hired by Petroecuador had been detained for twenty-four hours and released without harm by Cofan Indians and their chief—there it was in print—*Randy Borman*. The Indians were protecting their land against oil exploration, the article said. Immediately, I put down the paper and booked a flight back to Tarapoa.

Which is when the Hercules got lost. It got lost in a storm, in the clouds, above the trees, its navigation equipment down. While José stared out the side window, scanning the ground, I listened in stark terror to the cockpit communication until, finally we dive-bombed in a panic to the airstrip and the ordeal ended. I wobbled off the plane and set out to find the Cofan.

Russell was very surprised to see me on the Aguarico again. He was also a bit disappointed, having planned to stalk mountain trout in the Andes that weekend. I convinced him to change his plans.

"This man Randy Borman, whoever he is, has taken hostages, Russell. Grab your equipment."

A guide named Felipe offered his services, and the next thing we knew we were in a canoe heading back down the Aguarico, navigating the endless turns of the river current, unsure of what lay ahead of us. The long hours brought a heavy thunderstorm, then steamy afternoon light through which green parrots made their usual screeching way. Finally, we pulled up to a village clearing cleaved out of the profuse jungle near where the narrow Zábalo River flows into the Aguarico. We had arrived—the Cofan settlement. Felipe cut the outboard, then told us to stay in the canoe while he went ashore to find Randy. The Indians weren't expecting us and things had been tense the past few days.

Felipe returned ten minutes later accompanied by a man who—in some ways, at least—could have just as easily sashayed right out of a Des Moines café: White skin, blue eyes, thick mustache, baseball cap. But there were differences. Big ones. Randy was barefoot and wore the thin, gownlike cotton tunic typical of the other Cofan men standing around him. He also had around his neck a string supporting the tooth of a wild puma which, I learned later, he killed himself using only a machete.

"So you're journalists?" Randy said to Russell and me in perfect American English, fingering the puma tooth. "We don't get many journalists here, but I think we might need you now. Can you stay with us overnight?"

Russell and I looked at Felipe, who agreed to return the next afternoon to pick us up. Some men were gathering rocks along the riverbank to build a village well, and Randy, their leader, asked them in rapid Cofan to prepare a guest hut for us.

Now that I was finally in the presence of this chief, fascinated by him in every way, I had to overcome the urge to ask a thousand different questions all at once. I focused instead on the immediate situation.

"So what happened with the oil crew the other day, Randy? Did your village really detain them?"

He waved his hand in the air at this. "We'll discuss all that later," he said. "It's a long story. First, I have some fish nets I need to check. Want to come?"

We said yes, very much, and off we went, heading in a canoe up the smaller Zábalo River. Whatever crisis had come with the uninvited seismic crew, whatever sword of Damocles hovered over this Cofan world—it didn't seem to matter at that moment. The sky had broken clear, the sun was shining bright, and some fish nets somewhere needed checking.

Randy's Cofan brother-in-law, Alonzo, a short man with deep brown skin and flowing black hair, joined us. Along the way, Randy confirmed a few facts I'd learned about his life story, that he had been born to missionary parents and had spent most of his years in the forest. After taking a Cofan wife a few years back and fathering two sons he had made a final decision never to leave. Never.

Alonzo tied the canoe to a bank, and we set off through the forest toward what Randy called his favorite fishing lagoon. With nimble hands, Randy began gathering leaves and vines with which to carry whatever fish we caught. I asked him if checking the nets was a routine, something he did every day at this time. As I spoke, I noticed the only thing on his left wrist was a collection of colorful glass-bead bracelets.

"Time?" Randy said, looking at me rather puzzled. "No, there's no set time for this. We just do it. When you're hungry you check your nets or you hunt a peccary. You just do it. There aren't schedules for anything here. Sometimes the whole village loses track of what day of the week it is and we have to have a meeting just to try to figure out what it is."

As I listened to Randy say this, watching him pick more leaves in the process, I felt myself drifting deeper and deeper into one of the strangest cross-cultural experiences of my life. I was beginning to feel seriously off balance around this man. Forget the Des Moines face and the American accent. This guy was different. *Foreign.* Being with him was like watching a movie where the words have been poorly dubbed: What you're seeing and what you're actually hearing don't match up. It was more than just Randy's comment about time. The difference was there in his use of mostly simple sentences, in the grace and ease with which he moved through the forest, without shoes, picking leaves. Written all over both Randy and Alonzo was a demeanor of utter openness and guilelessness I've come to associate only with very traditional people in developing countries.

Alonzo plucked two peacock bass from the lagoon nets and Randy began wrapping them up. I decided to ask about his knowledge of medicinal plants. "I know a few," Randy said. "Maybe fifty or sixty that I use a lot. But don't ask me the scientific names because I don't have a clue." These plants included everything from certain leaves to combat fever to boiled roots for diarrhea. Russell perked up at this. He had developed a touch of diarrhea the day before.

"My special ginger tea is the best," Randy said. "If you drink it and your runs don't stop within an hour, you've got cholera, period."

Randy said his knowledge of plants was marginal, however, compared to other Cofan. Everyone in the village had a particular specialty, he said. For some it was medicine, for others basket weaving, for others harpooning fish.

"What's your specialty?" I asked Randy.

He thought for a second. "Blowguns," he said. "I probably make some of the best blowguns."

We returned to the village and went to Randy's house. His was the largest in the village and the only one with a tin roof. All the same, it had the general cluttered look of a jungle hut, with toucan feathers and old blowguns and blackened cooking utensils hanging from the porch eave amid a scattered assortment of Western tools. Randy's wife, Amelia, twenty years old and beautiful, with a baby sucking at her breast, began gathering plantains to accompany the fish. The baby was Federico, a boy seven months old, the couple's second child. Amelia imparted an air of calm shyness amid her purposeful activities. Her deep, dark eyes did not linger long on the newly arrived visitors.

"I wouldn't say they were hostages," Randy said, finally turning to the subject of the seismic oil crew as we settled onto the porch. "It was more like an arrest situation. We arrested them."

As he focused on this more serious matter, Randy simultaneously began doing a few odd chores. He pulled out a bundle of long knives, sharpening each one on a whetstone, stroking back and forth.

"One of our people saw the crew workers on the river. They were clearing one of our banana fields for a heliport. I showed up with six men behind me. I was prepared to go back and get more men and maybe an unloaded shotgun if necessary. But it wasn't. We asked the workers if they knew they were inside the reserve. They said yes. We asked them if they had permission from the head park warden. They said they weren't sure. So we told them they had to put down their equipment and come with us to the village. They didn't resist. We gave them a place to camp, and the next morning they got a radio message from their superiors in Quito telling them to evacuate, they didn't have permits. They got in their boats and we waved good-bye and they left."

Everyone was greatly relieved by the outcome, Randy said. It was, in the end, a rather gentle, Cofan-style operation—with results. But would it work the next time? I wondered. Surely there would be a next time.

"Enforcing the laws of this park is our only hope," Randy said. "So it's got to work the next time. The reserve's charter explicitly forbids the import of explosives or toxic chemicals of any kind. We may not have a title to this land, but we have legal standing within the charter to do what we did."

Now that the conversation had turned to oil, an entirely different side of Randy was emerging—and it was quite remarkable to watch. It was the side of him nurtured in a Quito high school and honed by a few years of college in the United States. His mind, out of abrupt necessity, was making a sharp Western turn right before our eyes.

"The problem," he continued, "is that there are conflicting laws here. The Ministry of Energy and Mines claims a legal right to drill wherever it wants to. The (government) park service, on the other hand, has set up laws to safeguard this forest. Then there's the economic pressure to drill. It's enormous."

Randy said fifty percent of Ecuador's export earnings come from selling oil abroad. Almost half of the government's total budget revenues come from oil sales, too. "But no money is being spent to enforce park laws," he added. "So we have to be the stewards. We have to uphold our set of laws."

It sounded like a tall order given all the circumstances, I said.

"Maybe it is," he replied. "But the least we can do is get delays. We can force the workers to get permits, if they can. Then we'll push for an environmental impact study. Then we'll use the time we gain to publicize the issue, to get more Ecuadorians and foreigners to realize that after ten years of pumping you don't have oil *or* a forest."

I recalled Roberto mentioning the appalling fact that all the suspected reserves in the lower Cuyabeno would meet U.S. oil needs for a mere ten days or so.

And what, I asked Randy, if the delays and the publicity don't work and encroachment continues?

"Then we'll draw a line," he said emphatically. "There are no other pristine areas left for us to go to. Not in this country. We have to draw the line here."

Did that mean, in the end, resorting to violence? Was that a real possibility?

A silence fell and Randy's face hardened when I asked this. He was still sharpening his knives, checking one now by running his thumb along the blade in a way that made me fear he was almost cutting himself.

"No," he said finally. "No violence. The lesson has been learned abundantly well by the Indians of Latin America: You can't fight Western encroachment physically. We have to stay within the spirit of the law. I wouldn't rule out some sort of civil disobedience, though. Definitely not. Sitting in front of bulldozers or something."

Randy decided to backtrack at this point. He described how seven years ago he had led this group of Cofan to the lower Cuyabeno forest. Four years after that he was officially voted chief. Two years after that, as chief, he helped secure establishment of the wildlife reserve, the clan's dream.

He pointed out that in the year 1500 there were an estimated 15,000 Cofan Indians in the Amazon rain forest. By the 1930s, owing in part to

the introduction of European diseases, that number was down to an astonishing 350. Today, the largest share of the 700 or so surviving members
lived in Dureno, surrounded by the Texaco oil boom, succumbing to a
familiar Indian pattern: Youth flight to the cities, rampant alcoholism, cultural disintegration. The Zábalo Cofan, eighteen families in all, were some
of the few remaining members still living the basic forest life of their
ancestors. Thousands of years of cultural knowledge rested on their survival. And their survival rested on an intact forest.

I decided to push things further. "Let's say civil disobedience doesn't
work," I said to Randy, "and the testing and drilling start."

"If it doesn't work, then we'll have no choice but to just watch and
hope and pray they don't find oil or that the oil is of a poor quality not
worth extracting. In the end it may come down to that: Luck."

And if the luck is bad, if the oil turns out to be good, and all the
destruction kicks in?

Randy didn't rush to answer the question. "I don't allow myself to
think that way," he said. "I just don't. I guess we've come too far now.
We've tried too hard for us to imagine the worst really happening. We've
just tried too hard."

An unmistakable note of sadness, laced with foreboding, infused his last
sentence. It hung on the porch like the midday heat, threatening to satu-
rate everything until, from the river, soaring like an eagle, a high-pitched
cry of joy altered the moment. It was Carlos, Randy's father-in-law. He had
just harpooned a large fish with his spear, and we went down to inspect it,
glad of the chance to break from so many bleak thoughts of the future.
Lying on the bank was a carplike colussuma, weighing at least fifteen
pounds. Carlos stood by grinning ceaselessly. He was a lean man of delicate Indian features who wore a headband interlaced with fresh flowers
across his brow. He had snagged the fish with a handmade spear whose tip
detaches upon impact, remaining tied by a string to a shaft that floats. An
ancient technique.

Squatting on the bank, Randy began cleaning the fish with one of his
just-sharpened knives. I sat on a stone next to him, and our talk continued, turning more personal. Despite the language and the dress and the
cultural knowledge he possessed, I asked him if he ever felt a little odd, a
little out of place, living this way day to day as the Caucasian chief of a

clan of forest Indians. Was perhaps part of it some sort of Western fantasy come true? A way of dropping out along Robinson Crusoe lines? Or did he really feel legitimate? Really feel authentic?

His answer came without hesitation. "The only reason I'm chief here is because these people absolutely see me as a Cofan. That's the only test that matters. Many of them were my childhood friends. I grew up with them. And as long as I'm one of them in *their* eyes and they want me as their leader, then that's enough for me. The rest of the world can say whatever it wants.

"And it's not a fantasy," he went on. "I don't wake up in the morning thinking, 'Wow, this sure is better than being a lawyer in Pittsburgh' or anything like that. I usually wake up thinking about the fish net I need to mend that day or the banana field I need to clean. It's not that romantic.

"But to be honest, for a lot of years, when I was younger, I don't think I really knew *who* I was or *what* I was. I went to a mission grammar school as a kid, while at the same time I was spending all my free time with my Cofan friends, doing what they did, growing up like a Cofan, playing in the forest.

"I think it really began to dawn on me just which culture was truly my own when I tried to go to college in the States. I missed the Cofan while I was at Michigan State. I missed the forest. I was also broke, so I did the only thing I knew to do: I hunted and gathered. My Cofan impulse took over. I had a pellet gun and I would go out in the morning and kill pigeons and rabbits in other people's yards before dawn. I would cook them and eat them with fruit I gathered like mulberries and blackberries and damaged apples from orchards. I also had a bicycle, which is how I got a lot of my food. I would ride it around on roads near my house and keep track of roadkills every day. Whenever I spotted a fresh roadkill, I'd pick it up and bring it home and cook it—raccoons and stuff.

"It was a real culture shock. I always felt like a foreigner in the States. Everyone is such a busybody there. No one slows down. And every time I thought I was getting the hang of things generally, something new would throw me off. Like 'streaking.' Remember that? I was there in the early '70s, and people were taking off their clothes and running around naked. It's so ironic how for centuries Western culture had been trying to force clothes on the world's savages. Then I get to the States and people were taking off their clothes and running around like savages themselves."

In 1974, after three years of school, Randy returned to Ecuador an "unreformed Cofan." He went back to the forest, living mostly around Dureno until 1984, leading this group here. I asked him what it was he liked most about Cofan life, what he would miss the most if it ended.

"Sometimes," he said, beginning slowly, "we make expeditions, some of the men, where we set off in a direction and canoe and walk for two or three days, hunting and camping as we go. And the whole time we won't see another human being. Not even the sign of another human being. The whole time. There might be a hill or a rise somewhere and you can climb to the top and look out and you see nothing but forest in every direction as far as you can see. Just trees—on and on and on. Then we'll come upon something simple, like a waterfall on a small creek. We've never been here before, never seen this waterfall, and it's beautiful. I look at it and I know there are other waterfalls in the world that are bigger and more spectacular. But we're probably the first human beings ever to see this particular one, after thousands and thousands of years. I don't know how to explain that feeling. I guess it's just knowing you live in a huge, huge forest and you live there in a very simple way. That's what I like. There's a joy in that."

The afternoon sun was sinking fast as Randy said this. He had finished cleaning the speared fish and was sitting on the bank, staring out across the river through the waning light of a blood-red sunset. Suddenly he had had enough of talking. "Come on," he said. "Let's go eat."

After a meal of fish stew, Russell and I retired to the guest hut on the other side of the village. It was one of three simple structures built for the groups of backpacking adventurers and wildlife researchers who visited the Cofan several times a year for organized treks into the forest. This small side business in tourism brought the Indians money that was used to buy the array of imported tools and goods that hunting alone couldn't procure: Outboard motors, shotgun shells, Western medicines to supplement herbal brews, and a fickle gasoline-powered electricity generator that juiced a lightbulb in each hut. The generator shuddered to a start—when it ran at all—from under a tumbledown shelter of banana leaves.

The next morning, the sky turned cloudy and Russell grew excited. Something about the diffuse light made him eager to shoot pictures.

Randy obliged us in our request, disappearing into his house and returning in full Cofan costume. He looked singularly resplendent with the streaks of red *achiote* paint across his cheekbones, the flower-laced arm-bands, the numerous bead necklaces that hung down across his traditional tunic topped off by one necklace made of nothing but peccary (wild boar) tusks, thirty in all. A village elder named Mauricio dressed similarly, adding a long and brightly colored macaw feather that protruded, startlingly, from one of his nostrils, the quill's stem pierced through a hole in his septum.

We went next to the home of Lorenzo, a man whose sons and daughters were Randy's godchildren. Burly and good-natured, with a round, full-moon face, Lorenzo sat straddling a hammock, applying face paint and beads and piercing his own nose with a red macaw feather. Russell and I watched the transformation as we drank gourd bowls of *chicha*, a home-made beer derived from fermented yucca. Now and again, Lorenzo looked over to make sure we had enough to drink. His almost shiny reddish-brown face was shaved of all facial hair, including eyebrows, as if to leave only the essential—a pure smile, pure black eyes.

At last everyone was ready. Russell set up his tripod on the riverbank, aiming the big 4-by-5 view camera back toward Lorenzo's long thatched-roof hut on stilts. His subjects gathered together. Knowing little Spanish and zero Cofan, Russell promptly employed the same quirky English commands that somehow served him photographing people around the world. "Scrunch in, everybody," he said. "That's it. Scrunch in close." He was looking through the lens, gesturing with his hands, and everyone scrunched in.

The Cofan men, with their beads and face paint, stood resolutely tall while children and scrawny dogs and chickens roamed about their bare feet. As I watched all of this from behind Russell's shoulder, taking in the whole village scene, an unbidden feeling came to me. It came quickly and inexorably, like the flow of the Aguarico River fifty feet behind me. I had the distinct, sad sense that Russell and I were recording—had been recording all along, despite Randy's hard-bitten words of hope—a world that truly would not be here ten years hence. These trees, these houses, these people would be gone if later we chose to return. Everything about the village seemed oddly ancient and temporary at the same time, giving the moment the feel of a very old memory even as it was happening. The feeling grew even stronger after Russell completed his work.

"Okay, you on the end, perk your chin up some," Russell said, walking around now, organizing a final portrait. "Perk it up a little. That's it."

In his soiled hiking boots Russell strode back to the camera, his long hair and his piranha necklace swinging as he moved.

The last shot had been taken and we were settling down to more *chicha* beer when we heard the hum of a motorized canoe on the river. It was Felipe, our guide, coming back to get us. As he stepped ashore, Felipe had an urgent, agitated look on his face. He walked straight toward Randy. "You have to come to Quito tomorrow," he said to the chief. "You have to fly to Quito and hold a press conference."

Felipe quickly explained: Petroecuador, the national oil company, had during the past few days begun blitzing the Quito media with lies, telling reporters it had conducted negotiations with the Cofan and had gained the Indians' full permission to explore for oil in the lower Cuyabeno forest. It was a falsehood so great, so outrageous, that it required that Randy and the other Cofan leaders go directly to the capital to deny everything firsthand. Transturi Touring would pay for the trip.

After conferring with Lorenzo and Mauricio, Randy agreed that the three of them would go, taking their families. They would do whatever was needed. The campaign would not be allowed to flag.

So we left, all of us, the very next day, settling into boats for the long trip up the Aguarico. The Cofan traveled in style, wearing the same tunics and woven headbands of the day before, the big difference being only the shoes they wore now—reluctantly—for the hard city sidewalks ahead.

At the Tarapoa airstrip the Hercules was already waiting, its propellers whirring loudly, prepared to go. Russell and I crossed the tarmac with the others, backpacks in tow, notebooks and film stored away as a chronicle of the endangered forest we had come to know and the clash of human wills we'd found in its dense, faraway clutches. Now we were returning home, our tour so brief as to seem nearly a form of voyeurism, a window opened and shut on a people and place we would not soon forget no matter what outcome prevailed.

Lorenzo was first to enter the plane. To the macaw feather pierced through his nose he had added long red feathers behind each ear. The feathers rose above his head like delicate horns, forcing him to duck down carefully as he entered the plane door. Then, one by one, the other Cofan followed, everyone looking grave and expectant and proud at the same time, everyone ready to sit behind microphones and TV cameras in the capital, trying to escape one more time—with a white man as their chief—a fate imposed on them by other white men beginning nearly five hundred years before.

Randy's oldest son Felipe, almost four, took my hand as we entered the plane. The rumble of the engines, I think, frightened him and he let go just before takeoff, scurrying back to his mother. I said good-bye, but he didn't hear me.

The plane then began to taxi. Everyone buckled in, and bolls of pink cotton were passed around. Then noisily, too soon, the hulking Hercules flew away, off to Quito, out of the jungle.

2

The very next evening, Russell and I were in a downtown Quito apartment visiting Dorys, the young doctor we'd met in the jungle. We were flipping through TV channels when suddenly Randy and the other Cofan appeared on the screen. The switch from jungle-hut scenery to cathode-ray imagery was something of a shock, but there they were: Randy and the others sitting on wooden stools, on a stage, dressed in tunics, peccary tusks around their necks, being interviewed by the host of a locally popular current affairs program.

Into a microphone Randy explained why the Cofan had detained the seismic technicians along the Aguarico, then argued passionately for rainforest preservation. In simpler Spanish, Lorenzo did the same. Then Mauricio. Then the program was over.

"Very good exposure," Dorys said, clicking off the TV. "Very positive. Half the people in Quito just saw that."

As the screen imploded to a lingering white dot, taking the picturesque Cofan with it, erasing them, I realized that perhaps all was not fixed on a course of utter doom as had seemed certain just the day before. Any group daring enough to pull off a virtual mass kidnapping, then suave enough to follow it up with the sort of burnished PR message we had just seen, was going to make a formidable foe for any oil company wishing to play outside the rules in the turmoil of a far-off jungle.

So on the day Russell and I departed, it wasn't for pure doodling purposes that I drew a fat, curlycue question mark on the last page of my notebook, underlining it several times as we soared over the Andes toward Miami. With the Amazon's greenery fading into the distance, I couldn't help tampering with Bovee's memorable line, "When all else *seems* lost, the future still remains."

Back in the States, Russell and I filed our story describing the endangered Cuyabeno and the Cofan Indians living there. But to our ire, *Travel Holiday*, the magazine that sent us afield, gave the piece relatively modest play, greatly reducing its impact. There was little time to remain frustrated, however, as we moved on to other stories, other places, time and distance gradually dimming in our minds the fiery urgency of the Cuyabeno struggle.

What remained for me, nonetheless, refusing to fade, was a real sense of wrecked innocence. In my office at home in the Washington, D.C., area I kept my own set of souvenir piranha teeth dangling from a spread of Russell's magnificent forest photos. This minishrine would have inspired fond feelings of an intense journey had it not hung so conspicuously on the wall of an old oil-burning house, to which a smelly tanker truck bellied up every few weeks to keep the tin-bucket basement furnace in bliss. This juxtaposition kept fresh in my mind the knowledge of where half of Ecuador's Amazon crude wound up. And that knowledge, with time, became personal to me in small ways. Light fixtures left on too long brought reminders of a specific village under siege in a faraway place. A badly cracked storm window meant more seismic trails across jungle paths I had walked myself. And gasoline flowing into my car each week— as if into a sinkhole, gallons and gallons of it—became an obscenity so hard to endure that when the old rattletrap was eventually towed from an illegal parking space, I never retrieved it, turning to subway trains and buses for almost all my travel.

The same jungle experience hammering me into these changes was also making it harder than ever to endure the native culture back home, where a central precept is to never admit the hint of a grain of a shred of responsibility for anything. Within months of my return, advertisements abounded in the States heralding a saving new product for American drivers, something called Crystal Clear gasoline. Using complex scientific methods, the producer—Amoco Inc.—had removed "harmful impurities" from its product, leaving the stuff you put in your tank, well, uh, crystal clear. With a background of chirping birds and gurgling rivers, the radio spots gave the impression that if you ever became lost in a desert wilderness without water enough to drink, you could simply siphon some of the liquid from your gas tank, pour it into a tall tumbler, pop in a straw, and sip mightily. Ahhhhhh! Cool and refreshing. Tastes good, too. How could anything so clean and wholesome, so crystal clear, possibly warm the planet or contribute to anything as untidy as deforestation in South America? Why would anyone listen to the hyena screams of wacko environmentalists bent on crippling the Ecuadorian economy—and ours—when we could instead keep doing the easy (and now responsible) thing of topping off our tanks with a smile: "Crystal Clear, please! Fill 'er up."

While I was getting reacquainted with such goings on back home, weeks and weeks rolled by, accumulating into months, and I received very little news of what was happening in the Cuyabeno. Dorys wrote after half a year saying she believed seismic testing was now under way throughout the area, but that I should write Randy for details. My letter to the Cofan chief, however, sent via a Transturi guide, went unanswered—or never arrived. So I remained in the dark and was not exactly braced for what I read a full year later while browsing through a copy of *The New York Times*. An article on the inside pages was titled "Oil and Tourism Don't Mix, Inciting Amazon Battle." It described the growing tensions across eastern Ecuador between ecotourism outfits and the ever-pressing petroleum companies. Toward the end, tucked inside a single paragraph, the article mentioned that three new oil wells were now under construction inside the lower Cuyabeno Wildlife Reserve. And at one of these sites, a place by the name of Zábalo, protesting "Cofan Indians (had recently) burned a Petroecuador heliport and placed obstacles on the landing pad."

I read the sentence again. *Burned a heliport?* I thought. The first news I get of the Cofan after so many months is that they've burned a heliport? What exactly did that mean? They took torches and actually set fire to the landing pad? It was quite a step beyond simply detaining people. Did it stop the well construction, at least? Were there any injuries? Were the Cofan arrested? The article said nothing more. No illuminating details. It was vexingly little information, but enough to arouse in me sharp feelings of recognition. A surge of memories came into focus. I *knew* these people, knew them individually, and judging by the short and dramatic news account, their lives had reached a new level of desperation. My hunch was that Randy would abandon his earlier pledge of nonviolence only as a last resort. A ring of wells was being built around the Cofan community. Was that enough to invoke a stance of last resort?

Fretting to know more, I wrote Randy a second letter, again failing to get a reply. By this point the second anniversary of my original Cuyabeno trip was fast approaching, and I began to strongly consider making a return trip, updating the story, urged on by the reported burning of the well site. Having pursued this jungle story once before, a reserve of momentum now kept me going. Why stop? I figured.

I tried my best to drag Russell back to the forest with me, but when other assignments prevented his return, I resolved to make a solo trip. Russell, at least, offered me the use of his battle-scarred tent. It would be a vital accoutrement since I planned to stay longer this time, six weeks in all, traveling throughout the reserve. I wrote Randy once again, informing him of my plans. But when a week before my departure I still had no response, I began wondering if, after all the troubles, he and the Cofan still lived in the reserve, if the village of Zábalo still existed. In a mild panic, I called the Quito office of Transturi, where a spokesman told me he too had been trying without success to contact Randy for the past two weeks. As far as the spokesman could tell, Randy had "disappeared into the forest to fight the oil company and hasn't come back out yet." The white chief was gone, in other words. Missing. Incommunicado.

I debated the significance of this development as I stared uncomfortably at my nonrefundable plane ticket. Forty-eight hours later, on the very eve of my departure, the mystery of Randy's whereabouts was finally solved. A California environmental organization I had written to for background information on the Cuyabeno forest had just gotten word from sources in Ecuador concerning the status of the Cofan. The organization issued the following emergency bulletin:

On Monday, November 1st, 1993, thirty-five indigenous Cofan men, women, and children occupied and temporarily stopped drilling activities at Paujil, an exploratory oil well located in Cofan territory and the Cuyabeno Wildlife Reserve in Ecuador. The Cofan hiked through swampy terrain to reach the remote well site operated by Petroecuador, the national oil company. Wearing traditional *"ondiccuje"* tunics and dresses, their faces and lance tips painted red, the Cofan ordered startled oil workers to shut the drill rig down.

The five-paragraph bulletin went on to say that the Cofan, whose weapons included shotguns as well as spears, had formed a circle around the well, refusing to retreat from their assertion that the operation was illegal. A tense standoff ensued and, at the time the bulletin was written, was still going on.

I spent the rest of the night packing—knife, boots, rope, tarp—and reading the extraordinary bulletin over and over again. I folded the notice into my pocket the following morning and, knowing nothing more than what was imparted in those five dramatic paragraphs, caught the next plane to Ecuador.

▼▼▼

It was a hot morning when I finally reached the Aguarico River after two days of traveling. Sunlight fell from the sky in a burning downpour, passing through steamy air. But there on the riverbank, clustered together, the butterflies had an incongruously cool look. There must have been hundreds of them, bouncing up and down, winging through wild orbits. They looked like specks of sherbet, every hue of sherbet you've ever seen in your life—green and orange and yellow and pink—all mixed together, each flavor given wings and told to fly. I made my way toward this blizzard, then through it, past it, waving my hands, carrying my backpack, reaching the small riverboat waiting to cover the final leg of my journey to Zábalo. The butterflies stayed where they were as the boat pulled away, a happy greeting party having welcomed me back to the Amazon—and now waving good-bye, seeing me off into its nether reaches.

It felt good to be on the Aguarico again, sliding down its current, even if this small wooden vessel was badly overloaded. A cargo boat owned by Transturi, it was sending crates of food and other supplies to camps far downriver. Besides the *motorista*, the only other passengers were two Ecuadorian biologists studying the eating habits of caimans in Iripari Lake. The biologists, in their twenties and working on dissertations, said the danger of wading through the lake with nets came less from the caimans (who rarely attack) than from the giant Amazon stingrays, whose long whiplike tails were capable of inflicting severe, gashing wounds across human flesh.

As we headed downriver, I noticed the clearings for small peasant farms—*fincas*—had increased in number on either shore since my last visit. Some even held cattle now, the beasts having been brought in by boat, bound in ropes and chains. Once released, they stomped about the river's edge, their hooves deforming and denuding the bank with a muddy jumble of pocked trails.

After three hours, the *finca* clearings began finally to fall away, allowing the jungle to strike its rightful pose on either shore, tall and green and dense, thick with chaotic vines and raucous, enchanting bird cries.

A violent, midafternoon thunderstorm blew overhead, dumping scattered rain before yielding to resumed sunshine and an enormous, utterly pristine rainbow. The rainbow began several hundred yards ahead of us, rising—according to my eyes—straight out of the middle of the river, straight out of the water. It then climbed high into the blue sky, forming a towering arc, before plunging directly into the shore to our left, spearing its colors directly into the clay bank, right into the earth. The whole rainbow was there, in other words. All of it visible. Nothing missing. A complete performance.

My thoughts turned to the Cofan as we reached the rich, blackwater Cuyabeno River, flowing like tea into the Aguarico. Here, the welcoming sign of a small military post featured a machete crisscrossed with an automatic rifle next to the words *"Ecuador: País Amazonas."* A fitting image, it struck me, as I thought back to the armed standoff between the Cofan and Petroecuador, a conflict I had learned about just two days before. Now, according to several people I had talked to along the river, the showdown was already over. The word, too, was that the Cofan had "won" somehow, had gotten their way.

But I was hesitant at this point to put too much faith in any of the information I was receiving, especially the suggestion that things were once again calm. I recalled the letter Dorys had sent me just before I left: "The best thing is not to take risks, Mike. Remember that even if it doesn't look like it at first, where you're going in the forest, it can be very dangerous."

An hour before sunset, the cargo boat rounded a bend, scattering a group of sand-colored nighthawks from their perch atop a gnarled, fallen fig tree. At the same moment, the village of Zábalo came into view on the far bank, thatched roofs getting closer—and the *motorista* headed that way. As he did, a young woman who had boarded upstream, a soldier's wife, turned to me in astonishment.

"You're getting out *here?*" she said. "*Alone?*"

I replied I was.

"You've heard about these people, right? *Están agressivo.* You're not afraid?"

I dismissed her questions with a wave of my hand, feeling her burning, incredulous stare follow me as the boat shoved off and I stepped ashore to the waiting crowd of Indians.

It seemed the whole Cofan village had turned out to greet me—adults, children, dogs, chickens—though I still wasn't sure any of my letters announcing my return visit had arrived. Mauricio, a stout, older man I remembered from before, a sort of lighthearted grandfather figure in the village, greeted me with a soft handshake that eased me back into the signature friendliness and grace of this village. He folded his calloused fingers across his belly in a polite way and then exploded in an eruption of noisy giggles when I told him nothing more than that my trip had gone very well. Recovering from his laugh, he announced that Randy was upriver visiting with Quichua Indians and would not be back till later that night.

A handsome young man in his late teens with skin the color of cinnamon stepped forward from the group. He was Randy's Cofan cousin-in-law Belizario, and he led me away from the crowd to the guest hut on the east side of the village, overlooking the river. We deposited my gear and walked to the water's edge. Both the veil of mosquitoes I flailed at uselessly and the violent, violet sunset sky, now dotted with giant striated herons, told me for sure I was back in this microdot village in the middle of a vast, trackless forest.

"Are you here because of Paujil?" Belizario asked, referring by name to the site of the Indians' most recent oil-well confrontation.

"Yes," I said, "that's one reason. What happened there, anyway?"

"The *petroleros*," Belizario said, "they came and made an illegal well on our land. So we made a circle around them and were ready to kill them all." He didn't pause to measure my reaction to the provocative phrasing. "We were strong. We had spears and guns. If they had refused to stop bothering us, we would have killed them all."

He made a thrusting motion with an imaginary spear. His longish hair swayed forward with the gesture, swinging around a face that had a sculpted beauty.

"Why?" I asked. "Why did you attack the well?"

"Because of what would happen if we didn't."

We were standing by a beached canoe with wide curving gunwales made dry and parched by the equatorial sun. Belizario dipped his hand in the river and began drawing a map using his index finger, leaving a wet trail on the bone-dry gunwale surface.

"Here," he said, "is the old Cofan land upriver where my father still lives, near Dureno." He drew a rectangle representing that tortured stretch of land 120 river miles away. "The oil roads Texaco built are here, here, and here." He rewet his finger and drew lines that enclosed the rectangle. "And along the roads there are wells here, here, here, and here," he said, drawing dots inside the lines. "And my father, he lives here." He put an X inside the dots. "He lives right in the middle of the wells and roads. We don't want to live with wells around us here like they do there. The wells smell and they kill animals and the roads are all slippery with oil. So we attacked the Paujil well before they could finish it."

"And what was the outcome?" I asked. "Was anyone hurt?"

"No one was hurt. And the outcome is that the well is shut down now, forever."

Before I could ask another question, he added, "And we get solar panels from the company."

"Solar panels?" I said, confused.

"Yeah, one solar panel for each house in Zábalo. The company's going to give them to us. We did a really good job at that well."

▼▼▼

I was fading into deep sleep under a mosquito net in the guest hut, surrendering to the drone of a million insects and the phantasmic grunt of a nocturnal curassow bird—hmmmmmmboom!, hmmmmmmboom!—beating its wings around the hut, when a canoe buzzed into earshot upriver. The outboard motor fell silent reaching shore, and in the late-night air, among the tired Cofan voices in the distance, I recognized Randy's. The chief had returned to his people.

Next morning, I traversed the village and was ascending the plank steps to Randy's porch, sidestepping a pet woolly monkey languidly scratching its ears, when Randy emerged from his front door. He was dressed in a light blue mud-stained tunic.

"Hi, Mike," he said. "Welcome back."

Even in the short moment before I replied, I noticed something was different about Randy. He had changed. It was his hair. The former blond-brown color was yielding to a surge of silvery white. And not just a little. Even the mustache was going. There had been a soupçon of silver before, but now he looked ten years older, not two.

I returned Randy's greeting. He had gotten my letters, he said, which accounted for his lack of surprise in seeing me. But he wasn't very good at replying to correspondence, he added casually, without a hint of apology.

Randy had come outside holding an enamel plate piled high with papaya rinds and seeds. He was on his way to feed his turtles, he said, so I followed him, stepping that quickly back into the rhythms of his village life before asking the first question about the oil situation.

Randy heaved the plate's contents into a simple pen next to the house where three clunky, dull-eyed turtles roamed. "Rainy-day food," Randy said, as if to himself. "For when you can't get out and hunt. You eat a turtle."

Then he turned to me. "You know how when you cut open turtles a lot of times and you find all those worms inside them, just tons of worms?"

I knew nothing of the sort, of course, but I nodded to keep things simple.

"Well, I've sort of experimented," Randy said, "and I've found that turtles given papaya seeds never have worms when you cut them open. Never. Based on what chemical principles, I'm not sure, but it's true." His tone was more one of consternation over not knowing *why* than satisfaction over a useful discovery. "I think fish scales help, too," he said, deepening the mystery.

We headed back to the porch, passing one of Randy's yard turkeys along the way, a plump female studiously keeping her distance. "Look at her," Randy said, pointing bemusedly. "She won't look me in the eye or come near me. Every few days she decides she's mad at me and ignores me." Then he laughed. "I think she knows what happens in the end."

I laughed too, tickled by the odd scene, and already I could see that the image my mind had built up for Randy—that of fierce warrior chief, of leader on danger's edge, all of it based on recent reports I'd received—was beginning to melt away. Whatever combative twist he had added to his role since last we met, the quotidian concerns of the small-scale farmer and hunter were obviously still central to his world, to who he was.

We took seats on the porch, on low-backed benches made from the gunwales of a retired canoe, while Randy's wife Amelia offered demure greetings and then disappeared to prepare morning *chicha*, the homemade yucca beer. The disorienting melange that was Randy's life was on view across the porch as if on a stage. On the floor, youngest son Federico, now two and a half, was busy talking to himself in Cofan while playing smashup with a plastic toy helicopter and four-wheel-drive truck purchased in Quito. Federico rose every few minutes, mouth imitating the putter of engine noise, and flew the helicopter past the bag of shotgun shells hanging on the wall and the crackling sound of a two-way radio spilling its chatter outside through the front door. He reversed directions only at the end of the porch, where his ancient, barefoot Indian great grandmother, Lucrecia, sat in casual repose, macaw feather removed from her nose as she made twine for a basket, expertly rolling palm-bark fibers together between her calloused palms in age-old fashion.

That the Indian world still had the upper hand in this mix of ways was clear.

When Felipe, almost six, came running out the front door headed for a neighbor's house, I waved to him. "Where are you off to?" I asked in English.

He looked at me blankly, his face a light-brown mix of Caucasian and Indian tones.

"Where are you off to?" I repeated.

"Fine, thank you," he said.

The *chicha* arrived, and after one bowl each, Randy began updating me on oil matters. A shine of satisfaction suffused his face as he confirmed the incident at the Paujil well, declaring it a Cofan victory, as had every-one else I had talked to. In the past six months, he said, the Cofan had managed to repel what basically constituted a frontal assault on their land by Petroecuador.

"We're still in danger," he confessed. "The forest is still in danger. But we've come a whole lot further than I ever dreamed possible." He paused. "No. Let me retract that statement, because we had to have big, big dreams to ever begin this campaign in the first place. I'd say we've done a lot more than I ever *thought* was possible."

Randy eased back against the bench just then, picking up the story at the point of my visit two years ago when the Cofan had detained and expelled twenty-four trespassing seismic technicians. A month after that incident, Randy said, in December 1991, the Indians confiscated the radio of another trespassing seismic crew, then detained the crew's boss until he agreed to evacuate his men.

But the setback came in early 1992 when the government issued explicit permits to Petroecuador's seismic crews to explore the lower Cuyabeno reserve. Forced to concede, at least for the moment, Randy demanded as a compromise that absolutely none of the objectionable heliports be constructed along riverbanks and that seismic trails be made significantly narrower than was usually company policy. As for material compensation, the Cofan would receive a small quantity of corrugated tin, plus five drinking wells constructed throughout the community and dug with the very same mechanical drill used to deposit dynamite twenty feet underground for the seismic booms.

Petroecuador agreed to Randy's demands. The Cofan got their five drinking wells and the technicians went to work across the reserve, making hundreds of miles of trails, clearing dozens of crude heliports, and detonating thousands of pounds of dynamite, affecting—at least indi-rectly—about a quarter of the Cofan land.

The process, at least, was blessedly quick. Six weeks after it began, the testing was over. The crews left the forest, and the Cofan, never informed of the results, clung mightily to hopes that nothing had been found. For a while those hopes seemed to bear fruit. All was tranquil for almost a year while the jungle began the gradual and thorough process of reclaiming the crisscrossing trails with new growth. At about the same time, after years of battling the park service bureaucracy, Randy finally secured for the Zábalo Cofan a title to nearly 200,000 acres of land within the lower Cuyabeno reserve. The title incorporated a short stretch of the Aguarico River, as well as much of the Zábalo River, reaching almost to its head-waters. But while it gave the Cofan greater legal footing to resist improper intrusions, the title did not supersede the government's self-declared own-ership of all subsurface mineral rights within the reserve.

Which is why, in February 1993, several Cofan men fishing about three hours up the Zábalo River began to hear strange noises in the forest distance. They heard chain saws and helicopters and falling trees. The Indians followed the sounds, walking two hours into the jungle until they came to the abhorrent site of hard-hatted workers chain-sawing 100-foot-tall cedars and kapoks, clear-cutting a six-acre area. In the middle of the clearing, felled trees were being used to construct what the Cofan recog-nized as a drill platform. There was going to be an exploratory well here, the first in the lower Cuyabeno. And almost as a dare, Petroecuador was placing it extremely close to the Cofan, giving the well the official name of "Zábalo" after the Indian community itself and the river near which they lived. It was galling beyond belief.

When Randy learned of this he was furious. He had agreed to seismic testing in the area, but not to wells. Who had authorized this operation? Why had no one contacted the Cofan? Where were the permits required under park regulations? What environmental impact study, if any, had been done?

As it turned out, no legitimate studies or permits of any kind accom-panied the well-clearing activities at Zábalo. Petroecuador, having taken over a huge area of jungle operations from Texaco, Inc.—after that American company left the country for good in 1992—was now using the brazen, long-running technique common to many oil companies in South America of never asking permission when operating on or near Indian land. The strategy was to barrel in and launch operations so quickly that the presence became a fait accompli, making it difficult for anyone to effectively protest and dislodge the company.

Randy knew the method, and went to work immediately, demanding a halt to the illegal operation. He dispatched letters to Petroecuador and to the Instituto Ecuadoriano Forestale y de Areas Naturales (INEFAN), the government agency overseeing park affairs. When his letters went unanswered, Randy led groups of Cofan men on several visits to the drill platform. The Cofan scolded the workers and their crew chief, explaining the illegality of their actions. On one occasion, Randy brought in the head warden of the Cuyabeno park, José Delgado, who made similar appeals. But on each return visit, the Cofan found the oil men still working, still chainsawing trees, now constructing a wooden heliport for ferrying in heavy rig equipment. Worse, they learned that the company planned to build a road from the heavily colonized Napo River directly to the well site should oil be discovered. A tide of settlers would then flow directly onto Cofan land.

With the stakes rising, the Indians got authorization from park warden Delgado to enter the site unarmed and confiscate all seven chain saws being used by the workers. This they did without incident, turning the saws over to the park. Yet on the Indians' very next visit, the workers had replacements. More upsetting, they were blatantly hunting the surrounding area. Hanging from nails in the camp were a pair of rare harpy eagle talons and a freshly cleaned jaguar pelt, the latter an enormous insult to Cofan culture, which holds the animal in high esteem, ascribing to it great power and intelligence.

And that's when Randy ordered an armed visit to the site. With twenty-two men behind him, half of them carrying shotguns, the Cofan chief emerged from the surrounding forest of the well site. He walked up to the crew leader and, with all the other workers listening, announced that since the men had decided to hunt the area, the Cofan were going to hunt it, too. Gripping their weapons, the Indians paced back and forth across the site several times before finally, quietly, withdrawing. As Randy told me later, "The threat was not explicit, but *strongly* implicit."

During these several months of visits, meanwhile, as progress continued on the drill platform and heliport, Randy and Delgado and officials at Transturi continued to press INEFAN to declare the well site illegal. A month after the Cofan's armed visit, INEFAN finally obliged, ordering Petroecuador to permanently suspend operations at Zábalo because of the area's great ecological delicacy and importance. It was an immense victory for the Cofan and for the park. Petroecuador withdrew its people, and several weeks later Randy and the Cofan made a symbolic comment by setting the site on fire. They took posts the size of railroad ties, chain-sawed by the now-evacuated workers, and placed them in several great piles across the rig platform and heliport. Using gasoline fuel and crank case oil left behind by the company, they set the first bonfire roaring and watched as it caused irreparable damage. Then, one by one, they set the others burning, cleansing the forest of the terrible intrusion, purifying the site with heat and flame. It was this angry demonstration that had been reported, in a paragraph, in *The New York Times*.

The original INEFAN decision to suspend work at Zábalo so angered Petroecuador that the company protested the decision directly to the president of the country, Sixto Durán Ballén, saying that for the good of the nation's economy the company needed to exploit oil reserves now known to exist in the lower Cuyabeno. To the dismay of preservationists, the president agreed, overturning the INEFAN decision and okaying oil operations at Zábalo and elsewhere in the park. (Never mind that the Zábalo work had now been set aflame by the Cofan.) Notified of this, Randy went to Quito and with the help of an American environmental lawyer, he and the Cofan filed suit against Durán Ballén in Ecuador's second-highest court, claiming the president had no constitutional authority to overrule INEFAN. Mauricio and Lorenzo and the others back in their riverside huts with the split-cane walls now had a lawsuit against the most powerful man in Ecuador.

As the charges and countercharges were being sorted out, meanwhile, the Cofan began in August to hear more sounds issuing from a different part of the forest. They heard the thump of more helicopters, the buzz of more chain saws. This time the clamor was coming from another side of the Aguarico, from the center of a tremendous swamp called Paujil. Though clearly on Cofan land, the sounds were difficult to track. Distance rendered them faint and distorted, and a neck-high soup of swamp water and tangled trees lay in the same general direction.

Randy wrote yet more protest letters, and Petroecuador acknowledged that a drilling site was under construction in Paujil, allegedly made legal under the same presidential decree the Cofan were now challenging in court. Randy was desperate to get to the well site and protest in person, but this remained impossible until October, when the Indians began to hear the low-pitched, constant rumble of their worst fears: A hydraulic drill. Enormously powerful, attached to a 100-foot-tall derrick, the drill had begun its work, pounding and tearing into the forest soil. Though unsettling in its significance, the sound provided the guidepost the Cofan needed to act.

On the last day of October, with Randy leading the way, thirty-five Cofan men, women, and children, ranging in age from spindly ten-year-old Valerio to portly and tuberculosis-weakened Lorenzo, forty-eight, set off into the jungle, all ears tuned to the awful, faraway reverberation. The Indians traveled light, carrying only a dozen or so shotguns, a few machetes, a change of clothes each, and bowls of mashed plantain pulp for making *chucula*, a thick, sweet beer that was the group's only sustenance for the next two days. Wanting outside observers to witness the expedition, Randy invited along a Reuter news photographer and two Western environmental activists—one equipped with a hand-held video camera.

The Cofan ran into difficulties almost immediately. The going was very, very slow, a sodden march through an obstacle course of swamp thickets and submerged fallen logs. The water was neck-high much of the way, and leeches attaching themselves to arms and legs had to be shaved off using the sharp blades of machetes. Still worse were the swarming red ants ready to attack any hand or arm braced in fatigue against a tree trunk. As nightfall came, the Cofan had covered fifteen excruciating miles and had to call the march to a halt, constructing a crude camp on a raft of dry land. To the drone of the enormous drill—much louder after the day's travel—everyone fell into exhausted sleep.

The second day was no easier. The dark, murky water deepened in places, forcing the Cofan to swim short distances amid the giant trees and hanging lianas. At several points, various members became lost, separated from the main group, forced to follow the drill sound on their own, stumbling and sloshing alone. Finally, around noon, all the Cofan came upon the great clearing of the exploratory well resting atop an expanse of dry land.

Secretly peering in from the forest's edge, the Indians saw the prodigious $4-million drill rig rumbling in all its mechanical complexity, groaning a constant, harsh, incredibly loud noise that gave the surrounding earth a palpable vibration and forced many of the seventy or so hard-hatted workers scattered about to wear ear protectors. The Indians saw the bunkhouses and the equipment sheds and the heliport. They saw the helicopters landing every ten minutes, conveying more casing for the drill and diesel fuel to make the whole operation run. On the far side, men with chain saws were felling more trees to widen the six-acre clearing, adding to the thousands of trees already cut.

The Cofan edged back from this scene and began preparing themselves in the surrounding forest. They changed into clean tunics and applied streaks of red ceremonial *achiote* paint to their faces. The men without shotguns busied themselves with machetes making long, sharp *nijon'cho* spears from the boughs of palm trees, then applying paint to the tips. As chief, Randy slipped into his bead and peccary-tusk necklaces before donning a headband of woven palm fiber, the light brown of the headband accenting the streaks of deep red *achiote* painted across his cheeks.

Finally the Cofan were ready. Spears and shotguns in hand, they emerged from the forest as a group, moving through the clearing and quickly forming a circle around the hulking drill rig. They marched wordlessly past stunned workers whose jaws dropped with the dawning realization that these people, whoever they were, with the wild paint across their faces, had arrived on foot, hiking through a thick forest swamp that the workers themselves, as a rule, feared to penetrate more than one hundred feet.

Reaching the rig, Randy told a thunderstruck worker he would very much like to have a word with the foreman of the operation. Randy spoke with utmost composure and courtesy despite having to practically shout above the drill's noise. While the foreman was being fetched, the Cofan began their maneuvers. To create the illusion that they were several times more numerous than they were, they began shifting and moving along the perimeter they had formed around the well site, with no one standing in one place for more than a few minutes. Such was the restless, moving stream of bodies and weapons confronting the saucer-eyed foreman as he reached the rig, greeted with a handshake by Randy Borman, chief of the Cofan.

Randy announced that because the well was in the middle of Cofan land, he would very much like a tour of the operations. Peering out at the Cofan still moving all around him, the foreman readily agreed, nervously leading Randy through the various parts of the compound, then up to the top of the drilling platform itself where roughnecks were throwing chains and sending casing down to a drill bit now 6,900 feet below the surface of the earth, heading toward the two-mile mark where they hoped to encounter oil.

When the tour ended, Randy thanked the foreman for his trouble, shook his hand again, then calmly and respectfully informed him that the entire operation was illegal and that he and his men were trespassing. No one had consulted the Cofan about any of this, Randy said. Where were the necessary environmental safeguards? What were the contingency plans in case of an oil spill? Didn't the foreman know he was on legally protected land inside a national park? The whole operation violated the national constitution. Consequently, Randy announced, the foreman must order his men to cease working immediately and remove the drill from the ground.

In disbelief the foreman stared at Randy until the white chief pronounced his instructions a second time: Shut down the drill and cease all operations. The foreman declared he didn't have the authority to give such orders, that he would have to radio his superiors in Quito. Randy obliged, listening as the foreman—deceived by the ring of armed Cofan still circulating around him—told his Quito office that he and his men were surrounded by no fewer than *sixty* Indians ordering them to shut down. The Quito officials, saying they needed time to digest the situation, radioed back two long hours later with the following instructions for the foreman: Offer the Cofan $10,000 to leave the site immediately and never return. The foreman relayed the offer to Randy, who relayed it to the rest of the Cofan, who followed Randy's recommendation that they reject it. Randy promptly told the foreman once more to shut down the well.

This time he obeyed, barking commands to his workers. Up the drill bit came: 6,000 feet. 5,000 feet. 4,000 feet. 3,000 feet. At 2,000 feet, with Randy's permission, the ascent was halted to avoid the complications of removing the drill shaft entirely. All the machinery was then turned off and suddenly an echoing quietude returned to the forest. The ground stopped shaking.

This over, a radio message arrived saying a high-ranking Petroecuador superintendent was being helicoptered in to negotiate directly with the Cofan. Ominously, the superintendent arrived an hour later escorted by a handful of soldiers who were themselves commanded by a colonel from a military base on the Napo River. The colonel, cloaked in army camouflage fatigues with combat boots and a camouflage cap, led the way, demanding of the first Cofan he saw the whereabouts of the Indian leader.

When Randy stepped forward decked out in his own costume, the colonel waved him away with obvious disgust, saying this was an Ecuadorian problem, not a matter for foreigners, for gringos. The colonel had never before heard of Randy or the Zábalo Cofan. He kept asking, yelling now, to meet with the real leader of the Cofan. When Randy stepped forward a second time, the colonel had had enough. He went nose to nose with Randy, aggressively yelling at the gringo to back off, to get out of his way. No doubt this bullying tactic worked well with peasants and Indians elsewhere, but in this case a half-dozen Cofan men rushed to Randy's defense, standing behind him, beside him, armed with spears. The Indians' normally serene faces became contorted with anger. They began yelling back at the colonel while gesturing to Randy: "He *is* our leader. He *is* our leader."

If there was any one moment when violence was truly close at hand, this was it. Fearing the colonel was about to strike Randy, several of the young men—Belizario, Bolívar, Roberto—admitted later they were determined to spear him immediately if he did.

But it never came to that. Sensing, surely, the danger he was in and the extent of the Cofan resolve, the colonel backed off a few paces, calmed down, and asked Randy why on earth the Cofan had come to this place and what they wanted. The Petroecuador superintendent, meanwhile, at last stepped forward. The company had tried solving the problem of the Cofan visit with money. It had tried solving it with army hostility. Now it was time to do what the Cofan had wanted to do all along: Negotiate.

And negotiate the parties did, for hours and hours, right there at the well site. As the sun began to sink into the surrounding swampland, Randy was still trying to get his central point across to the superintendent: The Cofan now had legal title to this land, and if the company wanted to drill for oil it *must* consult the community first. As it turned out, a very shrewd strategy informed Randy's demands here. Given the considerable clout of oil companies in Ecuador, he knew the Cofan would never be granted outright power to control oil activities on their land, to unilaterally authorize or veto operations. So he didn't ask for such power. He asked only that Petroecuador *communicate* with the community and that both parties come to an agreement on all activities. The superintendent radioed the demand to Quito and, after a long wait, returned with amazing news: The company agreed. The company would formally recognize the Indians' right to have full information and input concerning operations on their land. It was a truly historic moment. No oil company had ever made such a pledge to an indigenous group in Ecuador before.

Recognizing the power he had just won, knowing the potential it granted the Cofan to legally delay and upset future operations, Randy agreed next as a good-faith measure to allow the Paujil well to resume drilling. Shut down for more than six hours by Cofan order, it began coughing and wheezing into action again. Darkness had long since fallen by this point, and everyone was nigh faint with fatigue. The Cofan made camp at the edge of the clearing, drifting into sleep despite the earth's renewed rumble beneath them.

The negotiations continued next morning. There remained the tedium of putting the whole agreement into writing, of getting the words right. And there remained the issue of compensation. The Cofan wanted recompense for the company's prior transgression of drilling without consulting them.

Things dragged on until midday, when it was agreed to move the negotiations to the Cofan community at Zábalo. A helicopter was summoned and the Cofan piled in carrying their machetes and shotguns and now-empty tin bowls of *chucula*, most of them still wearing face paint, almost none having set foot in such an aircraft before. In no time at all the helicopter was landing on the Cofan's village soccer field, having covered in ten minutes what had taken the Indians one and a half days on foot, having breezed over the awful maze of turgid swamp water now glinting in the afternoon sun.

It was over a wooden table in the Zábalo village that the Petroecuador superintendent finally agreed to the Cofan's compensation demand. The Indians wanted solar panels. Lots of solar panels. Solar panels to go atop the thatch roofs of all twenty-two family houses. They wanted juice from the big equatorial sun so they could see at night, so they could clean the mess of fish or the freshly killed peccary they brought home after sunset with empty stomachs. Solar panels would let them do that—and Petroecuador acquiesced. Randy agreed to gather and submit to the company bids from manufacturers in the United States. The price would be around $20,000.

And then it was over. The agreements were set in writing, signatures were scrawled, and handshakes offered all around. A helicopter returned, whisking away the superintendent while the Cofan stayed behind clutching their copy of the agreement, their victory in hand.

But the victory wasn't complete. Not yet. For the very next day the story of the Cofan's Paujil raid broke in the Quito press. The city's largest newspaper, *Hoy*, ran a large front-page story with photographs of Randy shutting down the well and then negotiating a solution. The story was very sympathetic to the Cofan cause of rain-forest preservation and critical of Petroecuador's "environmental intrusion." Television and radio stations quickly followed with similar stories. Within hours, millions of Ecuadorians learned of the Paujil incident, and the Cofan couldn't have gotten better treatment had they crafted each story themselves. Petroecuador, conversely, couldn't have gotten worse treatment.

And then came the coup de grace. A few days later, on November 8, Petroecuador released a bombshell statement in Quito saying the company was permanently shutting down the well at Paujil, abandoning the site—unconditionally, forever. The official reason was the discovery of unusable heavy crude at the well. But a competing theory floating around Quito was that the company *had* found usable oil, but was forsaking it— at least for now—after the Cofan's surprisingly strong and sophisticated initiative. The well just wasn't worth the huge trouble the Indians were obviously going to make.

Whatever the reason for the shutdown, the rumbling in the swamp stopped once again—and suddenly the helicopters the Cofan heard in the distance were those carrying the edifice of a dismantled well, section by section, piece by piece, out of the forest. It was a sound the Cofan listened to with great interest, for several days, liking what they heard very, very much.

▼▼▼▼

"One, two, three, four, five, six . . ."

Randy paused. His eyes narrowed. Then it came to him.

"Yeah, it wasn't until number seven, the *seventh* visit, that we went in armed."

We were still sitting on Randy's porch, having spent the whole morning going over the recent Cofan protest actions. Now Randy was summing up, making final points. He was talking about the first well, the Zábalo well, the one whose drilling platform the Cofan had burned down.

"We did everything we could possibly do at that site—letters to Petroecuador, letters to INEFAN, suing the president of the country. When we ran out of options, that's when we went in with weapons. Same at the Paujil well."

Randy was eager to defend every last Cofan move. "We're talking about survival, remember," he said. "About avoiding extinction, for ourselves and this forest."

All the recent positive press seemed to have put the spark of a seasoned PR strategist in his blood, for his manner of arguing had grown discernibly more polished—and clever. "There's a simple three-point explanation for all our direct armed actions," he said, preparing to count on his fingers. "One: All the acts were unavoidable. Two: We pursued every possible alternative means before acting. Three: All the acts were unavoidable."

It was past noon as Randy and I sat down to a lunch of rice and boiled fish on the porch. His plate was loaded down with an enormous fish head. "It's my favorite part," he said when I inquired about the curious serving. "The eyes are best. I love the eyes."

Down at the river, meanwhile, a passel of village dogs was barking hysterically, having chased a deer into the languorous brown current. I went down for a look, watching through brilliant sunshine the deer's antlerless head bob and lurch in a curving trajectory toward the jungle foliage of the far shore.

I returned to carry my now-empty lunch plate inside Randy's house, passing a small and rather spartan living room that included two hammocks hanging from the ceiling and Randy's prized collection of about a thousand English-language books. A self-described "readaholic," he obtained the books from friends in the States and from English-language bookstores in Quito. The library included volumes on jungle botany and first aid, as well as science fiction and a copy of *Robinson Crusoe*.

Back on the porch, Randy's pet woolly monkey, the one with no name, the one Randy was raising after accidently shotgunning the mother for food, was trying to get at Federico's lunch plate. Federico preferred his rice incongruously splashed with ketchup (imported from Quito) and so did the monkey. Amelia shooed the animal away, chasing it off the porch in her unhurried way full of graceful movements and quiet laughter. She was wearing a brightly patterned red-and-green skirt of the sort favored by Cofan women.

I asked Randy if all the recent business with spears and guns at the wells meant he had surrendered the strict pledge of nonviolence of two years ago.

"But we haven't engaged in any acts I would call violent," he replied, offering a look of surprise. "We've used the *possibility* of violent action as leverage, yes, but that's all. Nothing more."

When I brought up the burning of the Zábalo drill platform, he countered with the sort of quick and handy moral rationalization I would hear more of from him on this trip.

"Is it an act of violence for the U.S. Drug Enforcement Agency to burn coca fields in South America? The fields are illegal. They cause harm. They have no right to exist. Why would burning them be an act of violence?"

"What about the weapons, then?" I said. "The possibility of violence as leverage? Is that just a bluff?"

"The only point at which I would use violent action against other human beings," he said, "is if other human beings attempted violence against us. That's why we carry weapons. Self-defense. If someone started firing at us while we made a visit to an illegal well on *our* land, we'd be pretty much in the right to defend ourselves, wouldn't we?"

Yes, I thought, but it was all a lot more complicated—and deadly risky—than he was making it out to be, and I knew he knew it. Rather than push the point, though, I roamed back to the issue of appearances. If the weapons weren't necessarily a bluff, the Cofan's stance before the Ecuadorian public *was*, at least in one respect: As Randy described it, the Indians' official position, the one they fed to the national press, was one of being basically *pro*-oil.

"We came to the conclusion a while back," Randy said, "that there was no way we could say we were flat-out against oil in the Cuyabeno. That would make us against what a lot of people see as the economic good of the country. So we say we have nothing against oil exploration as long as it doesn't harm the environment."

It was a simple declaration—and a masterstroke—and now it had been put in writing. In the Paujil accord, Randy had basically told Petroecuador it could drill on Cofan land—with conditions. Namely, the company would have to provide the Indians with information, lots of it, including an inventory of all chemicals, toxins, and machinery used at well sites, and a list of contingency cleanup plans in case of spills. Upon receipt, the Cofan could meticulously pick the material apart, asking for clarifications here, more information there, raising various objections along the way, perhaps requesting a full environmental-impact study for a particular well site. They would always be able to file suit, meanwhile, using the legal footing carved out in the signed Paujil accord.

In short, the Indians could put up a whole host of bureaucratic and legal obstacles that would cause delays and force Petroecuador to produce either extraordinarily well managed rigs or, better, the Cofan's ultimate goal, abandon the lower Cuyabeno forest altogether.

Indeed, the process of pulling up stakes had perhaps already begun with the Paujil well, though Randy was far from convinced of it. His hunch was that the company was still very much committed to drilling throughout the area. All he knew for sure was that Petroecuador owed the Cofan twenty-five solar panels and he meant to collect them soon, while the momentum was still with the Indians. His plan was to head to Quito at the end of the week and, while there, contact manufacturers in the United States for bids. These he would present in person to company officials at Petroecuador's national headquarters in downtown Quito.

Randy said I was welcome to accompany him on the long canoe and truck ride to the capital. But first I told him I was interested in visiting the Zábalo well site, the one the Cofan had torched, and perhaps taking some photographs. That is, if I could find someone to guide me there.

"Ask Bolívar," Randy said. "He knows the way. He lives on the other side of the village. He's the one building the new house."

Randy then broke things off in an abrupt way that was almost brusque. It was midafternoon. "I'm tired," he said sharply. "I'm sorry. So much English makes me tired. My language is Cofan. I've got to rest now."

I rose, slightly startled, having forgotten for a moment, lured into unawareness by his midwestern U.S. accent, that the man across from me was suspended between states of being: Caucasian-Indian, American-Cofan, Westerner-savage. One consequence of the dichotomy was that I, the one-hundred-percent unadulterated gringo, was work for him.

I took my leave, ambling across the village till I found twenty-six-year-old Bolívar hanging from the skeletal outline of his new house. He was perched high atop the support beam of a second-story wall. He had a lean, angular body that seemed a model for the sturdiness of his carpentry. Across his forehead hung slanting black bangs shiny with sweat. We had met before, briefly, so Bolívar wasn't shy about exploring my usefulness.

"Can you hand me that pole right there?" he said in Spanish, peering down, gesturing toward the ground. "No, not that one. That's for the roof. The other one. From that pile of hardwood poles."

I hoisted up the heavy piece of wood, and Bolívar, with his friendly but somewhat taciturn father Elías perched beside him, lashed it into place using a ropelike vine. The wood they were using—*congiocho* in Cofan—was exceptionally solid and good for building, Bolívar told me. It came from a special stretch of forest upriver, on an island, past Randy's banana field.

Finishing their work, the two men shimmied and swung their way to the ground for handshakes. I noticed that the house they were constructing, though possessing a small foundation like those around it, was going to be the only two-story structure in the entire village.

"I have three sons," Bolívar said when I mentioned this, "and I want many more, maybe ten children altogether. This way they can all stay upstairs while my wife and I, we are downstairs. *Mucho mas tranquillo, no?*"

His square, handsome face gave way just then to a burst of laughter, sending ripples rolling down his loose-hanging tunic all the way to his knees.

It came to me that any man erecting such an ample, solid house for a prospective brood of ten children was not exactly walking weak-kneed into the future. Bolívar, sweat on his brow from the day's work, obviously intended to remain where he was, to prosper where he was, without major changes in the scenery around him. It was such a change from the bleakness I remembered here two years ago when all everyone knew was that the oil company was coming. The company was definitely coming. And sure enough, the company *had* come. But the results were so surprising—one well site in ashes, another abandoned—that for the first time in a long time a man could build a house in Zábalo with some confidence that he'd be around to live in it ten years hence.

"We want to hurry and finish the frame," Bolívar said, turning to survey his work again, "and then the roof, putting on the thatch, so we'll have a place to tie on a solar panel as soon as it arrives."

Like a gleaming, bright hood ornament, I thought.

Bolívar knew I was a writer, and was happy to have me visiting the village. "Randy says *periodistas* are our friends," he volunteered. But when I told him I was interested in making the half-day journey to the Zábalo well site the next morning with him as my guide, Bolívar and his father looked at each other with pained expressions.

"You want to go to the site *in person?*" Bolívar asked.

"Yes," I said. I then watched as my comment set off a fast and spirited conversation in Cofan between the two men.

"Is there a problem?" I asked, not understanding a word they were saying while having to practically duck from all the punctuating hand gestures.

"Oh no," Bolívar finally said. "There's no problem. We should be able to make it there. Don't worry."

It hadn't occurred to me to worry.

"We should be able to make it," he said again.

Then both men turned, looked at each other directly, and added in unison, "If we're lucky."

3

Mauricio thought it was very funny the way I tipped back the calabash bowl of *yoco* tea, swallowed hard, and then did my very best imitation of a wrinkled prune—lips puckering, cheeks puckering, my entire face a maze of crazy folds.

It was 5:30 A.M., barely light, and somewhat naively I was plunging into the Cofan version of a morning cup of java. Made from the shavings of a vine by the same name, *yoco* tea is sickly orange in color, bitter as pure sin, and utterly saturated with caffeine. In Zábalo, Mauricio was the master brewer, rising before everyone else to collect and prepare the vines. Between five and six A.M., all takers teetered sleepily to his house near the center of the village where Jaguar, Mauricio's bossy, pale-eyed cur growled a crotchety greeting to drinkers one by one. I growled a greeting back to the dog, then took my turn at the trough. In his generous, grandfatherly way, Mauricio handed me the calabash. I began drinking. An instant later my mouth and palate were in utter turmoil. I returned the bowl to Mauricio, parting my puckered lips only enough to rasp an insincere thank-you.

When the last of his great undulating laugh had percolated from his chest, Mauricio said in Spanish, "One bowl of this, Mike, and all your sleepiness and night dreams are gone. You've got great force. You move through the forest with power."

My sudden urge to do fifty pushups seemed to confirm the point. I practically sprinted to the river, where Bolívar and Elías were already waiting in their forty-foot canoe. As the amphetaminelike buzz reached full force, I could feel my stomach floating in a pool half tingle, half nausea. Like the outboard motor now rumbling and ready to take us away, Mauricio had pulled my rip cord—and everyone else's. Off we went through the early morning forest, charging wide-eyed with power down the Aguarico.

We were going to need every bit of the energy, too, it seemed. I glanced at our cargo. Bolívar and Elías had littered the canoe front-to-back with the following items: Two wooden paddles, two shotguns, two machetes, three bundles of fishing line with hooks, one handmade harpoon, one heavy, big-bladed ax, and one portly pot of *chucula* guarded by Bolívar's wife, Norma, a quiet, corpulent woman with kind eyes. Clearly we were going to do more than just inspect a well site that day. The purpose of all the items seemed pretty much self-explanatory, except one. The ax. What did we need an ax for?

We reached the Zábalo River ten minutes later, gliding into its narrow width and black tannic murk, pointing ourselves upstream. Veils of faint morning mist lingered in the trees, and in the air hung a smell almost like fresh bread dough, though more refined than that, sweeter, like the thick, pleasant smell of cake batter. Orchids were the source of the fragrance, and now I could see them, dozens in several directions, red and blue and pink, homesteading on the boughs and trunks of trees, offering their nectar wells to passing hummingbirds and thirsty bees.

I was able to enjoy this sight for only a moment before we rounded a bend and it became ruefully clear why we had brought the ax. Randy had told me that, under good conditions, getting to the Zábalo well site involved about two hours of river travel and an hour and a half of overland hiking. But we weren't facing good river conditions that day. The dry season, normally extending from mid-November to mid-February, had arrived a bit early this year. No significant rain had fallen for several weeks, dramatically lowering the water level of this tributary and leaving the impression that some giant hand had gone up and down either shore in cosmic mischief, deliberately pushing trees into the water to keep us from reaching our destination. The trees were harmlessly underwater most of the year, wholly submerged, having fallen as the result of bank erosion or natural death. But with the low waterline they were now visible as far as we could see upriver, ours to get past, around, and over for the next fifteen miles. A smaller canoe might have been more helpful, but it was regular practice in Zábalo to use the village's longer community-owned canoe for guiding visitors through the Cofan forest.

After a few crafty S-turns past clumps of debris, we came quickly to the first real impediment. Bolívar stopped the canoe. He stood up and with his trim, sinewy body seemed to lean into the scene, eyes squinting below his bangs. A partially submerged tree trunk was lying horizontally three-quarters of the way across the river, its protruding edge rising a good twelve inches above the water. The rest of the river's width was gummed up by the upturned root system of another tree. It was a wall, in other words, from shore to shore. I groaned at having to turn back so soon, stymied right out of the block.

But neither Bolívar nor Elías prepared me for what happened next. Indeed, I thought something was terribly wrong the way Bolívar, after assessing the situation, sat down and began gunning the outboard, sending us racing directly toward the horizontal trunk. The closer we got, the more diabolically insane I realized he was. We were going to smash head-long into the trunk. Instinctively, I began bracing for the collision. But upon impact, instead of collapsing in an explosion of splintered wood, the tapered hull of the canoe rose up out of the water and began climbing the trunk. Elías and I, sitting in the front half of the canoe, were suddenly air-borne, literally riding through air as the vessel continued gliding up and over the trunk. Reaching the halfway point, we began to descend just as Bolívar and Norma, who were in the rear, began to rise, the canoe pivoting in a giant seesaw fashion. Bolívar instantly unlocked the motor and tilted the shaft out of the water so it wouldn't strike the trunk as momentum carried us the rest of the way over. Elías and I, gripping the gunwales tightly with our hands, smacked sharply back into the water with a splash, followed by Bolívar and Norma sliding down behind us.

The bizarre, unexpected maneuver left my heart pinwheeling inside my chest. Water dripped down my shirt from the splash. "Bolívar!" I said. "Is that . . . is that *safe*?"

"Why?" he asked calmly. "Did you almost fall out of the canoe?"

"No. But . . ."

Before I could finish the sentence, Bolívar was speeding up again, heading toward another half-submerged tree trunk, and the whole process repeated itself, the big seesawing motion to the other side. As odd as it seemed, this procedure was clearly going to be routine for the trip, and with effort I tried adopting my companions' obvious equanimity with the method.

We received the gift of perhaps one hundred yards of clear passage before hitting the next obstruction: A rotting trunk that required a few thundering ax blows from Elías leaning over the bow. A hundred yards more and we came to a real shocker. A gargantuan mahogany had fallen all the way across the river, too big to chop in half, too high out of the water to seesaw up and over. There was absolutely no way forward this time, nothing that could be done, and again I heaved a groan of pained disappointment.

But Bolívar, on a hunch, maneuvered toward the base of the fallen tree on the shoreline, where we discovered the tree's uprooting had left a crater so huge it had filled with river water, forming a sort of small bay. With a lot of pulling and paddling, we managed somehow to float the canoe through the crater, literally steering it around the root end of the tree, an act that gave me a new sense of the scale of the Amazon's handiwork.

No respite followed. We came next to a shore-to-shore mess of thin trunks and tangled branches that forced us all into the chest-high water to push and prod the canoe through. We'd been struggling upriver for more than an hour now and we'd gone only a few miles—and I was beginning to face the fact that the whole process was getting very much on my nerves. My Western need for brisk linear progress toward a specific, guaranteed end was taking a whipping. Bolívar and Elías had no such problems as far as I could see. "Three or four hours, maybe," Bolívar said cheerfully when I asked him how much more of this we had to look forward to. Elías, who was handsome in an aging, rugged sort of way, nodded in agreement. He was generally less talkative than his son Bolívar and simply nodded several more times to tell me not to worry. The idea of a journalist photographing for the world to see the righteous ashes of Cofan protest had caught hold of them, I think, and now they were determined to see the thing through. So we kept pushing. "Not to worry," Bolívar said.

For the next hour we did so much seesawing up and over trees—the trunks were growing more numerous the farther we traveled—that I started getting a sort of wobbly-headed seesaw sickness. I was able to recuperate only when obstructing trunks too high to pass over forced us to stop for ax work. One exceptionally large tree held us up for quite a while, with everyone taking whacks in turn. Only humor assuaged the difficulty of the work.

A loud splash sounded upriver while I was chopping, and I turned to investigate.

"Jaguar!" Bolívar said excitedly. "Very big jaguar!"

"*Really?*" I replied, crooking my neck to see. I felt a prick of fear, and then heard nothing at all for a long moment before my companions dissolved into gales of laughter at my panic over nothing more spectacular than a diving bird.

Later, a similar splash sounded. "Jaguar!" I said, hip to the gag now and playing along for a laugh.

"No, no, no!" Bolívar said with sharp and startling seriousness. Lines of fear crossed his face. It was no joke this time. The Cofan men stared at each other. "Caiman!" they said in unison. "Caiman!"

Again I crooked my neck wildly, trying to catch a glimpse of the giant reptile. Again my companions melted into uproarious laughter at my response—this time over a big, bad falling branch.

I feigned a sulk that was half smile, trying to be a good sport, then took a seat on the shore. Bolívar had a go with the ax, meanwhile, and as he worked I noticed the tattoo on his left arm. It was a sleek, black condor with wings extended in flight. He had made the tattoo himself, he told me, using a needle and his own ink. The almost sinister-looking bird actually helped him through his hitch in the Ecuadorian army, giving him an added look of strength and courage during that longest, most unhappy year of his life, he said. He had joined the army out of curiosity mostly—and to improve his Spanish—but he spent most of his time on tedious guard duty in Lago Agrio, the biggest, filthiest, most raucous of Ecuador's jungle oil-boom towns. He left a year later wanting nothing more to do with that world of loud bars and dirty roads and pushy whores and honking horns and swindling merchants. A *blanco* merchant can smell a forest Indian coming from ten kilometers off, Bolívar said, and assumes he's too ignorant to notice the suddenly doubled price or the last-second switch to shoddy goods.

Not that Bolívar had much money to begin with. A scam among army officials required recruits to recycle three-quarters of their seventy-dollar monthly paycheck back into the pockets of staff officers for the bad food the army provided. It galled Bolívar to have to pay for his food. He missed the world of his fellow Cofan. He missed hunting and fishing for his livelihood.

"Do you know what the two favorite ways to fish are among *colonos?*" he asked me. "Poison and dynamite, that's what. Can you believe it? I've seen it. I've seen a man toss a stick of dynamite into water to kill fish. I've seen one pour a cup of tick poison into a stream and then all the fish die as far as you can see, hundreds and hundreds of them die—and the *colono* collects them. But then the whole stream is dead too, everything poisoned, for maybe a year. It's terrible."

Mustered out of the army in 1987, Bolívar moved directly to Zábalo, where Randy was just getting the new Cofan community started, leading willing families away from the oil depredations around Dureno. Randy had always been an uncle figure to Bolívar. The two had hunted and fished together since Bolívar's earliest years, and in the early 1980s, when Randy began bringing in groups of gringo backpackers and scientists for forest treks, Bolívar served as a steadfast aide-de-camp, filling roles ranging from guide to stevedore to cook. In the process, Randy more or less helped raise him to adulthood, serving as a sort of second father. The loyalty and affection were fierce and obvious in Bolívar's eyes as he spoke of these ties. Not that the relationship was surprising given the common cultural footing. According to Bolívar, Randy knew as much about Cofan ways as most of the Indians and actually spoke the language with greater breadth and fluency than did Bolívar himself, a blood Cofan.

As he continued to chop, I asked Bolívar some pointed questions about the future. His two-story house notwithstanding, what realistically were the Cofan's chances of continuing their forest way of life at Zábalo? Was he optimistic about the odds?

His response was to bring up the subject of poison again.

"If Petroecuador ever finishes a well here," he said sullenly, "and builds a road into our forest, then the *colonos* will come here. That is certain. And sooner or later, one of the *colonos* is going to pour a cup of tick poison in our river, our Zábalo River, and there will be no more fish. And then we will be hungry. And then we can't live here anymore the way we do now."

Which is precisely why Bolívar helped burn the Zábalo well platform.

"We have to show Petroecuador that the Cofan people are a very brave people, or else they won't listen to us seriously about anything we say. Whatever happens in the future, we have to stay brave. We have to make them fear us. When they look at the Zábalo well now, all burned down, that's what they do: They fear us. And if they feel that way, we might have a good future."

Progress continued on the downed tree, meanwhile, with Elías taking over. He kept spitting in his hands, rubbing them together, and then chopping away like some brawny lumberjack cliché. Finally the log creaked and cracked and gave way, and we were off again.

The midmorning sunshine was pouring down hotly now, giving an extra brilliance to the yellow-blooming mimosa trees on each shore and an extra edge to our thirst, which we doused with a round of *chucula*.

Our moods soured dramatically, despite the refreshment, as we rounded the next bend.

"This one we'll never get past," Elías said in disgust.

"This one's impossible," Bolívar said.

Before us was an obstructing tree twice as thick as the last, its top side thrusting a good eighteen inches out of the water, too high to seesaw. There was only one possibility.

"Can't we chop it?" I asked Bolívar as we pulled to a halt on the adjacent bank.

"You try," he said, handing me the ax.

Never in my life have I even dreamed of wood so hard. The ax blade literally bounced off the trunk, leaving my arms stinging from the positively rebuffed blow.

"*Chuncho*," Bolívar said. "That's what it's called. Hurt your arms, didn't it? It's a type of cedar tree. Just like a rock."

And like a rock, my spirits plummeted. We were really finished this time. KO'ed by a *chuncho* tree. Bolívar and Norma sat morosely atop the offending log. Elías stomped off dejectedly to take a pee in the forest. I lay on my back on the sandy bank, hat over my face, resting up for the grinding trip back, deflated beyond measure. Even this far upriver it would take forever to proceed on foot to the well site, Bolívar said. There was nothing to do but turn around—period—and my brain shuddered at the thought: All those trees we had crossed, all the chopping, all the hours of seesawing—only to be redone in empty-handed return.

We'd better leave soon, too, I realized, if we wanted to make it back before sunset. But Elías was taking an inordinately long time relieving himself. He seemed to be dawdling, in fact, something that upset me, given the work ahead of us. Then, inexplicably, I heard a chopping sound from somewhere in the direction he had wandered. A machete was striking wood. When finally Elías emerged from the forest, he was carrying a bright orange, one-by-three-foot piece of what appeared to be a kind of tree bark. He held it up to show Bolívar, and there was a quick conversation in Cofan followed by a sort of "why not?" shrug from Bolívar.

"Sometimes we try this," Bolívar said to me, wading into the river and draping the swatch of mystery substance over a central spot atop the blockading trunk. The substance was indeed tree bark, though very peculiar. Its interior side was the slickest, wettest, slimiest, spongiest thing I had ever touched in my life. The bark was from a cycopria tree—*dondo fa* in Cofan—a softwood whose leaves are favored by Amazon sloths, Bolívar said.

Just how it was supposed to help us was unclear until, with Bolívar directing things, we positioned ourselves two on each side of the very long and heavy and wide canoe. The goal was to grip the gunwales firmly with both hands and, on command, begin pushing with all our might. We would rush the canoe bow toward the bark, hoping that with enough muscle power we could glide the vessel up and over the lubricant to the other side of the tree. It would be seesawing without the inhibiting weight of passengers—but also without the assistance of a motor.

I had my doubts even as Bolívar gave the order, "*Uno, dos, tres—ivamooooos!*"

We made our charge. We rushed toward the downed tree, aiming carefully for our target. Skeptical to the end, I had the sense of approaching a brick wall. The tree was much farther out of the water than any we'd faced before. I was girding for a crash, afraid the canoe would crack and fall to pieces, when suddenly the one-ton vessel hit its mark and, magically, dramatically, began to rise as if of its own power. The Vaseline-like properties of the *dondo fa* bark truly defied belief. Indeed, the bark seemed to offer less resistance than the water, meaning the pushing actually became—for a moment—*easier*, even though the canoe was now being forced uphill, as it were.

But within seconds gravity caught up with the proceedings, and we began struggling mightily to maintain our forward motion. Our initial progress forced us into a steady grouping toward the rear, where we now pushed madly, trying to reach that midway-point-plus-one-inch when the canoe would slide down the other side on its own.

But we failed. The canoe sputtered to a mind-paralyzing halt two feet from the pivotal center. Straining just to hold this position, to keep the canoe from sliding back toward us, required supreme effort. Yet somehow Bolívar found the breath, and the rest of us the strength, to address the situation: *"Uno, dos, tres—¡Vamoooos!"*

Reserve muscles I didn't know I had came into play—panic power, adrenalin fuel—and I pushed harder than I'd pushed anything in my life. The sounds of my Cofan companions, pained mutterings vague in my ears, let me know they were doing the same. Our progress was measured in inches now. Closer and closer, inch by inch, we drew toward the critical divide. And when we hit it, we knew it. The rear of the canoe began to thrust sharply upward, out of our hands, and the whole vessel slid away from us with absolute ease, splashing into the water on the other side as we watched.

Then we screamed. In triumph. In delight. We exchanged back slaps, and with cupped hands I launched a pool of river water into the air that rained down upon us in cool, sparkling congratulations. We clambered over the downed tree, another challenge met, and prepared for forward movement. At the last moment, wisely, Bolívar reached back and tossed our saving, slippery tree bark into the canoe. "In case we need it again," he said.

That one little sentence was enough to yank me down from the giddy high of the moment. It turned my thoughts from celebration back to boiling worry. From trip's start, I'd been unable to avoid viewing all the fallen trees in our path as double-edged swords, each waiting to draw blood upon the second chance of our return. The farther we went, the more they accumulated behind us, of course—and the thought was really gnawing at me: Weren't we covering more ground than we could hope to retrace in a day?

"Not if we hurry," Bolívar said when I asked. He then pulled the motor's rip cord to send us again on our way.

But instead of rumbling to a start, the motor did nothing—and for some reason Bolívar's effort at pulling almost sent him flying backward into the water. He regained his balance in time for the rest of us to see, with horror, the problem: He was holding the entire rip cord in his hand. He had yanked it off the pulley, detaching it from the motor completely.

The wailing began.

"Oh, no," Elías said.

"I'll be damned," I stammered in English.

Bolívar pried off the motor cover and stared at the machinery in disbelief. A quick inspection made clear the impossibility of repair. There was no way to start the motor now. My worst-case fear of heading back without even the help of a little underwater horsepower began pounding at my temples.

But just then, with incongruous calm, Norma motioned for Bolívar to hand her the cord. While we men kept up the groaning over our loss, over all the wasted work of coming this far only to turn around empty-handed, she quietly went to work. A look of complete focus suffused her big, round face. Her cheeks, smooth and ruddy and fleshy in that way common to many Cofan, grew moist with perspiration as her fingers busied themselves with the task at hand. It was never entirely clear to me what she did, but after a few moments, by some mystical combination of tying and weaving, she seemed to have put some sort of knot at the end of the cord.

She handed it back to Bolívar who reinserted it and pulled. It worked. The engine started. We were off again, whooping with relief. I might have been forgiven for thinking us invincible by this point. We seemed destined—cosmically preordained, our stars lined up—to reach the well site that day. So when we arrived in short order at another huge, blockading tree, I didn't panic. With the aid of the slippery bark and some more resolute pushing, I knew we would make it over.

And we did. But this time when the motor wouldn't restart on the other side, it wasn't the rip cord. It was something worse. Again Bolívar pried loose the cover and looked inside. After a few minutes he replaced the cover and I knew it was over—*really* over. At several points that morning, facing the worst obstacles, he had said things like, "This is impossible," or "We'll never get past this one,"—which I soon grew to understand meant, "This will be hard, but I think we'll make it."

On this occasion, though, Bolívar broke out the paddles and said, dispiritedly and with certitude, "Time to go home."

The problem was small, basic, and devastating: The spark plug was dead. Bolívar had pulled it out and replaced it with a backup he'd brought along. But it, too, was dead. There was nothing to be done. It was that simple. "Time to go home." I would have gladly gone aft and axed the motor into tiny pieces had I not known I would need every last particle of my energy for the awful return trip. Bolívar, prince of understatement, kept saying, "Bad day, Mike. Bad motor, bad river, bad day." I think he thought he was consoling me.

We were all in a torpid state of shock now, mentally numb and disbelieving of our changed fortune. No one said much, consequently, as one after the other, using the slippery bark, we heaved the canoe up and over the two very difficult trees we had just surmounted going the other way.

It was past noon, and sunlight was pelting the river with blistering intensity. Even if we paddled steadily, Bolívar said, there was exactly zero chance we'd reach the village before nightfall. We had no flashlight, matches, or candles, either.

To adjust, mentally and physically, to the altered circumstances, I suggested we take a brief shore break. Bolívar agreed, beaching the canoe in a deep pool of riverside shade. We decided to fish for a while, casually tossing out line, but my heart wasn't in it and I kept getting my line hung up on submerged branches, making my mood worse.

It was then that Elías began signaling for silence. He detected some sort of noise in the forest.

"Monkeys," he said, cocking his head to one side. He was sure of it.

He and Bolívar grabbed their single-barrel shotguns, and Norma and I followed them into the jungle interior. Shotguns had become an increasingly popular hunting weapon among the Cofan in the past twenty years, in part out of necessity. Curare, the tree resin used for poisoning the tips of blowgun darts and historically obtained from jungle traders in Colombia, was now in great demand as a medicinal muscle relaxant in the West, making it scarce and expensive for the Cofan.

Elías led the way into the forest, shotgun on one side, machete on the other, singlehandedly cutting a trail through the undergrowth as fast as he could walk, slicing and slicing, never breaking his stride. He was almost too efficient and flawless to be real.

We were hunting now, and for a moment the sudden excitement of the quest, combined with the sun-dappled grandeur of the verdant forest, restored my flagging spirit. Fragile beams of light fell all around us, streaking through the luxuriant canopy overhead to illuminate epiphytic mosses spread like watercolors across trees—red and orange and yellow and violet.

But we soon lost the sound of the monkeys and came to a halt. The river was no longer in sight, and I wasn't sure in which direction it lay. As we stood at the end of this blind alley, wondering what had gone wrong, Bolívar detected the grunt of a tapir somewhere in the distance—and suddenly we had another mammal to pursue. He and Elías put keen ears and eyes to work, probing in all directions, casting about for more clues.

Standing apart from the men, watching as now they gestured and discussed in spirited Cofan which way to go, I realized that with the physical switch to the forest interior the Indians had made a shift in states of mind as well. At warp speed their senses processed hundreds of bits of data altogether hidden from me, the visiting gringo, the man doing all he could just to keep up. A vague hoofprint on the forest floor, a broken stick in an unnatural posture, a line of droppings here, a whiff of odors there—all were part of the expert tracking that led them to their prey as well as led them back out of the jungle, never getting lost on return. The Indians' presence here was as natural and graceful as the spread of monstrous trees in every direction. These were not visitors, not in a forest hosting Amerindian inhabitants for perhaps as long as 50,000 years, a stay which had nearly the aspect of geologic time. It would have been as easy to contemplate the absence of kapok trees and macaws and river dolphins here as that of Bolívar and Elías in their *ondiccuje* tunics, cupping their ears to better hear their prey, wrinkling their noses to smell the forest's clues. The men were part of the scenery. They *belonged*. It wouldn't have been a proper rain forest without them.

Bolívar chose a direction and off we went in pursuit of the tapir. It was a good sign that we passed half-devoured fruit from mauritia palms along the ground, a favorite food of both tapirs and peccaries. And now the hoofprints were so clear even I could see them. For a long time we followed the prints, pushing farther and farther into the forest, which became denser the deeper we traveled into it—and concomitantly darker. It became so dark at one point that usually nocturnal mosquitoes, thinking it their witching hour, began attacking us in swarms each time we paused.

This deep forest dimness didn't last long. Up ahead a wide band of bright sunlight was gushing down through the middle of the forest. It was a clearing of some sort, and we were getting gradually closer to it. At first I thought it was the river, but when we finally reached the space, I was completely perplexed, unsure what I was seeing. It seemed to be a road of some sort, a very narrow, perfectly straight road, with neatly chain-sawed tree stumps left unaccountably in place all across its surface.

"Seismic testing," Bolívar said, looking over his shoulder just then to explain to me. "The company did this. It's the trail they used for their explosions."

So this was what it looked like, I thought. The trail was wider than I had imagined, measuring more than ten feet from side to side. It stretched as far as I could see in both directions, the sawed trees themselves felled into the adjacent forest. I understood now, as never before, the warnings of rain-forest biologists who emphasize the strain such trails cause in the form of plant-population fragmentation and the long-term dispersal of certain canopy-dwelling animals and insects and birds. The trails were an utter eyesore to the Cofan, besides. Cleared strips like this ran in a loose grid across large portions of the Indians' land now, totaling several hundred miles. In their geometric exactness and steamroller completeness, nothing could have looked less natural in the free-for-all poetry of the forest.

The job of making these trails wasn't an easy one. At very low wages, oil companies operating in the Ecuadorian jungle regularly employ unskilled Indians from nearby tribes to perform the task. Equipped with machetes, chain saws, and rarely more to eat than just rice and beans, the Indians are dropped into the forest by helicopter and left for weeks at a time to slash miles of trails under primitive camp conditions. Dysentery, accidents, and exposure to chilling rain are common features of the work.

Once the trails are complete, the explosions begin—one explosion every 300 meters, detonated in holes twenty meters deep. The huge eruptions of sound give a seismic profile of oil reserves below ground—and wreak havoc on wildlife above ground, injuring and/or scattering a myriad of species that break away in mad, panicked flight. Along lakes and rivers, as many as 500 fish can be killed from the shock waves of a single seismic explosion.

Once the blasts are over and the seismic crews have vacated the jungle, the remaining trails in their unnaturally naked state are often susceptible to severe erosion, which further compounds the disruption to the forest. After plant life finally takes hold, the results can be equally problematic. The uncustomarily wide and uniform openings along continuous lines foster rapid and fantastically dense growth among young plants vying fiercely for sunlight. The plants eventually succeed in forming literal walls of tangled, dense vegetation inpenetrable by men with machetes, much less forest animals roaming in search of food.

These disruptive "fences," which can last for years, are a final, lingering wound in the assault that is seismic testing. The whole process—a step-by-step, comprehensive trauma to the forest ecosystem—happens before the first exploratory well sinks its drill a single foot into the soil.

By chance, the tapir tracks we were following that afternoon spilled for a short distance onto the seismic trail we'd just stumbled onto. As we walked along the cleared avenue, following the prints, we passed several small metal signs nailed at intervals to trees. The signs bore company measurement numbers and code letters related to the testing. I noticed that over several of these signs, using *achiote* paint, the Zábalo Indians had written in tall letters: COMMUNIDAD COFAN. It was another way of making their presence felt. The color of the paint was blood red.

We soon left the seismic trail for some very hard tracking back into the forest. The tapir was now taking us in and out of steep-banked, muddy streams and standing pools of swampy water. Up front, Elías continued his brisk machete work, leading us to all manner of naturally fallen trees which we crawled over or under, according to the trees' size. My eyeglasses kept fogging up badly, meanwhile, like a mirror after a shower—a condition brought on by my own heavy perspiration and the almost soupy forest humidity all around.

Then the tapir tracks petered out. We lost the animal. There were no more sounds to follow, either. Another dead end. Given how far we had strayed from the river, I was almost glad for this second dose of failure.

Just how we would have gotten a 200-pound tapir from this distant spot to the canoe was beyond me.

Yet no sooner had we made an about face, retracing a few of our steps, than Bolívar and Elías stopped and began taking deep breaths through their noses. "Smell that?" Bolívar asked me, still inhaling deeply. "Smell that? Peccaries. Lots of them."

I used my nose to its fullest capacity, but failed to detect anything in the air indicating that a bevy of large-tusked, wire-haired, piglike creatures was near. Not that anyone was seeking my confirmation. The next thing I knew, Bolívar, Elías, and Norma—without any notice—were disappearing in a virtual sprint to my right, fading into the jungle. Here we go again, I thought, as I commanded my legs to do everything they could to keep up.

Our quarry was very close this time, the pursuit red hot. There was no time for clearing any semblance of a trail with the machete. The rules changed to every person for himself. Leafy branches whipped across my face. Hanging vines nicked my shoulders and arms. Unseen divots in the soil caused missteps. I was aware of vague human figures bounding and darting up ahead of me, and, for fear of being abandoned more than anything else, I stumbled and bumbled my way forward, staying more or less within sight of the figures.

Then, abruptly, the Cofan stopped and I reached them. Bolívar and Elías cocked their ears and whispered to each other while I tried catching my breath. But too soon, they were off again, bolting away. We splashed through a swampy area, then plunged into some very thick foliage that left an odd scratchy feeling in my throat as if, in the act of plowing face first through the branches and leaves, I had swallowed some delicate, feathery forest thing.

We came to another steep-banked stream across which a fallen tree acted as a convenient bridge—for the Cofan. For me it was impossibly narrow. The Indians scurried across with mystifying dexterity while I threw myself into a crashing slide down one bank, sloshed through the current, then flung myself up the muddy far slope before redoubling my running pace to catch the others.

Then we stopped again. We really stopped. We stopped because we were almost on top of our prey. Bolívar and Elías stood stock-still, fingers to their lips to indicate silence as they surveyed the surroundings with their ears. It was clearly the point at which absolute stealth and quiet were at a premium, but the vexing hair ball or whatever it was lodged in my throat was threatening to jeopardize our cover. The urge to clear my windpipe with a huge, satisfying cough was almost overwhelming, and repressing it literally brought tears to my eyes. I held out as long as I could for the sake of the group, but then a short, muffled cough escaped.

Everyone turned to me with fingers pressed to their lips, eyebrows arched in irritation, silently telling me that the peccaries were oh so close. I shrugged apologetically just as three very loud, full-bodied coughs burst forth which were no doubt at that moment scaring away every peccary with functioning ears for miles around. Bolívar gave me a disgusted look just before leading us on another short sprint. We stopped again, and again I coughed idiotically, but by this point it didn't seem to matter because we were so close that even I could smell the peccaries. It was a thick, mildly unpleasant scent that filled my nose, a muskiness mingled with what vaguely resembled the pungent bite of human body odor.

We were moving again, this time through thick mud. Bolívar and Elías, shotguns drawn, were running in a crouch, so I did the same. I could hear animal grunts up ahead now, and when I looked I saw pig figures flashing and scrambling, running away. Bolívar turned sharply to the left and disappeared at the same moment Elías stopped, stood, aimed, and fired. The explosion reverberated through the forest, drawing shrieks from a group of toucans overhead. I followed Elías forward to a downed peccary weighing at least eighty pounds. It lay on its side, rear legs twitching violently from a bleeding, mortal wound to the head. Its cylindrical black snout was stained red with blood just above the long, curving yellow tusks with the pointed tips.

Panting from the run, my chest heaving, I took in the sight while Elías grabbed a long, thin branch from a nearby palm tree. He jammed the branch into his shotgun muzzle, ejecting the spent shell from the breech end of the barrel—a necessity with this simple model. He reloaded, but by now the rest of the peccaries were gone—as was Bolívar, who was in hot pursuit.

Elías and Norma busied themselves gathering vines of varying widths and lengths to tie the now-motionless pig into a crescent shape, a hind leg threaded through the tied-shut jaws. A thicker vine rose from either end of this arrangement and formed a U that served as a sort of carrying handle or sling. This allowed the peccary to be carried on Elías' back, anchored by the slinglike vine, which would be looped over his head to come to rest across his front shoulders.

As the peccary was being so prepared, another shotgun blast sounded a short distance away. Bolívar had finally drawn a bead on others in the pack. We set off in that direction as a second shot boomed, then a third—and by the time we arrived, three peccaries lay dead at Bolívar's feet, victims of flawless marksmanship. While they collected more vines for transport, all three Indians burst into their native Cofan, reliving the hunt several times over with descriptive hand gestures and theatrical speech—the benedictory habit of newly successful hunters everywhere.

It was probably just as well I couldn't understand the particulars of what was being said. My brain was elsewhere, already focused on the disturbing arithmetic and geography of our situation. With his deadly aim, Bolívar had dropped two adult peccaries indistinguishable in size from Elías'—about eighty pounds—plus an offspring caught in the melee weighing roughly fifteen pounds, a poodle-sized runt. So there we were with our game more than a mile, it turned out, from the river. In all, there were four of us human beings, three men and a woman. And there were four peccaries, three adults and the poodle-sized pip-squeak baby.

In one respect, the Cofan Indians were different from most of the traditional peoples I had visited in my life. Women were not exploited here as de facto mules, routinely given the hardest physical labor, as in, say, most of Africa. Cofan men tended to share in the heaviest lifting, the toughest grunt work. More than this, though, it was my own vanity, my own old-fashioned or New Age (take your pick) sense that a man was a man with certain responsibilities no matter what the culture or situation, that led me to reject two possibilities. I would not watch Norma moan under the heft of a brawny adult peccary while I skipped to the river with the lithe poodle dangling around my neck. Nor would I abide the sight of Bolívar or Elías making two trips in order to transport all three adult peccaries between the two of them.

That left one option.

"I'll carry a big one," I told Bolívar. "Give it to me."

The same question had been on his mind, I could tell, as he finished tying up the last peccary. Both he and Elías had been casting speculative glances my way in an apparent effort to assess my mettle. Was the gringo going to resolve this awkward situation with honor? their eyes seemed to ask.

"It's very heavy, Mike," Bolívar said, skepticism in his voice. "Are you sure you want it?"

"Give it to me," I repeated.

Bolívar lifted one of the peccaries, and I slipped my head through the vine loop, the vine itself coming to rest across my chest and around my shoulders. When he let go completely, I grew very confused. It was an eerie shock to feel the warmth of the peccary's body heat, not yet diminished, spreading across my back. But it was the weight, the astonishing leaden weight resting suddenly on my spine, that made me think for a moment that Bolívar, too, was piggybacking atop my frame as a prank. When I swung slowly around, however, and saw Bolívar standing five paces off, staring back at me with a look of deep concern, I knew I was in a fix of Mayday proportions.

The problem wasn't the weight alone—though the weight *was* like carrying a small person on my back. The problem was just as much the technique. I could already feel the anchoring front vine of this minimalist Indian backpack digging sharply into my shoulders. The vine had a discomfiting straightjacket effect, lashing my upper arms like cement to my torso, leaving my limbs all but useless for maintaining balance. I found that in order to walk at all I had to lace my thumbs through the front of the vine and lean significantly forward. But then the awkward shape of the peccary itself came into play, the contours of whose skull I could feel in painful profile against my upper back.

Carrying so much weight in such a fashion for more than a mile might have been a survivable ordeal had the land before us been flat, dry, and unobstructed. But of course it was none of these things. All I had to do was walk one hundred feet with the peccary—struggling in a waddling fashion through thick mud and around a fallen tree—and I knew I'd never make it even halfway to the river.

But I tried. I put one foot in front of the other and followed Bolívar, Elías, and Norma to the last stream we had crossed. There, despite their own charges, the Indians tightroped along the same narrow log as before. Then I crossed my way. Without the use of my arms, I somehow slid down the near bank to the stream and entered the water. Wading through, though, the mud was so thick that my left foot, with a protracted sucking sound, came sliding completely out of my boot. The boot itself remained mired in the gook. Bolívar had to retrieve it and put it back on my foot for me when—by some miracle—I made it to the top of the far bank on my own.

Everything became a blur after these ugly opening moves. It was a strange slow-motion torture of forward movement full of blood, sweat, and mosquitoes, of long waddles through stagnant swamps, of tricky footing on strained knees, of almost, almost, almost falling with every tenth step. I slipped badly coming out of the next stream and only at the last second freed my thumb from under the straightjacket vine in time to grab the closest tree around to steady myself. But the narrow trunk I reached for was a peculiar species of palm with needlelike thorns protruding thick as hair from its bark. Bolívar turned around just in time to see me pulling three of the thorns from my palm with my teeth—and I realized I was embarrassing myself more with this mammoth adult on my back than if I'd carried the poodle.

Bolívar couldn't have agreed more, I'm sure, though he was trying to be delicate.

"Just put it down," he kept saying, only a soupçon of scorn in his voice. "It's heavy. Let my wife carry it for a while. It's okay."

But idiotically, the weaker I became from the beating and the fatigue of the march, the more obsessed I grew with making it to the river. I've long since given up trying to explain it, for the drive far outstripped any Western sense of finish-what-you-start Puritanism. Some shmo in a lab coat might have homed in on an inordinate fear of failure—and been close to the mark. But whatever the case, my thinking grew as piggish as the meat on my back: I *had* to reach the canoe with this lashed-on cargo or I'd never be able to face myself in the mirror reflection of the Zábalo River again.

"I'll make it," I kept telling Bolívar after each of his appeals. "I'll make it."

But to continue trying I had to resort to an even slower pace, a walking crawl, really. Elías and Norma broke off for the river, leaving Bolívar behind to tend to me. Every time I looked up he was standing still, waiting for me, barely stooped under the weight of his own pig, his taut body a work of steel that silently mocked the wreck of my own arms and legs. I began resting every fifty yards now, discovering that if I stopped and bent far forward, I could table the peccary on my back, relieving the pressure on my shoulders and neck. As for the carrying vine across my front shoulders, which was now digging and scraping into my skin to the point of drawing blood, I tried padding it by stuffing copious amounts of leaves between it and my flesh. That this didn't help wasn't important after a while when the entire area became utterly numb. I lost all sensation across my shoulders.

I'm not sure how I made the last quarter mile. We crossed the perverse sunlit scar of the seismic trail, then entered the dense, dark stretch of trees where mosquitoes attacked us without pardon. With my arms immobilized by the vine, I could do little to swat the insects away. Nor could I reach up and remove my glasses when they again became fogged to uselessness. Bolívar removed the glasses for me, an act that dramatically reduced my ability to see the approach of face-level branches and other nuisances. My head became a punching bag.

In the deep mud of the next creek bed I lost my boot a second time. I pulled myself out of the creek with enormous effort, one foot exposed, and called up to Bolívar. He turned and stared—and despite obvious effort he couldn't stifle a laugh at the hump-backed, mud-splattered, half-blind gringo covered with mosquitoes limping toward him with just one boot on, cursing a wild streak of English bad words. It was my rock-bottom bottom. I didn't try to hide it. Bolívar went back to fetch the boot, still chuckling to himself, while I paused to table the peccary on my back for a breather.

And that's when I quit. I tossed in the towel—finally. This was preposterous, I realized. I was faint with exhaustion, close to collapse. What exactly was the point?

I was just about to sling the lead-weight peccary onto the ground when, still hunched over, I saw two muddy feet step into my frame of vision. They were Elías' feet. He had reached the river, deposited his peccary in the canoe, and come back.

"How far is it?" I asked him, still bent over, still staring down at his feet, unable to stand just yet.

"Close," he said. "Give me your animal."

Somehow I straightened my spine. Still carrying the pig, I stepped back into the boot Bolívar was now holding for me like Cinderella's suitor.

"I'll make it," I said. "I want to make it."

Bolívar grimaced. "But Mike, you can't . . ."

I started walking.

Cruelly, just as victory seemed nearest, the pain was greatest, cracking out all over my body during those last few stubborn steps. Up ahead, I could see a clearing. It was getting closer, bigger. There was more sunlight. Then the river was before me, down one last sloping bank, which I negotiated in one last rump slide, reaching the beached canoe. I maneuvered my fanny to a gunwale, wobbled slightly, and then unloaded my charge in a loud thunk to the floor. I then made my own thunk on the sandy shore, lying on my back, limp with relief, smiling despite the lingering hurt. I was too spent to whoop or otherwise vocalize the fact that, inwardly, my soul was doing a pirouette of utter joy against a backdrop of happy, booming fireworks.

I looked up and saw Bolívar and Elías bending over me, silhouetted against the sky, grinning down at me.

"*Gracias,*" Bolívar said. "*Muchas gracias,* Mike. *Muchas gracias* for carrying the pig."

"*De nada,*" I managed.

"Rest now," he said. "Rest a long time. It's okay."

"I'm not a Cofan," I whispered back.

The men were still peering down, straining to hear. "What?" they asked.

"I'm not a Cofan," I repeated. "I don't know how you do these things."

This comment struck them as absolutely hilarious for some reason and the men laughed uncontrollably, and for the rest of the day they kept asking me, "Mike, are you a Cofan?" and I'd say "no" and they'd laugh some more.

We all rested there on the riverbank for a while, reposing long enough to face up to the implacable fact: We were still a long way from the village without a motor and now with 250 pounds of added peccary meat to contend with. The latter point became a factor the instant we got underway. The paddling grew so much harder that even when we weren't snagged on something below, it felt like it to me. The process of seesawing, meanwhile, of pushing and pulling the canoe up and over trees became a long series of minor miracles.

Just before sunset, a terrific rainstorm of brief duration left us thoroughly drenched. My teeth began to chatter. Then the lights went out. We could scarcely see a thing. Elías leaned over the bow, squinting his eyes, trying to detect and steer us clear of avoidable stumps and logs. Tired, wet, and hungry, we preceded this way until the lights *really* went out. We entered a stretch of very dense forest just as full nightfall descended—and suddenly we couldn't see anything. It was a total, inside-a-cave sort of darkness. I put my hand in front of my face and saw black. I looked all around and saw black. We were in the center of the river when this happened.

But we didn't stop, which was the strangest part. We kept moving forward, floating in a bizarre, disembodied way through both water and darkness. Everyone fell silent in the canoe and stopped paddling, knowing that at any moment we were going to hit some obstruction without warning. Forward, forward, forward we went, gliding through the blackness—and still no obstruction. The absurdity of our predicament, cruelly prolonged as it was, spurred a great deal of tension, and right in the middle of it, Norma, of all things, let go a giggle. It was just a little twitter of a giggle, but a giggle nonetheless—and to my surprise, I could feel a grin playing across my face. Forward, forward, forward we floated. It was a scary situation, really, given the certainty of impending collision. But then Bolívar giggled, then Elías. My grin grew bigger.

I wasn't a Cofan, it was true, but on this occasion I was starting to feel like one, giving in to that impulsive, fatalistic sense of humor that led the Indians to laugh at the obvious and unchangeable, the unfixable. In a tight spot, you might as well seek out and surrender to whatever humor may be there.

Which is why, as we continued our glide through nothingness, I was the first to pass the giggling phase to plunge in with a raving, full-bodied, hollering laugh. I laughed and laughed and laughed, so hard I almost startled myself, overcome with the irrational certainty that the dreadful fix we were in was positively, unbearably comical. Pausing between hoots to catch my breath, I heard Bolívar and the others doing the same, laughing boisterously. We were a lunatic boat of raving crazies now, rudderless in the Amazon night. I was wiping tears from my eyes. Elías was snorting between long howls. Norma was cooing her loud, steady coos without pause.

And then it happened.

Whaaaack!

We stopped laughing. The sharpness of the impact threw us all slightly forward. The canoe came to a jolting stop. There was silence now. It was still pitch dark.

Bolívar called out to make sure everyone was okay. Then he called up to Elías, a sober tone coming to his voice. "What is it?" he said. "What did we hit?"

Elías began leaning over the bow, probing with his hands. Then he got out of the canoe entirely, and we could feel the bounce and sway of his departure. Then a rumbling peal of laughter split the silence. Elías was at it again, frantically, uncontrollably.

"What? What is it?" Bolívar asked.

Elías kept laughing, howling now.

"What? What? What?" we all kept imploring. "What did we hit?"

Finally a voice came from the dark. "The shore!" Elías managed. "We hit the shore of the river! We were so totally off course we hit the shore! I can't believe it!"

I'm not sure why, but never in my life had I heard anything so devastatingly funny. We had hit the shore. With tired arms inside my wet T-shirt, I gripped my empty stomach and laughed until I nearly fell out of the canoe. Bolívar and Norma were doing the same, I could tell, because the whole canoe began to sway and everything in it—fishing line, ax, paddles, peccaries—jiggled with the vibrations of our delight.

It was a good feeling, a great feeling, and it lasted a long time. We carried it all the way home to the village, in fact. It carried us home too, safely, through the moonlight that eventually emerged, allowing us to see again. We paddled past remaining trunks and branches until the huts of Zábalo finally took vague shape before us. We hit the shore with purpose this time, then teetered off to soft beds and an exhausted sleep that was deeper than the Amazon night.

4

"Good morning, Randy," I said, depositing my gear with a jangle outside the chief's house. It was 7:00 A.M. and time to begin the two-day journey to Quito to check on solar panels. I was packed and ready to go.

But Randy barely acknowledged my presence that early morning. He didn't even look at me. In a tone so brusque it was almost baleful, he said only, "Hello." The word came out like pure ice.

Had I done something to offend him? I wondered. Was I misreading his tone somehow? I was sleepy, after all, having skipped the paroxysm of *yoco* tea that morning and having no coffee backup of my own. I picked up my pack and followed Randy to the river. He was bearing supplies from his house to the canoe. I decided to try again.

"How are you today?" I asked, trailing after him.

"Alive," he snapped in the same frosty manner, without turning around. "Alive."

No ambiguity there. Something with muscle was eating the guy—and a thousand miles away is where he wished I were. Silently, I took a seat on the riverbank while Randy, Belizario, and two other Cofan men finished loading the canoe.

This wouldn't be the last brush-off I'd receive from Chief Borman. During the dozens of hours I'd spend with him over the next several weeks, the episodes would come regularly. Upbeat, voluble, almost manic in his hospitality and willingness to answer questions about his life one day, he'd be a pure stone wall the next. Or it would change from moment to moment, as when two days before he dismissed me almost angrily, saying he was tired of speaking English after several lively hours during which he seemed happy to go on forever. A casual observer would have thought us best of friends—then sudden antagonists after the glum looks of our sharp breakup.

"Toss your pack in here," Randy was now saying this particular morning, almost barking the order at me on the riverbank. I did as instructed without comment.

Randy Borman was inconsistent. He was moody. Smiles and frowns came in streaks with him. All of which actually made a strange sort of sense when one considered that nothing in his life was consistent. Nothing. It was as if being half-Western and half-Cofan in his personality left him predisposed to be on both sides of every divide, constantly crossing back and forth, never content to act the same, to hold the same views, to be the same person all the time. Here was a man who two days before had described to me the enormous degree of patience he was trying to instill in the Cofan in facing the legal and procedural matters related to fighting Petroecuador. Patience, patience, patience, he told me with perfect conviction. Then ten minutes later, he was switching perspectives entirely: "A militant approach is what I'm trying to encourage among our people vis-à-vis Petroecuador. Our traditional lack of militancy is what has cost us so much of the forest already. We've *got* to be more aggressive." And before I could point out the evident contradiction, Randy was changing course again, reemphasizing his earlier point that South American Indians could never fight Western encroachment physically and win. In virtually the next breath he was countering himself a third time, offering detailed and almost boastful descriptions of his visits to the two oil-drilling sites flanked by Cofan comrades toting shotguns, their purpose to present an "implicit" message to the startled workers.

The verbal lawn tennis would go on like this for long stretches, back and forth, back and forth. I wasn't panting to anoint myself judge of

Randy's overall campaign tactics, to be sure. The antipodal mix of pacifist patience some days and de facto aggression others had so far brought lots of success and no injuries. And success for the Cofan, as with any people anywhere, succeeded like nothing else.

It's just that it was frustrating, for me, trying to get purchase around a guy for whom no behavior fit dependably into any solid category. At times it was altogether maddening. There were his various acts of cultural preservation, of encouraging Cofan men to wear traditional *ondiccuje* tunics much of the time, for example, while at the same time he was selling to the community *Kuchitos* cheese puffs and bottled sodas from stashes inside his house. The snacks themselves, of course, could soon be enjoyed at night by the light of the solar panels Randy was hotly negotiating to have delivered. And yet every time that thought threatened to become too flat-out bizarre for my brain to handle, I'd feel the sharp pain in my back reasserting itself, making things even more confusing. The back pain was there from carrying the chubby Amazon pig the day before, a pain that now seeped deeply into my muscles, unpacking for a protracted visit. The pig was the same sort Randy hunted every week like Bolívar and Elías and everyone else in the village. Stalking, killing, and transporting the beasts with vine backpacks, sauntering over log bridges with magical skill—that was one way Randy provided for his family. You had to be the real thing for such feats. That much I knew for sure. The acrobatic poetry of an Olympic ice skater would have been easier to feign.

Randy was presently returning to his canoe, loaded down with more cargo. In one hand he gripped a collection of ceremonial bead necklaces for the trip and in the other a black, use-worn Echolac briefcase filled with important oil-company documents and correspondence. My eyes widened at the sight of the briefcase: One of the limitless props of Randy Borman. So many roles to play.

I continued to keep my distance on the riverbank, meanwhile, per "implicit" directions. Apparently Belizario, Randy's cousin-in-law, had neglected to have the canoe packed and ready to go that morning as previously agreed. That accounted for Randy's tailspinning mood—a mood that allowed some of the chief's true feelings toward journalists to rise to the surface as well, I think. "*Periodistas* are our friends," he had told the village. But *periodistas*, he certainly knew, could also be intrusive, and they could sell you short in their work if they chose. The two sides of this particular coin seemed to affect Randy strongly enough that I never felt entirely comfortable in his presence, entirely welcome and relaxed, befriended by him—or if I did, it never lasted more than a few hours, quickly replaced by his intermittent and unpredictable stoniness verging on insult.

"Time to go!" Randy yelled over just then, motioning me into the dugout.

Dutifully, I climbed into the vessel, avoiding eye contact with the chief. I focused my gaze on the canoe itself instead. It was huge, carved from a true forest giant. It was wider and even slightly longer than Bolívar's forty-footer of the day before. But despite the size, congested conditions quickly prevailed. I was trailed on board by six adults, six children, one infant (five-month-old Herman, Aguinda's son), two fifteen-foot pieces of sugar cane, a fishing net, various satchels of clothing, and an eight-week-old mongrel puppy named Machete. Machete wound up next to me near the bow and promptly earned his name, chewing on my sandals as if starved for the damp leather sprinkled with jungle mildew.

Getting to Quito was going to take two full days of travel, the first by canoe up the Aguarico, the second by truck slithering into the Andes. The river portion would be a marathon, 120 miles, nearly the equivalent of riding a crowded, thirty-six-inch-wide dugout from Washington, D.C., to Philadelphia, PA. Our destination that day would be the community of Dureno, a collection of huts along an upper stretch of the Aguarico I'd never visited before. Dureno was the oil-drenched traditional homeland of all the Cofan—where 300 of the Indians still lived. Hence the stuffed conditions aboard our canoe that morning. This covey of Zábalo Cofan was converting chief Borman's solar panel excursion into a chance to visit friends and relatives upriver. Riding with them, I was about to venture farther into the region of established oil exploitation—and forest mauling—than I'd done so far.

Our little floating village made its start with Randy at the stern, manning the outboard. If I still felt the discomfiting sting of my reception that morning, the bad feeling didn't last long, yielding within minutes to the balm of the forest's beauty. Rounding our first bend, we watched as forty red-bellied macaws—*forty* of them—lifted in unison from a gnarled riverbank tree. Together they beat their eighty wings in retreat, flashing their colors—maroon, gray, green; maroon, gray, green—like streaks of velvet passing through fog. I leaned over the gunwale and felt the hair rise on my arms while a silent smile formed on my lips. In the Amazon, I found, I experienced less of travel's periodic bouts of loneliness and depression than any place I'd visited before. In all their sublime grandeur, macaws and kapok trees, dolphins and sherbet butterflies have a way of chasing away dark turns of mind the way a great painting often can or, say, a Ravel piano concerto. You simply have to work hard to stay crotchety in the face of such intricate and fragile excellence.

We must have been near Baltimore on the D.C.-to-Philly scale when someone aft broke out the *chicha* for a late-morning snack. My portion came in a wide tin bowl passed, one by one, through a half-dozen hands up to the bow, where Belizario and I sat. The yucca had been mashed the day before and allowed to ferment in water till now. When I suggested to Belizario that it was perhaps too early in the day for so much beer, he said, "No, drink a lot. It's good for the heart. *Chicha* is good for a strong heart."

He thumped his chest for ventricular punctuation, exhibiting that same young-warrior zest I'd seen in him three days before when he imitated the act of spearing an oil man. Despite his odd dress combination that day of high-top tennis shoes below an *ondiccuje* tunic, Belizario remained consummately handsome, brave, and strong in appearance— and irresistible. I obeyed his direct order. I tipped back the bowl of *chicha* in a rush. There's no waiting with *chicha*. You down the half-quart serving right away, gulp after gulp, hurriedly freeing the communal bowl for the next thirsty palate. It actually made the perfect travel companion, this libation, quick and convenient, both a drink and a food in one, the residual yucca pulp a real stomach-stuffer gliding down with all the liquid. The attendant light buzz rising to the head also blunted some of travel's niggling physical discomforts. In fact, *chicha* was going to be the sole food, as it were, we would have during the next two days of traveling. The only downside was that a canoe in the middle of a river wasn't the optimal spot for quaffing huge quantities of liquid of any kind. I was nigh suicidal with pain when, an hour later, Randy beached the canoe on a small island and we all dashed madly into the trees to relieve ourselves. Everyone dashed except Machete, that is, who had already relieved himself adequately all over my knapsack and was now sleeping serenely.

I was stepping off the island back into the canoe when I heard the helicopter. We were well past the mouth of the Cuyabeno River, so all the
land on the south bank of the Aguarico was now outside the reserve. And
that's where, looking up, I saw the aircraft floating above the trees.

"They're building an exploratory well," Belizario said, noticing my
stare as he padded back to the canoe in his tennis shoes. "It's over there.
Right under that helicopter." He pointed.

Sure enough, looking closely, I saw the summit of a drilling derrick
obtruding above the forest canopy, metal braces crisscrossing up its sides.
Ironically, a squadron of common black vultures had taken wing around
the drill site, riding thermals in wide metaphorical swirls overhead. We
were reaching the far outposts of the oil-industry killing fields. Round and
round the vultures went.

"There's nothing we can do about this one," Belizario said with deepening disconsolation. "It's not on our land. It's not in the park." He
shrugged his shoulders and shook his longish, shaggy hair as we pulled
away in the canoe. Everyone on board turned around for a final glance,
leaving the helicopter to do its job. I recalled Carlos, one of my guides
two years before, and his loathing for such company helicopters. They
represented the start of a repulsive, predictable chain, he said, their job "to
deliver equipment to complete the wells to drill the holes to find the oil
to pump it out to send to America."

As if to offer solace for this dour construction site and the increasing
number of *fincas* on either shore, a quick and noisy thunderstorm hastened
across the sky just then, followed by not one but two rainbows. It was a
rare double beauty, literally one spectral arc atop the other. This being the
dry season, storms tended to be small scale and short lived along the
Aguarico now, often occurring with luminous sunshine still pouring down.
Hence the recurring iridescent spectacles. The Season of Rainbows, it
seemed to me, would have been a better name for this time of year in this
part of the Amazon.

We were now more than seven long hours into our journey, and I was
farther up the Aguarico than I'd ever been, when up ahead we saw three
elephantine dump trucks plowing through the river on five-foot-tall tires.
I took off my glasses, wiped them clean, and put them back on—and still
the trucks were there. They were moving along a shoal near where an

equally large machine vaguely reminiscent of a farm combine was dredging gravel from the water. I asked Belizario about the vehicles.

"Maxus," he said, shading his eyes as he looked out. "It's Maxus that owns those. They need the little rocks for the new roads they're building to get to the new oil in the forest."

He was referring to Maxus Energy, a Dallas-based American oil company which in recent years had become heavily involved in the region's pell-mell scramble for oil. That it took a road to get these road-building machines here in the first place summarized the stark change from the trackless ocean of green infinity downriver, where wheeled vehicles were a physical impossibility.

The props greeting us on this altered terrain continued to multiply just before Dureno. Up ahead, a taut suspension bridge came into view. Its narrow frame carried just one passenger across the Aguarico: A natural-gas pipeline made of sleek galvanized steel. Before I could blink, there was a second bridge, this one holding up a set of high-voltage electrical wires stretched between metal support towers. Each bridge had such a hard, angular look so violent and out of place on this previously untamed river, that I had the strange urge to duck as we passed under them despite their being at least fifty feet aloft. The bridges put on display the life-giving tubes, the very blood veins, of what Randy was fond of calling the Occidental Juggernaut. With them, obliterative modern change was made as easy as putting a scythe to grass.

The scenery declined still further as we reached the outskirts of the Dureno village, pulling up to one of the first huts we saw. On the shore, a Cofan man in hip-hugging '70s-style bell-bottom jeans waved with clumsy vigor, welcoming us to this community of seventy-one families, the ancient center of Cofan life. Mr. Bell-bottoms had the vacant eyes and unmistakable sway of alcoholic consumption. Next to him, inside a small beached canoe, his wife was using an already-fouled disposable diaper to wipe excrement from the buttocks of the couple's baby son. The diaper—donated by an oil company doctor, I learned later—was then tossed casually into the river current, where it lost buoyancy after twenty feet and disappeared.

I was still watching the bubbles when Amelia's brother Loriano came down to the riverbank to welcome us from our long trip. We would be passing the night with this man, sleeping in his riverside hut. Covering Loriano's moderate build was a blue T-shirt announcing: "H.R. Smith/Ford Trucks #1." No one, it seemed, wore tunics here.

And that wasn't the only difference. Something else was missing. In the sky. I noticed it right off. It was something I had grown accustomed to downriver. I recalled the day two years before when I first arrived in the lower Cuyabeno reserve. My guide Roberto had assured me then that I'd become bored sick of macaws within a week from seeing so many. He was right in one sense: It was almost impossible to go more than a few minutes without observing or at least hearing these flamboyant seed-eating denizens of the forest. Such a burst of fireworks it was when a pair or more took flight with their long tails and big hooked beaks. But the thrust of Roberto's prophesy turned out to be false. I never tired of beholding the endless permutations of blue and yellow, red and green, green and scarlet. The exhilaration was there that very morning near Zábalo as forty of them, maroon stomachs and green tails, had burst from the riverbank like a rising painted curtain in a wash of soft sunrise light.

But not in Dureno. No macaws lived anywhere near this place. None. Like so many Amazonian birds, these required a fully intact forest in order to feed, to reproduce, to elude predators—to survive, in short. Their absence was a sure snapshot indication that the forest around us now was fragmented and scarred, wheezing its final breaths. I did a 360° scan of the horizon without luck. "You never see them here," Randy told me later. "Macaws? No macaws of any kind. Ever." Trapped, caged, sold off, rifled, chased off—they were gone. The sky had a lonely aspect without them.

It turned out that the map of Dureno that Belizario had drawn for me a few days before with his wetted finger across a canoe gunwale was accurate. This 22,000-acre patch of traditional Indian land—now more or less a reservation—was indeed surrounded by oil roads. The Indians had managed to retain a small green enclave of still-standing forest in the center. But if you traveled far enough in any direction, you came eventually to the gravel avenues and attendant black ruin of oil operations, something we would do the very next day en route to Quito.

Loriano, presently, led us up the bank to his small house on stilts surrounded by yucca and coffee plants. Given the manifest glut of cultural change all around, I was half-surprised to see Loriano's hut crowned with the traditional palm-thatch roofing. When I mentioned this to Randy, he quickly said, "Oh, no. Tin is on the way. All the roofs here will be tin in a few months."

The problem, again, was the declining forest. Where before bound-less resources had lay ripe for the picking all around, the Dureno Cofan in recent years had found it harder and harder just to find enough palm trees with enough fronds to cover their roofs. Even basic materials required a sweaty scramble now. So when a Maxus oil representative arrived three months earlier saying the company wanted to dredge this stretch of the Aguarico River for gravel, the Dureno Cofan listened closely. The gravel would be used to surface the company's approach to its wells to the south. In return, each Cofan household would receive thirty sheets of corrugated tin. Deciding they could scarcely decline if they wanted to keep rain away from indoor food supplies and off their own beds while they slept, the Cofan accepted.

Loriano led Randy and me to a pavilionlike porch area of his house overlooking the river. There we sat down to a restorative round of *chicha* as Randy's sons gamboled off to play with their cousins out behind the hut. I used the moment to ask Loriano how the fishing was this far up the Aguarico. He retorted with an outpouring of mock laughter. The fishing was so bad, he said, that he was trying to build an inland fish pond near his house for food. The tributaries of the upper Aguarico had become fouled with oil and garbage in recent years to an extent that most people here were afraid to eat the fish. Forest game was nearly nonexistent in the vicinity, too.

"From here," Loriano said, "if I walk all morning, then I walk all after-noon, then I camp, then I walk all morning again—then I *might* find a peccary in the afternoon."

With the spinal trauma of my outing the day before, I tried not to imagine the horror of a successful return from such a trip.

"The only game around here closer than that," Randy added, "has four wheels for legs or has a rotary blade on top." He grinned devilishly, and imitated the sound of a gun going off. The joke was slightly morose, perhaps, but funny nonetheless. Randy's mood was improving. The frostiness of that morning was finally falling away. We both had a second bowl of *chicha*.

Not all aspects of forest-bound culture, it turned out, were vanishing from Dureno. Amelia, barefoot and exuding her usual quiet cheer, was at that moment outside arranging several termite nests into a tin bowl for use later that night. The rock-hard, dried-mud, roughly oval-shaped nests would be set afire at dusk and left to burn slowly next to the house, the faint smoke acting as a slammed-door repellant to mosquitoes, a perfect fumigator. I'd seen the Zábalo Cofan use the same method. I asked Randy how it worked.

"It's the enzymes and other chemicals the termites secrete into the mud when they're building the nest," he told me. "They do it to keep predators away from the nest, as far as anyone knows. When you burn it, it has the same effect. No mosquitoes come near."

He sat up in his hammock as if a great thought had just come to him, and added, "That's one thing about the rain forest that's been badly overlooked by scientists: The chemical world of insects. Everyone's concerned about plants in the Amazon, about ethnobotany, but insect chemicals have to be just as valuable for medicinal purposes. But they've been poorly mined. I mean, the degree to which chemical manufacture and use by insects goes on here is unbelievable—for defense, nest building, digestion, predation, nocturnal illumination."

I remembered reading about one particular beetle that combines volatile chemicals inside a hard-walled chamber in its abdomen. When disturbed, the beetle secretes a catalyzing enzyme that leads to an actual chemical explosion, which is in turn shot from a swiveling cannonlike duct, sending attacking toads into agonizing seizures.

"All of which is too bad," Randy continued, speaking of the dearth of study in this field, "because it's so fascinating. If I could clone myself and somehow start over in another career, I'd get the scientific training and set myself up to do studies of chemicals and poisons in the insect world."

Randy's sudden passion for this unexpected topic was intriguing. What would you call it? I wondered. Ethnochemoentomology? But what interested me even more was his last sentence about changing careers. I couldn't quite make sense of it. What sort of career, as he put it, did he have now? What was his job? Before I could ask the question, he answered it.

"No doubt about it," he said. "If I weren't operating an indigenous community, insects are what I'd want to be into. I'd study them all across this forest."

My mind jumped back a sentence. What did he say? "Operating an indigenous community?" Hmmmm. So that was it. I couldn't think of a less romantic way—nor perhaps a more accurate one—to describe Randy's life given the layers of outside threats and complications besetting the Cofan. We *were*, after all, on our way to visit a government agency to procure solar panels for a people who, for purposes of survival, Randy was trying to make both militant and patient at the same time. That was high-octane management, to be sure.

And it wasn't a huge surprise to me, given his back-and-forth ways, that Randy's four-word job description seemed to contain a central contradiction. If a community is indigenous—that is, native, natural, of time-honored ways—doesn't it run itself according to an internal collective dynamic? The moment any single individual begins self-consciously controlling and operating it, the community stops being indigenous—at least in any true and significant sense. If Randy saw any validity in this point, he didn't let on. But the truth was simple all the same: Randy didn't run anything indigenous. He was providing guidance toward preserving an Indian culture's core, yes. In that sense he was "operating" his butt off, keeping alive a reasonable copy of the original. But as on the canoe ride earlier that day, he was just one man in the rear, steering. And he almost never steered in a straight line, forced by obstacles and uncertainty into shifting directions of thought and motion. It was a very tough career he had chosen for himself.

Randy wandered off for a moment to help Amelia with her chore, and I stayed behind, pondering how differently Randy's life had turned out from that of his father, the missionary, the one who came first, the one who had made initial contact with the Cofan right here in Dureno in 1954. Sitting alone on Loriano's porch, looking out, I tried to imagine that first missionary pontoon plane gliding down to this very spot, scattering macaws, descending into the greenery that fell away toward every horizon. My mind lingered on that image for a long while.

I thought of how Bub Borman, then twenty-seven years old, paid a pilot to take him and his duffel bag to the upper Aguarico, where he'd been told a small clan of Indians lived on land as thickly forested and pristine as any on earth. But on that day almost forty years ago when the plane landed there was much confusion. The Cofan women and children fled in terror, I learned later, leaving the men behind banded together to confront the strange Caucasian striding up to them. Using limited Spanish picked up from far-roving river traders, the Cofan told Bub that, yes, he could stay and live with them and learn their language if that's what he wanted. Not knowing whether this was true or just a ploy to put spears through him for his gear the moment the plane left, Bub waved good-bye to his pilot, and the plane vanished over a distant tree line.

The invitation, it turned out, was sincere. That first exchange led to nearly three decades of mission work along the south bank of the Aguarico. Bub Borman built a small house, brought in his wife Bobbie, and began raising a family in the jungle, Randy being the eldest of four children—three sons and a daughter. Bub and Bobbie, meanwhile, pursued step by step the credo of the Summer Institute of Linguistics, their evangelical sponsors: Learn the native language, give it an alphabet, translate the Bible into it, and teach the local people how to read. After that, in theory, the people could decide their spiritual fate for themselves through direct encounter with the holy text. By the late '50s, Bub was spending the long, sultry tropical days, morning to night, poring over his translation of the New Testament, page by page. It was a tedious, exacting process made more knotted by the difficulty of the Cofan language itself—where, for example, the same word was used to connote faith, love, and hope. Not until 1980 did Bub complete the translation, a milepost received with much celebration among the Borman family and their Cofan followers. It took another dozen years to complete a condensed version of the Old Testament, most of it written in the ten years after Bub and Bobbie's 1981 retirement from the Amazon.

In sharp contrast to almost all Christian missions the world over, including some within their own sect, the Bormans as Summer Institute Bible translators elected to forgo as a central objective the transformation of the local culture along Western lines. Their preferred approach was to simply live with the people with minimal interference while, again, learning the Indian language. The plain fact of the Bormans' presence introduced incremental cultural change, to be sure. But "operating" the community, whether as a proactive assimilation goal or a reactive preservation strategy, simply wasn't on the docket. Indeed, by 1993, it was oil, much more than Christianity, that had gone far to transform and pervert the Dureno culture, an interesting fact, given that some Ecuadorian Indian tribes refer to oil as "the excrement of the devil."

A small wooden church erected by the senior Bormans still stood near the center of the Dureno settlement, and Randy's younger brother Ron still served as a missionary there. But Randy rarely set foot in the building. He wasn't a missionary. Definitely not. To hear him tell it, studying insect chemistry was higher on his list of preferred things to do. True, each Sunday under a crude palm-thatched pavilion downriver in Zábalo, Randy led a brief church service for his own clan of Cofan. But while most of the Zábalo Indians maintained a faith in Christianity, they possessed a parallel faith in an animist world replete with forest spirits and thinking jaguars and village shamans with supernatural powers. Such was the context and tepidity of Randy's involvement in these Indians' religious lives.

What Randy reserved his ardor for instead was seeing to it that the old Cofan world, the world of his childhood, the one he knew from fishing and carving blowguns and gamboling barefoot through the forest while his father worked his way through Matthew, Mark, Luke, and John—what he saved his ardor for was seeing to it that that world didn't die. Because if it did, a big part of Randy would die with it. And that was the cause for which, finally, he could work up big doses of real zeal. Randy was, if anything, a sort of cultural disciple, a preservationist missionary. The gospel was secular but no less fixed on the idea that a just and final kingdom awaited the dedicated and believing follower.

Back at Loriano's house on stilts, meanwhile, Amelia had finished arranging the bouquet of termite nests for ambush duty later that night on mosquitoes. Randy had already returned; and with the sun lowering in the sky behind her, Amelia climbed the wooden ladder up to where we sat, then coquettishly plopped down next to Randy in his twine hammock. Both husband and wife chuckled as she insinuated herself in an amorous tight fit under one of his arms. Many times before, I'd seen such tender moves from this couple—the affectionate embrace after a momentary absence, the meaningful glance at the end of a sentence. Indeed, despite the peculiarities of their union, Randy and Amelia seemed as happy a pairing of man and woman as one could find. Always, if one member was reclined atop a bench or a canoe gunwale or, their favorite, a hammock, the other was sure to materialize quickly, sharing the space with a where-have-you-been-I-missed-you smile, consistently giving the impression that they'd gotten married just yesterday instead of six years before.

It all added up to make Randy's decision to take an Indian bride seem utterly natural, as fluid as water. This was no small point, given that it was the marriage itself that cast Randy's lot fully and permanently with the Cofan, sealing his impulse to go native, to go deep, to forever live the culture and defend it—the cultural missionary. Randy was who he was today, and could only be who he was, because of Amelia, his Cofan bride. To marry her had been a risk, one as fruitful now as it had been daring then.

Some reasons for the success were easy to see. For starters, there were Amelia's personal grace and physical beauty. Her dark hair and dark skin and dark eyes were accentuated by arching eyebrows and a full, sensuous smile. She was the granddaughter of an equally beautiful Indian healer, and Amelia herself was known as "a woman of herbs," expert at gathering, blending, and preparing forest plants for all their copious uses.

Despite attempts, I'd had little success conversing with Amelia in any substantive way. Part of the reason was that she spoke no Spanish and I no Cofan, and much was lost in translation. More than this, though, was her almost painful shyness toward strangers. For reasons never fully clear to me, Cofan women are extraordinarily reserved and aloof in the presence of visitors—more so by far than women in any culture I'd ever come in contact with. In Zábalo I was doing well to get a woman to respond in the slightest way to a simple "good morning" voiced in Cofan (my total vocabulary). The usual reaction was a nervous giggle and averted eyes. Could the deeds of those original outsiders, the conquering Spaniards, have doomed male visitors here forever?

I turned to others for a profile of Amelia, including Randy, who stressed above all her fierce intelligence. Though bereft of Western education, she was highly educated within the Cofan system, he said, with a special interest—besides herbs—in the nesting behavior of birds. She enjoyed harvesting eggs for food and spending long moments watching mating rituals. "She's taught me a great deal about nesting," Randy said, not seeming to grasp the double meaning. "We're both naturalists."

When in 1987 Randy told his parents, who were then living in Quito, that he planned to marry Amelia, they were not especially keen on the idea. They knew the culture and the potential consequences of a union within it. Bobbie was particularly concerned about the gulf in education between them. She worried too that Amelia wasn't a true Christian. And what if, per an Indian custom, the bride's parents exercised their option to raise one of the grandchildren?

Randy himself anguished over the marriage for different reasons. Even after dropping out of college and returning to the Amazon and establishing the Zábalo community and launching the nature tours, he'd held onto the idea of marrying a nice missionary's daughter, an American girl raised abroad, a "third culture" kid, as he put it, and with her making a life among or near the Cofan. For sure, it was a safer and easier strategy, one that avoided the deep plunge into blood ties a Cofan marriage would bring. Randy even met the woman he thought he wanted, an American in Quito, and all was nearly set.

But then Amelia Quenama strode into the picture. Over the years, dozens of eligible Cofan women had postured themselves to accept a pledge of marriage from Randy, all viewing him as a fine catch with his mix of Indian and Western ways. Amelia, however, was cut from cloth different from the rest. She was extraordinarily mature for her fifteen years—the traditional marrying age for Cofan women. The easy conversations Randy had with her, the long walks in the forest together, the spying on favorite nesting birds—all persuaded Randy to think harder about a roost of his own set squarely inside this same forest, built with native care on a fully Indian foundation. In the end, he told me later, it came down to, "Which world do I really belong to most?"

It was in March 1987, while Randy was inventorying his deepest feelings on this issue, ruminating on every possibility, the need to decide bearing down upon him, that the ground shook violently beneath his feet. An earthquake struck. It was a powerful quake, hitting the upper Aguarico valley hardest, collapsing parts of an Andean mountainside into the river and then inundating miles of the valley with biblical-scale flooding. Mud slides ten feet deep erased entire *colono* towns and Indian villages, killing several thousand people and emptying vast gallons of black crude into rivers from broken oil pipelines. By chance, the Zábalo Cofan, farther downriver, were spared the worst of the destruction. They huddled together on their bank of dry land and watched as six-foot waves littered with dead cattle and human beings churned down the river past their village. The exigencies of crisis, the working together and coming together of the Zábalo community to protect and preserve itself, also brought Randy and Amelia closer together. The goal of survival kept emotions raw and stripped down and exceedingly honest. Randy now says it was almost like a sign, that earthquake, jolting him into realization, moving the tectonic plates of his soul in the right direction. He figured out, at last, who he was and where he belonged.

A few months after the earthquake, Randy, thirty-one, and Amelia, fifteen, were wed in a simple Cofan ceremony. Only afterward did Randy inform his parents, who acquiesced amiably to the news. "If he followed his heart, it'll work out," Bub Borman said later.

During the first couple of years of marriage, Amelia suffered some of the slings and arrows of petty village jealousies and grudges over her prize fetch. But these gradually passed, as did certain fears Amelia herself harbored. "[Randy's] a gringo," she told an Ecuadorian journalist not long after the wedding, "and before I married him, his eyes scared me. But after we were married, I came to consider him a Cofan."

As did Randy himself, of course. But what, I wondered, does a man who reads science fiction fantasy for pleasure and who has worked in a modern assembly-line factory in the United States (for college tuition money) talk about with a wife, now barely out of her teens, whose sole language is spoken by only 700 people in the world and who, until she met Randy, had never ventured more than a few miles beyond her birthplace?

"Small talk, mostly," Randy said when I broached the issue on Loriano's porch that day. "We discuss our version of the little things all married couples discuss." That included where to fish on a given day, what yucca plants to harvest, and what time to go visit the set of handsome new twins born in the village. "Nothing earth-shattering," he said. "Not at all."

But surely there were moments when the chasm of education and experience frustrated more intellectual communication between them or made such communication impossible altogether.

"If you're asking," Randy said, "whether I seek out Amelia to discuss Rousseauean philosophy, no. We don't sit around discussing whether man corrupts society or society corrupts man. But my dad doesn't discuss that with my mom either, and they're both college graduates. How important are such topics in everyday life anyway? I just don't feel I'm missing any-thing with Amelia."

When it came to oil, however, Amelia *was* at a technical disadvantage. She couldn't read up on the safest way to dispose of toxic mud composi-tions from drilling shafts or do research on which features were most efficient and cost-effective in solar-panel manufacture. But like most of the Cofan, she understood clearly why the drills had to be monitored for envi-ronmental damage and why solar panels were fair and necessary compensation for damage already done. From this base of understanding, she supported and advised Randy to the extent of her ability in every step of the resistance campaign.

"I'm closer to Amelia than to anyone else," Randy said, summing up the half-dozen years of mixed-race unity. "It just feels so natural I can't imagine not having done it. I can't."

The initial difficulty in making the decision now struck him as bizarre and distant, he said. Amelia, who had had her own reservations six years ago, showed the same assuredness and satisfaction with the outcome. If further proof were needed, the two of them, again, seemed congenitally incapable of spending more than fifteen minutes apart. "More than that and we just don't feel right," Randy said. Ergo, the frequent and often humorous act of piling double onto the nearest bench or riverbank perch or, as in the present moment, hammock.

Husband and wife were still suspended in a slow-motion sway of relax-ation as Randy and I finished our talk and sunset approached over the Aguarico. Glancing out, Randy announced it was time to unload the canoe and take a bath in the river. At that, we all rose and began descending the steep clay bank, our movement hastened slightly by the sound of grum-bling storm clouds to the east.

After a quick swim and bath, I offered Randy a hand in emptying the canoe. He was wearing at the moment only a pair of blue shorts and the necklace with the single small puma tooth dangling across his bare chest, the puma he had killed himself with a machete. We hauled a few wood planks onto the shore, then a crate of empty soda bottles, then a harpoon and some calabash bowls and a steel propane gas tank to be refilled for the stove Randy kept inside his Crusoe house. All the while the storm clouds to the east drew closer, billowing into irregular black ovals that stretched across a violent, lumpy line. Over the river, the wind picked up and the trees swayed on either shore as if tremulously waving to one another.

I was reaching into the canoe for more gear when I noticed that Randy, water up to his thighs, had stopped. He was staring at the oncoming storm. He was silent for a moment. It seemed sort of strange. Then finally he spoke.

"I almost died three months ago," he said.

There was little emotion in his voice as he spoke these words, pulling them out of what seemed like nowhere. He at first volunteered no further comment or explanation. His eyes were still on the sky.

"How?" I asked after a lapse of a few seconds. "How did you almost die?"

He pointed in the direction he was staring. "Lightning," he said.

We were both standing still now, wind sweeping over us as Randy sketched the story. It happened on the Aguarico River, near Ecuador's border with Peru. It happened on a sandy, open riverbank just before dusk with a thunderstorm approaching. Randy and several other Cofan men, hired as guides by a group of Swiss naturalists, were making camp, setting up a line of tents, when a blinding blast of light drenched the air. There was a simultaneous explosion, a sudden cracking boom immediately overhead, sending Randy, Belizario, and Lorenzo landing on their backs after flying a full ten feet through the air. The tent poles, long spikes of pure aluminum, had drawn a powerful bolt. By some fantastic chance, though, everyone in the group shook their heads and brushed themselves off, shocked in more ways than one but basically unhurt, still alive, okay.

Randy let go a sort of "and that's that" sigh after the brief story, giving no more details. He resumed lifting material from the canoe. Felipe and Federico, by this point, had wandered down to join us, carrying light loads in their small arms to help their father stay ahead of the rain, which was still getting closer. Both boys were still shirtless from bathing. Their feet left tiny footprints on the sandy bank.

I resumed my own lifting, but my mind stayed focused on the lightning story, unable to let go of the strange event. For me, it brought up both a fact and a question. The world down in Zábalo, so deep in the forest, so far from roads and telephones and hospitals, so full of hunting trips and insid-

ious serpents and sharp-toothed mammals and the vagaries of intestinal par-
asites—that world was not a place, as Russell would say, for "sissies." The
potential health perils were as varied as the flora and fauna all around. That
was the fact. Just six months before, Randy had spent four weeks in bed in
Zábalo virtually comatose from a combination of pneumonia, malaria, and
an acute allergic reaction to the antimalaria drug Fansidar. A few years
before that he nearly drowned navigating the flooded Aguarico in a small
canoe. A few years before *that* he lost nearly a third of his right index finger
in an accident while crossing an upriver canyon. Then, of course, there was
the minor stuff: The stitches, burns, broken bones, and parasitic diseases
that with time come to anyone living in daily contact with machetes, shotguns, harpoons, river rapids, floods, and impure drinking water.

I glanced across the shore just then to see Felipe and Federico had
already lost interest in unloading the canoe. They were chasing each other
now on the sandy shore, smiles shining across those bright faces that so
handsomely melded Caucasian and Indian features.

And then the question.

"Do you ever worry," I asked Randy, "about your kids? I mean, about
what could happen to them from accidents or their getting severely sick
way out here so far from emergency medical help?"

He was lifting another crate of bottles from the canoe, the stub of his
truncated forefinger laced through a handle. I went on to suggest that perhaps it was one thing to accept risks for oneself, and another to impose
them on one's children. My approach was blunt, perhaps, but Randy's
quick response made me think he'd thought through the issue long before
I ever came around to bring it up.

"Am I concerned that there's no hospital for my sons anywhere near
where we live?" Randy said, setting the crate on the shore before proceeding to set me straight on a couple of points. "Sure, I'm concerned.
And am I concerned about them getting hit by a car or shot by a drug
dealer or getting AIDS or being trapped in a burning office building? No.
In any situation, you see, there are always going to be positives and neg-
atives. Always."

I wondered if grandparents Bub and Bobbie felt the same way—a
thought that crystallized for a moment the oddity of Felipe and Federico's
world, where one set of grandparents wore nose feathers and made hand-

woven baskets, and the other—now retired in Dallas—dashed across five-lane highways and browsed through air-conditioned shopping malls.

Randy continued talking about his sons.

"I'll put it to you this way," he said. "If there were ever an accident in Zábalo or a sudden illness of some kind, and I did all I could possibly do to save my kids with the resources I have available, and they didn't survive, I certainly wouldn't have feelings of self-incrimination. It's all a trade-off, again. I accept that."

The sky had darkened severely now, bruised black by the curtain of swollen, onrushing clouds. The wind and thunder kept up the pace, moving in coordinated waves from the east, getting stronger, barreling toward us. Randy told Felipe and Federico to go up to their uncle's hut. I wanted to do the same, but the canoe was not quite empty and Randy seemed to want to finish. There were no aluminum tent-poles lying around, so I decided to trust him.

We doubled back in our conversation, meanwhile, back to the subject almost too well tailored to the blustery moment at hand.

"So, really," I said, scanning the sky again then turning to Randy, "in that little lightning episode you had a while back—nobody got seriously injured?"

Something about the story's original version had left me skeptical.

"Little?" Randy shot back. The word was so sharp it seemed snatched from his mouth by the wind. "It wasn't *little*," he said.

Randy allowed the story to unfold, now sending a shower of details pouring out.

"When it first happened," he said, "I remember a sort of explosion and then being thrown backward by the lightning, literally flying through the air, and thinking at that moment, 'What jerk dropped dynamite into the campfire?' That's how big it was. I thought it was a dynamite explosion."

Not a farfetched thought, perhaps, in a forest so recently peppered with the TNT of seismic testing. But Randy's initial fears were off base.

"After I landed on my back," he went on, "and was able to pull my head up and look around, I didn't see the carnage and blood from that type of explosion. We were just all flattened. Lorenzo—and you know how big he is—was thrown two-and-a-half meters before landing. He was okay, thank goodness. I saw him start to get up. But me, my right arm and left leg were completely numb, and the muscles were all cramped up. I managed to get up after a minute and, with Lorenzo, go over to Belizario, who was barely moving. Belizario got the worst of it. He was obviously having a little heart arrhythmia. For about an hour he was semiconscious, which scared me. But then he came out of it. He was okay, on his feet, feeling better. My numbness went away too, although I had a weak leg for a few days afterward."

To my surprise, Randy grinned after he said this and then started laughing. As if on cue, a ripping burst of thunder exploded very close by. It really was time to go in.

"What's so funny?" I asked Randy after a glance in the thunder's direction. "Why are you laughing?"

"Because," he said, "once we realized no one had been hurt by the lightning, the whole thing struck us as kind of funny, flying through the air like that. We were just flying right through the air."

He laughed some more. I suppose it was something like being in Bolívar's canoe when the lights went out. A bad situation, but not much you can do about it. Only, given the extraordinary seriousness of Randy's violent near miss, I sort of expected a summing up from him a little more profound than that it was "funny."

"Didn't your world flash before your eyes or something?" I asked. "Didn't the experience, you know, kind of leave you taking stock of your life?"

"Huh?" he said.

I stared back at Randy's puzzled face. His eyes were dull with incomprehension. His Cofan side was completely out now, as bare and stripped down as his near-naked body. I could see it. I was losing him. I repeated the question.

"Nah," he said. "Take stock of my life? Why? I figure, if you're not constantly taking stock of your life as you go, it's too late to start when you get hit by lightning."

Scattered drops of rain began to fall. They came at a hard angle, whipped by wind through the darkened air.

"So that's all?" I said. "Just something humorous? Something to laugh about?"

"What else is there?" he said with a hint of impatience now. "When it comes down to it, you're either dead or you're alive, right? I mean, that's it. Period. Dead or alive. So why not laugh?"

Why not? I thought to myself. Because contact with lightning—the numb legs and arms and all the rest—really *wasn't* the same as canoe foibles after a hunt. Not for me. Not even close. You had to live in a forest, I suppose, to view yourself so casually attached to a cold natural order where everything was easy come, easy go, and you were just a speck of matter on the grand organic chain of life, easily flicked aside. This was fatalism writ extreme—and it left me feeling at that moment further away from Randy culturally than at any point before. No wonder he didn't mind lingering in a thunderstorm so soon after nearly paying the price in an earlier episode. Suddenly I wanted to go. I didn't trust Randy. I wanted out from under the open sky.

And at last I got my wish. The rain began falling harder all around us, forcing us to turn toward the steep riverbank and the shelter above. The sound of drops hitting the water behind us, falling in sheets, made it harder to hear Randy's voice as we climbed the bank. He was still talking, still answering the last question. I had to strain to listen.

"Dead or alive," he said again. "That's all you are. Period. One or the other."

We were both wet, our feet smudged with mud as we reached the hut above. Randy ran his fingers through his wet hair.

"Period," he said, louder this time.

▼▼▼

Loriano was still wearing his "Ford Trucks" T-shirt that evening as he lit two candles in his small hut. A textured luminescence flared yellow and gold across the split-cane walls, allowing us to stay awake talking deep into the night.

I was stretching out on a wooden chair when Loriano, this time with heightened urgency, mentioned again his desire to build fish ponds. The chronic shortage of food in Dureno, he explained, was getting worse with each passing year. Wild game was becoming nothing but a memory, dreamlike images from the past. I wasn't too light-headed from lack of food myself just then to realize Loriano was indirectly explaining why I'd been offered no dinner that night, just more *chicha*. I learned later that the Dureno Cofan eat cheap canned sardines and store-bought rice almost every day when they can afford it, and papayas and watery soups when they cannot.

Early in the evening, Randy's younger brother Ron, twenty-nine, came by for a short visit. The spirited round of greetings passing through the room began with Randy and Amelia swinging and waving *a deux* from their hammock. In his flip-flops and gym shorts and T-shirt and ambitiously unkempt beard, Ron looked like anything but the missionary he was. The blood connection to Randy wasn't obvious either. Ron's hair was darker and curly, his build much leaner, and he almost never wore the traditional Cofan tunics favored by his brother. He had the same fluent command of the language, though, and the same emphatic, alluring eyes—something I noticed even in the dusky hue of candlelight as he took a seat by my side.

Ron told me that since he began work in Dureno in 1989 as a Plymouth Brethren missionary, his central achievement had been the establishment of a "youth center" for the community. The center offered children a sweep of recreational activities from cards to dodge ball as "an alternative to drinking themselves brain dead every night."

The alcohol problem in Dureno, Ron went on to assure me, was very big and very real—and it was partially rooted, paradoxically, in Cofan tradition. The Indians had always brewed their *chucula* and *chicha*, of course, the mild beers of custom that could be downed in largeish doses to subdue thirst and hunger while socializing with village compatriots. You'd have to tip back nearly a vatful to get really tanked, so debilitating addiction was rare. But the story was different in the new shanty towns clustered like barnacles along the oil roads. There the descending legions of *colonos* had brought with them a rival drink of choice: *Cristal*. This blue-tinted, 180-proof cane liquor brewed in Colombia packed a potency tantamount to rocket fuel. The Cofan men in Dureno had taken an unfortunate shining to *Cristal*, throwing it back the only way they knew how with libations: In the same huge quantities they downed *chicha*. The result was a daily spectacle of pickled men staggering about in epidemic numbers, frittering away what little cash most households had. Not only was the booze stronger, but with so many traditional activities now extinct, there was a surfeit of time to wander through the deadening haze.

I asked Ron what percentage of the seventy-one Cofan families here was burdened by a problem drinker. His eyes narrowed and he grimaced in a contemplative way, suggesting he'd never been asked the question before. He reflected for a long moment.

"To be honest," he said, coming up from his thoughts, "I can't think of a single family that *doesn't* have a problem drinker."

A scratchy, scurrying sound rose from the edge of Loriano's candle-lit floor as Ron finished his sentence. I glanced over in time to see a thick-bellied mouse, eyes narrow and black, disappear into a wall crack, its foot-long tail slithering behind. I shifted my weight in my seat and turned my attention back to the group.

Randy and Loriano had been discussing for some time the details of the recent deal permitting Maxus Energy to gorge its dump trucks with thousands of tons of gravel here in Dureno. The vehicles were already stripping the river of the small, perfect-for-road-building stones almost around the clock. I thought back to the brawny dump trucks we'd seen that same afternoon, and I could almost hear my old guide Carlos' memorable words shifting with the circumstances: "Get the gravel to build the roads to maintain the wells to get the oil to send to America."

As it turned out, in addition to thirty pieces of tin sheeting per house-hold, Maxus was giving the Dureno community as payment for the gravel one fifty-pound pig, fifteen chickens, a few dozen machetes, and an out-board motor for the village's communal canoe. Modest though it was, this compensation constituted lucrative payment compared to the outright thievery of Amazon oil companies in the past. It reflected how quickly and how badly the American company needed the stones for the one-hundred-mile road it was constructing from a point south of Dureno to the heart of its operations inside Ecuador's other great rain-forest sanctuary, Yasuní National Park. Maxus had leased from the government a half-million-acre parcel of land stretching across the Yasuní park and endowed with enough known oil reserves to busy 120 wells laboring around the clock. And there, spread across the same stretch of jungle land, lived a tribe of Huaorani Indians, ancient forest inhabitants like the Cofan, some having made their first sustained contact with Westerners no more than ten years before.

Maxus, in other words, was right on track to do to the Huaorani in the 1990s what Texaco did to the Cofan in the 1960s and '70s: Put a road through their homeland, opening their forest to an onrush of settlers and their waterways to the assured stranglehold of toxic oil spills. Hence the company's noisy trucks, like giant worker bees, slaved away in full view of some of the Cofan riverside huts in Dureno. All the while, Maxus' press officials were busily telling the outside world not to worry: The company was going to exploit oil in this portion of the Amazon without significantly damaging the forest. However, this was something no other company in the last half-century had managed to do, and environmental groups both inside Ecuador and abroad weren't swallowing. The groups continued fighting the road bitterly, labeling as utterly suspect the sudden forest-preservation interests of a company that, during the Vietnam War, under the name Diamond Alkali, manufactured the defoliant Agent Orange for use across thousands of acres of Southeast Asian grasslands and forests. Some of those areas are still graveyards of bare, seemingly fossilized trees. They may never recover.

I asked Randy if, given these circumstances, it wouldn't be a good idea for the Dureno Cofan to refuse to sell their gravel to Maxus. Weren't the Indians here, having been victimized themselves in the extreme, now becoming shareholders in a fresh round of genocide elsewhere?

"Maybe," he said. "But I have no control over events in Dureno. A lot of the people here assume that Maxus will get the gravel somewhere else—or just outright take it here—so the Cofan might as well get paid. Maybe they're wrong. But I can only focus on what affects the Zábalo Cofan. The odds are bad enough against us. If I tried to fight everyone else's battles, I'd lose all sanity."

Actually, there had been some talk of spurning the Maxus proposition on moral/environmental grounds, but with their own environment despoiled beyond redemption, the Cofan really did need the sheets of tin to keep roofs over their heads—literally. More than this, though, it was the ironclad support of Dureno's eccentric, increasingly Westernized chief that sealed the Maxus deal. The chief's name was Ermenegildo Criollo, and by many in the village he was viewed as a man virtually incapable of abandoning traditional ways fast enough, personifying the wholesale social demise around him.

Ermenegildo had a nickname: The Big Mouth. A quirky manic-depressive equally prone to both swings, he was all over the village during his manic phases engaged in ceaseless stream-of-consciousness prattle. One of his favorite chatting points was the upcoming end of the world. He lived in near-debilitating dread of a violent, unforgiving apocalypse arriving at any moment, an understandable fear perhaps in a culture so thoroughly garroted by worldly forces beyond its control in recent decades.

Ermenegildo's other major concern was much more pedestrian. It was his hair. He was regularly trying new fashions to alter those straight black strands he found so dull and unattractive and, well, so Indian. He eventually decided on a perm for himself. While others in the village watched and giggled, he let the lovingly combed curls grow to about medium length. He did all the perms himself, fretting over them, attempting with his own hands each week to look less and less Indian while, conversely, down the river in Zábalo and up a notch in irony, Randy Borman was taking long, determined strides in a jog the opposite direction.

From my seat on Loriano's porch, I saw another rat just then, smaller than the first one, scurrying noisily across the far edge of the room—this time in plain view of everyone present, though no one said a word. I'm not sure whether Loriano's family threw their garbage directly under the house or what, but now, in addition to the rodents, I saw cockroaches flitting through the peripheral shadows all around. The more I looked, the more roaches I saw—and suddenly I felt the blood leave my face. To avoid rudeness, I had to force myself to stop gaping and fix my attention back on Loriano, who was then telling the story of how Chief Ermenegildo had recently traveled all the way to North America, to a city with big, big buildings called Baltimore, Maryland.

The chief had gone by invitation to a special leadership conference, Loriano said, sponsored by an economic development organization in the United States. It wasn't clear just how much Ermenegildo gained from the experience beyond two elementary insights. The first was that a haircut in big-city America was unfathomably expensive. It depressed Ermenegildo very much that he couldn't afford one while he was there. The other was that the world was so much bigger than he had previously believed—it took eight hours to *fly* to Baltimore—that even if the end of the world came tomorrow, it would take so long working its way down to Dureno that the Cofan had nothing to worry about for at least several more years. That fact was a fantastic relief to the chief. It countered the depression of the missed haircut and left him on a manic high for several weeks after he returned home to Ecuador.

Loriano comically slapped his palms against his thighs as he finished the story, and there was laughter. Everyone laughed, in fact, laughed hard, laughed at the crazy chief, but not hard enough to wipe away the touch of pity on every face in that room. A listless and awkward moment of silence came as the laughter at last ebbed away. Then, finally, Randy stood from his hammock and stretched his arms. He let go a long yawn. It was time for bed, he said.

I unfurled my bedroll on a porch hammock while the others padded off sleepily to the back rooms of Loriano's house or to other houses nearby. I turned to see Randy, his tunic dirty from the day of travel, following his Indian wife through a door to a guest room where Felipe and Federico already lay stretched out on their own woven hammocks.

The door shut behind him, and as I settled in for my own sleep, I thought again of the Dureno chief's bizarre trials. If it made sense to ponder whether Randy was or wasn't a true Cofan (and by extension a bona fide chief), it made just as much sense to ask the same of Ermenegildo Criollo of Dureno. Legitimacy was the sole currency of genuine leadership, after all. But then, what did it mean to be a true Cofan these days anyway? I recalled a previous conversation I had had with Randy wherein, trying hard to justify his native lifestyle, he had told me that the original intent of the word "Cofan" was simply to signify "people of the Aguarico River." That's it. That was the original meaning. And by that definition, Randy seemed very much more a person of the Aguarico—fishing in it, hunting around it, assailing oil wells to preserve it—than did his "blood" counterpart, the Maxus gravel broker with the much-fussed-over 'do. One could forget the world of wildlife in this complex Amazon region, it seemed. It was hard enough just keeping track of the human picture, where the closer you looked, the more the colors and images melted together, running all over—and off—the canvas.

I blew out the last candle and climbed into my hammock. In the surrounding moonlit air, the world grew suddenly quiet. Downriver, the dredger and dump trucks had ceased their work for the night. But before I could enjoy this relief, the sound of hundreds of tiny scampering legs filled the void. Directly below me and around me in every direction, roaches and mice now dashed furiously about, leaving me suddenly glad I was elevated two strategic feet above the floor. But ripples of nausea passed through my stomach as the sound continued. Mice couldn't jump this high, could they?

I was in no mood to ponder the answer, but neither could I sleep without one. My mind tottered off to other thoughts as a diversion, sifting through the day's events, landing—no doubt thanks to the eeriness of the moment—on the most unsettling image my eyes had yet to take in during this zigzagging journey through the rain forest.

The moment had come earlier that evening. The twilight rainstorm had passed and night had fallen, and I was just finishing an extended tour of the Dureno community provided by José Criollo, the community's young assistant chief. Through the ghettoized center of the village, José led me, as if through a gauntlet. We passed the group of sullen two-year-olds dressed in charity diapers around a water well that didn't work. We passed the boisterous "drinking party" where more men in bell bottoms sat around a hovel stoop making *Cristal* disappear. We passed the hut next to it with the boom box blasting bad and scratchy disco music up to a sky long since bereft of macaws. Then came the wood-plank Christian church with the rusting tin roof, and the village elders with their "Maxus Energy" baseball caps (courtesy of the gravel deal), and the ten-year-old boy with his toy helicopters made from fresh sardine cans.

But then something different came into view. Something very strange. We rounded a path near the village periphery, and I saw it up ahead, beyond a spread of trees. There was a small, abrupt clearing, and inside the clearing was a small Cofan house. And inside the house was nothing— nothing at all. There were no people, no voices, no candlelight, no wood smoke from a cooking fire. Just a dark, empty, shadowy shell of a structure in the gray glow of moonlight.

"That's Mauricio's house," José said to me in a voice cold and stark. "He used to live here. He lives in Zábalo now. Do you know Mauricio?"

I nodded my head as I stared in fascination at the abandoned house. The front door hung crazily from rusted hinges. The entire right wall was missing, the wood planks long since cannibalized by other members of Dureno, José said.

We were soon moving again, arriving eventually at the shattered remains of another house—Lorenzo's house. The thatched roof of this one was cratered with multiple holes, allowing a forest of moonbeams to pour through, soft and silvery, spearing an interior devoid of anything or anyone. Another ghost house.

Then came Elías' house, then Alfonso's, then Luis'—all the Cofan who in fear and disgust had fled this place called Dureno, with its dearth of food and abundance of force-fed foreign ways. In canoes they had gone, down, down, down the Aguarico, 120 miles down, almost to Peru, to make the final stand. There they found clean water and game and trees enough to sustain them while they beat back, again and again, the encroaching germ of Dureno's killer. Again and again.

"There are more houses," José said. "Many more. Come this way."

He showed me all the others, one by one, vacated and forgotten. Each was as distinctly chilling as the one before, each a testament to a family afraid to perish and so willing to disappear, setting off for a reinvented life, leaving behind only the skeletal houses, the unburied bones, of the old one, the dead one.

5

They came from the sky, those first Texaco oilmen. One by one, step by step, they scrambled down rope ladders, down from the clouds, hanging, swinging, swaying below hovering helicopters. Their boots touched soil and they entered the Amazon, gods of a strange new land, ready to bend to their will all that they saw. Which wasn't much. Not in 1965. Not really. There were no roads along this stretch of the Aguarico basin then. No clearings. Not even a place to land a helicopter. Just trees. Everywhere, trees.

But Texaco had a hunch and it proved to be right: Below the dark jungle surface lay even darker riches. A well was flown in preassembled from Colombia. It struck oil. Another was brought in. Then another. Same results. Soon supplies and men were arriving by barge along the Aguarico. And soon, inside the growing constellation of new wells, Texaco set up a bustling and brazen field headquarters. It called the camp Lago Agrio—"Sour Lake" in English. Not that there were any big lakes in the immediate area, much less foul or malodorous ones. The name came from Sour Lake, Texas, a dusty speck of a town east of Houston where Texaco made its first fortuitous strike in 1902. Two thousand miles away and more than sixty years later, poking deep holes along the equator, the company had found a follow-up profit fountain so thick and generous it evoked fond memories of home. Lago Agrio it was. Ecuador's oil boom had begun.

But there was a small problem. No doubt those first American *petroleros* flying around in their helicopters saw the lithe, red-skinned bodies far below them, skirting to and fro in the downpour of chopper noise. And had those *petroleros* paused to ask why this was the case, why these scattered Indian men like streaking apparitions were fleeing in apparent confusion, they would have learned this: The growing Lago Agrio oil camp had been set down in the exact center of a rich and important Cofan hunting area. Some of the region's largest herds of peccaries roamed there, a valuable source of protein for the community. But company workers were far too busy to ask, much less care. Business was too good. By 1972, wells were going in by the dozen across the region. Helicopter pilots fresh from war in Vietnam, steeped in new skills, pitched in—and soon the company was reaching even the most remote forest spots with new and daring quickness.

Next came the bulldozers. Getting the oil out of the jungle meant miles and miles of pipelines—and roads to maintain them. One of Texaco's first major pipeline roads ran just north of the Cofán settlement of Dureno. Then came roads to the east, west, and south. With time, the company actually tried building a road running right through the village itself—an erasure dragged across the community's heart—until Cofan men felled trees and seated themselves with shotguns in the path of the bulldozers. Texaco, with a huge fuss, finally backed off.

Over the years, sole compensation for the Cofan's mangled territory came in the form of a Texaco emissary pulling up in a pickup truck each Christmas with bonbons and pats on the head for all the darling little Indian children. True, there was that one time in the late sixties when twelve-year-old Randy Borman and three other Cofan youth came upon a new well site while hunting monkeys in the forest. The camp cook gave the boys rice to eat and then let them keep the four steel spoons they used. By 1992, when Texaco turned over all its operations to Petroecuador, its 400 wells had been pumping an average of 220,000 barrels of oil per day for twenty-plus years—a roaring, spewing, nonstop river of dollars. The Cofan, meanwhile, still had their four spoons, nothing more. It was their first and last cut of the pie.

But the bargain wasn't enough. Not for Texaco. To keep operation costs even lower in this middle-of-nowhere jungle so far from the eyes of the outside world, the American company trimmed corners. Lots of them. For more than two decades, it failed to reinject unprocessable crude oil and toxic production wastes into its well holes—or to otherwise dispose of them safely—as was the routine industry practice back in the United States. To save money, it rid itself of these virulent substances—in extraordinary quantities—by alternative means. It dumped them into open-air pits and into streams and rivers and delicate wetlands; or it simply set them on fire in huge pools without any controls or safeguards whatsoever, letting them burn for days.

At least these are some of the claims made by virtually every national and international environmental group ever to set foot in the region. "Nothing in my experience prepared me for the scenes . . . in the Ecuadorian Amazon," wrote Robert F. Kennedy, Jr., after a July 1990 visit to the upper Aguarico valley sponsored by the U.S.-based Natural Resources Defense Council. What environmental lawyer Kennedy saw, among other things, was the "tragedy" of Texaco-built production pits that *each day* helped dump "an astounding 4.3 million gallons of toxic production wastes and treatment chemicals into Amazonia's rivers" while virtually assuring the destruction of the region's aquifers at the same time. A 1993 team of Harvard-trained scientists studying inhabited areas adjacent to former Texaco production facilities found drinking- and bathing-water sources tainted with oil-related carcinogens—including highly hazardous polycyclic aromatic hydrocarbons—at levels from two to 2,793 times the maximum accepted by the U.S. Environmental Protection Agency. Astonishingly, even rainwater samples in some areas along the Aguarico were found to be unfit to drink, the result of what locals call "black rain," or rain contaminated by particles from burning waste pits.

Texaco, it should be noted, denies the charges of rampant pollution made against it. All the charges. Emphatically. "We have always placed a very high premium on environmental safety in Ecuador," a spokesman later told me.

The Ecuadorian government itself, nonetheless, admits that many times more oil has been spilled in the country's Amazon rain forest since the boom began than was spilled in the Exxon *Valdez* disaster in Alaska.

The actual total comes to thousands of gallons of oil per day for twenty years in an area barely larger than the state of Mississippi.

I saw several gallons of the noisome liquid myself the very next morning after crossing the Aguarico by canoe with Randy and his now-pared-down entourage of Cofan family members. We were climbing out of the Dureno River, a side stream of the Aguarico, and were about to hike up to the oil road that would lead us on to Quito, when I spied an evanescent sheen of petroleum atop an eddy of dingy water.

"That's from the most recent spill," Randy said, pointing to another spot where a stringy black strand of oil was corkscrewing up to the surface. "The oil's still all around here."

I poked a stick into the water. Faintly, more oil floated up. A large catfish lay dead nearby, bloated and belly up. "Welcome to Dureno," Randy said.

This particular spill had occurred twelve months earlier. A squad of company workers deployed to manage the crisis had done a farcically half-hearted job of cleaning things up, I was told. The workers scooped up only part of the oil, mostly along the shore, then poured it into plastic bags and placed the bags in unlined pits just a few feet from the river. Predictably, the foul stockpile of oil was now leaking back into the surrounding soil and water, methodically poisoning everything with a saturating thoroughness guaranteed by the slapdash disposal method.

The air around the river reflected this condition, smelling like hot asphalt after a summer rain shower as we ascended the bank to the barrio town above. The town itself lay straddling a dirty gravel road, offering to the eye a wreckage of low-slung cinder-block houses topped with cheap roofing tin. This *colono* enclave of 2,000 settlers, also called Dureno, was situated almost directly across the Aguarico from the Cofan village. Even in the bright morning sun, the place looked insufferably dreary. A towering construction crane, abandoned and left behind by a Texaco subcontractor years before to disintegrate in place, the word AMERICAN painted neatly across its side, stood at one end of town, dominating the scenery and bestowing a junkyard appearance over the whole community.

And then there was the pipeline. Blackish-brown and fat, braced atop ugly steel support bars, it slithered along the main road a few feet above the ground, ferrying Amazon crude to Pacific tankers 320 miles away. The oil I'd just seen in the Dureno River had been disgorged from this very pipeline. Several of the *colonos* in the town who witnessed the disaster later told me how it happened:

A hulking Caterpillar front-end loader working for an oil-company subcontractor was mending part of the pipeline road when the driver, bending over to light a cigarette, accidentally backed his machine into the pipeline itself. There was a chilling ripping sound right before part of the pipe erupted with terrible force. Oil shot twenty feet into the air in a thick black stream, propelled like a rocket by the pipeline's great internal pressure. As it happened, the oil came out at an angle, choosing as a target the nearest roadside house. It landed in torrents on the roof and against a side wall of the structure, literally pounding the house. Inside, a woman and her children frantically slammed shut doors and windows to keep oil from blasting in and coating interior furniture and walls and the prone body of a sleeping infant. The hum of pressurized oil splattering against tin and concrete, meanwhile, could be heard a half-mile outside of town.

An incensed crowd soon gathered around the spectacle, demanding the driver do something. Never pausing for a second, the oil soared and gushed forth still more, now forming huge pools in the road. Desperately, the driver used his front-end loader to dig a trench beginning at the point of rupture and running directly to the Dureno River itself a few hundred feet away. He then used the vehicle's shovel bucket as a sort of shield, deflecting the trajectory of the oil away from the house and into the trench. A foot-deep stream of black liquid at once began roiling and gurgling into the river, which rapidly turned soupy and jet black as a result. A similar spill a few years earlier along a river south of Dureno actually led to a fire. For miles from bank to bank, the river's surface burned, a rolling, boiling field of flames. That didn't happen to the Dureno River. It slipped into a deep coma instead. Virtually everything in it, drenched black with sludge, died.

You have to give oil its due: Even in very small quantities it packs a toxic punch of remarkable power. A gallon of oil will kill fish in a million gallons of water and adversely affect aquatic life at concentrations as low as one part per hundred billion. Minute quantities of its constituent parts (benzene, toluene, xylene, polycyclic aromatic hydrocarbons) will cause cancer in humans and animals. That day on the Dureno River, perhaps as much as 10,000 gallons of oil cascaded into the water.

DANGEROUS and FLAMMABLE read the warning signs plastered across tanker trucks barreling through town the morning of our arrival. The trucks, headed to nearby wells and processing facilities, rumbled so loudly that Belizario had to shout as he pointed out the exact spot where the oil pipeline had ruptured twelve months before. As usual, Belizario was dramatic with his gesture, his fingertip resembling an angry spear launched at a distant target. For eight long hours that day last year the horrid spill had continued into the Dureno River before the pipeline was finally shut off. By then the disaster was complete, years of degradation assured.

A major criticism of the Texaco-built pipeline, now operated by Petroecuador, was its basic design. The night before, Randy's missionary brother Ron had showed me a copy of a $1.5 *billion* class-action law suit recently filed by lawyers in New York against Texaco on behalf of the roughly 30,000 Indian and *colono* inhabitants of the company's former Amazon production areas. The suit claimed that hundreds of miles of pipeline snaking through the region had been negligently constructed with an inadequate number of shutoff valves. Consequently, "when a rupture occurs, oil will (often) flow unchecked for days." A quick shutdown of the Dureno pipeline might have saved the river, for example, but delay brought ruin. According to the suit—itself an historic document for its sweeping environmental scope and hefty compensation demands—the pipeline design, combined with the routine dumping of toxic well wastes into streams and open-air pits, constituted "outrageous" behavior on the part of Texaco of treating "the pristine Amazon rain forests of Ecuador and its people as a toxic waste dump."

My senses were still processing the opening doses of this surreal oil culture as Randy led the way up from the river to his vehicle, a liberally dented Toyota pickup truck he and Ron shared and kept parked behind a building in town. Amelia and the boys joined Randy in the cab while Belizario and I took the bed. From my seat, I noticed that the bizarre, rusting, three-story construction crane was the tallest thing around, the land in every direction having been strip-mined entirely of trees that could offer any sort of rivalry. A shame of nakedness seemed to hang over everything—and over my Cofan companions themselves. Their unusually urgent movements seemed to say it all: Flight from this place couldn't come fast enough for them.

We lurched onto the pipeline road and instantly the chemical smell of oil intensified. The reason was simple: The road itself was thickly coated with the stuff, this time by intent, not accident. Petroecuador, following the practice of Texaco before it, regularly sprayed the dirt-and-gravel road with thousands of gallons of unprocessable crude to keep down the dust its drivers complained bothered their eyes. This incredible practice left toxic oil lying wet and gooey and in places hardened like tar across the pock-marked two-lane road. As a result, everyone who could afford them in this settlers' town, from young children to old women in dresses, wore high rubber boots against the small sea of filth they trod through each day just crossing the street.

A Latin culture dominated here. Groups of men in straw cowboy hats stared out from the town's concrete storefronts and plank walkways as early-morning salsa music bellowed here and there from cheap radios. Most of the men were campesino farmers or oil company hands waiting to be picked up for jobs on nearby wells.

A predawn rainstorm had left the road blotched with large oil-and-water puddles that Randy swerved to avoid as the pickup pulled out of town. For the first time in my presence, Randy wasn't wearing a tunic that morning. He had on a pair of tired and faded blue jeans, a Washington Huskies football T-shirt, and a baseball cap. Also for the first time since I met him, I noticed a watch on his wrist. Outwardly at least, the chief was metamorphosing right in step with the scenery. His briefcase lay securely stored in the cab, just below the dashboard.

When we first jumped into the truck, Belizario had gone straight for the front of the bed, sitting with his back against the cab wall, facing rearward. There seemed to be no reason for this beyond personal preference, so I thought nothing of sitting on the edge of the bed above a wheel well, a more comfortable perch.

Just outside of town, we picked up a group of six hitchhiking campesino men carrying sacks of corn and trussed-up chickens. The first two men to board went straight for the cab wall with Belizario, filling that space. The rest joined me along the bed edges.

Things finally became clear the first time a truck, heading the other way, passed us while plowing simultaneously through an extended puddle in the road. I tried ducking out of the way, but it was too late. Suddenly, the whole left side of my shirt and upper pants was splattered with oil drops. My stomach fell with revulsion. I reached up to touch my tingling left cheek and pulled away fingers smudged with grimy oil. I touched my hair. The same. My glasses were splattered. I couldn't get my handkerchief out of my pocket fast enough. I wiped furiously, trying not to think of the carcinogenic possibilities of this insidious minishower. Everyone in the pickup bed had taken a similar hit save Belizario and the other two men against the cab. I should have seen this coming, I suppose, but some sort of warning would have been nice all the same. My clothes were completely ruined.

I pulled a plastic tarp from my pack. There was no threat of rain at that moment. The sky was blue overhead. The tarp came out to fend off the idiotically oil-sprayed road. The vulnerable farmers and I huddled underneath the plastic, draping it over our heads like grim, hooded monks in a medieval scene.

Protected so, I surveyed the countryside, my eyes colliding first with the relentless, omnipresent oil pipeline. It ran in ugly, blackened tandem with the winding road, curve for curve, absorbing various subsidiary pipelines that emerged along the way from unseen wells operating nearby.

Beyond the pipeline lay the small farm holdings of campesinos, the plots stitched together like parts of a ragged quilt one against the other in an almost unbroken spread along and beyond the road. Most of the farmers were immigrants from Ecuador's land-poor highland and piedmont regions, the pipeline road having offered them free and unhindered entreé to a vast land once the exclusive domain of the Cofan. Everywhere I looked now, in every direction, the land was fully—or nearly so—cleared. Haphazardly laid out plots of corn, coffee, and cacao plants, interspersed with the rotting trunks of innumerable chain-sawed trees, filled the clearings. Equally haphazard in manner were the tiny wood-plank houses where families of ten to fifteen people lived without plumbing or electricity.

The strategy here, the reverse of life in Zábalo, was to dominate the forest, to make it heel completely. Trees were leveled and soil beaten into service to produce wealth measured in metric tons and board feet. There was no braiding of human needs into the forest's life-giving balance of wealth the Indian way. One's livelihood here preyed upon the defeated, obliterated remains of the forest.

But my eyes didn't miss the hand-painted signs peppering both sides of the road, telling the full story: FARM FOR SALE. The paradoxically thin and feeble rain-forest topsoil, dependent as it was on constantly bio-recycled nutrients, was depleted after just five to ten years of typical cultivation. Families then sold off their degraded properties for a pittance, routinely moving on to new plots, new patches of forest, migrating in massive slash-and-burn waves radiating out from the Texaco road. Dead and denuded, the land left behind often succumbed to erosion on a scale so appalling that elaborate sandbag walls were needed in some places to keep gullies from gobbling up the oil road itself.

At that moment Randy passed a second truck heading the other way through a big, inky pool in the road. I dropped for cover as fast as I could, hearing the rat-tat-tat of oil drops against my tarp shield. The overkill of this place was becoming almost too much to comprehend. Some psychopath's torture victim hacked to tiny pieces then lavishly coated with gasoline and set afire—that's what this nearly clear-cut land slathered generously with oil and other toxic wastes brought to mind. I peered out just in time to watch another wetland pond pass by, its surface gummy and black, lying prone below a span of pipeline. That macaws evaporated entirely from this scenery seemed the only possible response. That any living creatures of any specification—humans included—could survive the withering effect of so harsh a wasteland is what, in the end, truly astounded me.

A while later, the pickup slowed to a crawl, then stopped completely. I stood up to investigate, looking over the top of the cab, and was deflated to see an actual traffic jam. Ahead of us, a paralyzed string of cattle trucks, oil-company tankers, bush taxis, and buses disappeared over the next hill, a hundred yards away. Zero traffic, meanwhile, was approaching from the other direction. Randy got out to inspect the situation, disappearing over the hill himself. When he still hadn't returned ten minutes later, Belizario and I went to find him. We reached the crest of the hill, then looked down upon a small nightmare. An eighteen-wheel logging truck of massive dimensions, piled high with the trunks of thirty-four freshly chain-sawed forest giants, had jackknifed on the oily, slippery-wet road. There were no injuries, but during the accident the gigantic trailer had slid a long distance before coming to rest in a perfect blocking formation from roadside to roadside. The trailer's rear axle had actually come to a halt just feet before it would have struck the pipeline itself, narrowly averting yet another catastrophic spill, no doubt. We could see Randy standing near a group of other onlookers, everyone gaping at this giant cork in a bottle.

Belizario continued toward the wreck while I decided to take a short break, discreetly sidling off the road. So much morning *chicha* was again to blame, leaving my overburdened bladder suing for peace. I found a spot overgrown with tall grass right next to the oil pipeline. There, laminated in my oil-splattered clothes and sticky hair, cursing a derelict logging truck in this gloomy ex–rain forest, this dark cartoon land of ecodoom, I prepared myself, taking aim. Some wild hope told me that it was worth a try, that with enough accuracy I might feel better. And it worked. I turned and headed back to the road after a long moment of savored satisfaction, a steaming, watery mark of revenge left lying across the pipeline.

There was no change in the situation by the time I caught up to Randy and Belizario. The enormous logs, perhaps living trees just days before, might as well have been bricks in a wall the way they blocked everything. Trailer chains thick enough to have been swiped from the *Queen Mary's* decks, meanwhile, strained to keep the logs in place. The hard-hatted driver, sitting roadside, had given up entirely trying to move the truck. With dozens of vehicles stretching away in either direction he seemed to want nothing so much as to disappear.

Looking back, I'm sure it was Randy's switch to more Western clothes that made me think he'd be a little more like me that day, that is, rousingly uptight in the face of this traffic bottleneck. But the crisis had no apparent effect on him at all. If anything, unaccountably, it seemed to relax him a little, easing him out of one of his signature bouts of stay-away-from-me stoniness that had kicked in briefly earlier that morning.

"What a pain," I said, standing next to the chief now, gesturing toward the truck.

He looked at me. "This?" he said. "Oh, this isn't so bad."

He must have known something I didn't, I decided. "Has someone announced a tow truck is on the way?" I asked hopefully.

"No."

"But one will be coming?"

"It could take a while."

"Like a few hours?"

"I don't know," he said. "Maybe. But they'll get it out of the way."

I walked away from the scene scratching my oily head. Hitting a mire of morning traffic for a few *hours* was tantamount to death by a thousand cuts in the fast-moving milieu of my own country. And here were Randy and Belizario chatting together with little emotion in Cofan, even smiling now and again as I walked away. I tried to remind myself of the central fact: Either the logging truck was in the road or it wasn't. One or the other. It was that simple. One or the other.

Three very long hours later a mammoth Petroecuador cargo truck with a heavy-duty winch finally emancipated the logging vehicle and we were again on our way. I resumed my tarp crouch as we entered the outskirts of Lago Agrio, Texaco's once-small jungle headquarters founded by those men from the sky twenty-five years ago. The place was today a very bad hallucination of a city, squalid and nearly treeless, jammed full in frontier slum fashion with a population of 15,000 people, a good quarter of whose women were prostitutes servicing the run of oil men passing through. Merchants along the oil-splashed main street sold shotguns by the discount dozen and dynamite by the quarter stick. Others offered stuffed macaws with haunting marble eyes and giant tarantulas pickled in Colombian whiskey. Grizzled men donning Petroecuador baseball caps romped in and out of myriad bars—we passed three bars with honest-to-god swinging saloon doors—while less fortunate laborers pedaled rickshaw bicycles burdened to the breaking point with sacks of beans and rice. During a brief halt, I purchased a pair of the locally de rigueur black rubber boots to protect my feet and pants from further ink-black ruin on the noxious roads.

Degraded land continued to mark the way as we pushed on to Quito, crossing the equator on a southwestward course. Campesinos with thundering German-made Stihl chain saws made quick work of whatever trees were still in need of slaughter, while large petroleum processing stations began showing themselves behind double-helix strands of concertina wire. An ugly jumble of graffiti, meanwhile, intensified the eyesore of the oil pipeline along the road. One message stood out from all the others, penned in the blood-red paint of dissent. I tried to recall ever seeing environmental protest graffiti anywhere else in the world, including spray-paint paradise New York City. I couldn't. But there it was over and over again on the TransEcuadorian pipeline:

$$
\begin{aligned}
&\text{T ERRORISMO} \\
&\text{E COLOGICO} \\
&\text{X} \\
&\text{A} \\
&\text{C} \\
&\text{O}
\end{aligned}
$$

Not everyone in Ecuador, it seemed, was content to let a class-action law suit do their talking. A tempest of anti-Texaco sentiments building in recent years among intellectuals, labor groups, and conservationists in Quito was now spilling into the countryside just like the black stuff.

Our climb out of the Amazon basin was at first slow and steady, almost imperceptible, before giving way to the sharper rise of Andean foothills. Then came the real assault, accelerated and steep, past the peaks themselves. We followed winding asphalt roads through deep valleys and past heart-stopping overlooks, all the while crossing and recrossing the shimmering headwater tributaries of the Aguarico. The crystalline alpine air sent Belizario and me scrambling for blankets, squeezing closer together in the pickup bed as snowcapped pinnacles, getting closer, marked the way ahead. The TransEcuadorian pipeline kept up all the while, mile after mile, looking ridiculously cumbersome and inefficient somehow as it traced steep hills and mountains—up, up, up, up; down, down, down, down—then followed its own bridges over river canyons.

Randy pulled up to a strictly guarded army checkpoint in the road— the third we'd encountered since leaving Lago Agrio—where soldiers in polished combat boots and camouflage clothing demanded identification from all in our party. I produced my passport while one teenage soldier rummaged purposefully through my pack. Though we were waved through without incident, I kept wondering who—or what—the soldiers were looking for. Drug smugglers? Fugitives? Guerrillas? Ecoterrorists? A glance at the accompanying pipeline seemed to bestow worth on the last possibility. For the multitude of people whose health, homes, and hopes had been smashed to splintered misery by the country's Amazon oil industry here lay an extra-

ordinarily vulnerable target. A whole barge of contingency-crazed
Pentagon strategists couldn't protect every foot of this pipeline twenty-four
hours a day through jungle and over mountain passes for 320 miles. Simply
put, any ongoing series of hit-and-run explosions could have bottled up this
flow of Amazon oil to the sea as effectively as the logging truck had blocked
vehicles on the road earlier that morning.

I mentioned this thought to Randy later on, making the obvious com-
parison to the environmental "monkey-wrenching" popularized by
American author Edward Abbey and now a tactic in the repertoire of Earth
First! disciples and various other ecocop outfits worldwide. I was surprised
to learn, however, that terrorist threats to the pipeline, portentous graffiti
notwithstanding, were pretty much nonexistent here and weren't taken seriously as a future possibility by the Ecuadorian government. More surprising
still, given the breadth of his reading and his own seemingly prototypical
impulses, was Randy's admission that he'd never heard of Earth First! or *The
Monkey Wrench Gang* or Abbey himself, for that matter. Here he was, way
down in the Amazon, on his own, reinventing a wheel that had already
been put to repeated use elsewhere. The great difficulty and loneliness of
that task, I think, is what led him to accept so eagerly when I offered to ship
down from the States a parcel of Abbey's books full of monkey-wrenching
target ideas and philosophical justification for going on the attack.

On the scale of an ant trickling into an immense and magnificent
cathedral, our pickup finally descended the last stretch of bending mountain road into Quito, city of one million people hemmed in by mountains
at the top of the world. The mix of centuries-old churches and modern-
glass office buildings lay touched by glittering sunset light as we made our
way past ponchoed Indian beggars and *blanco* corporate bankers in glossy
Italian suits. To the west, through a haze of auto exhaust that never quite
seemed to leave the city, old colonial Quito rose up on hills with its maze
of whitewashed copulas and Spanish-tile roofs. Farther away still, overlooking the whole city display, was eighteen-thousand-foot Mount
Cayambe, a glimmering extinct volcano whose halo of snow and clouds
lay tinged indigo by the approaching twilight.

The warmth of Randy's small modern apartment, shared with missionary Ron in an upper-income Quito neighborhood, was pure luxury
satisfaction after the windswept cold of the truck ride. I used a phone in a

well-equipped sideroom office to make overnight arrangements with a nearby friend. Flanking me were a computer, a fax machine, and a filing cabinet, Randy's replacement weapons when he hauled his jungle quarrel to Quito. The apartment served as a sort of urban campaign headquarters for the chief. And there on the office wall was the prize itself: A map of the lower Cuyabeno Wildlife Reserve with the village of Zábalo highlighted in yellow Magic Marker. I stared at the map for a moment with a new appreciation of conservation's central challenge: Making an endangered place vivid and specific in the human imagination—and keeping it there. After two days of travel, that Day-Glo bar across the map already had something of the aura of an abstraction, real in its essence but nearly as indefinable and amorphous as the SAVE THE RAIN FORESTS bumper sticker next to Randy's desk or the stack of exotic jungle books on his shelf, headlined by Zikmund and Hanzelka's travelogue thriller *Amazon Headhunters*. Maybe it was the brain-numbing temperature of the truck ride, but suddenly the jungle and all we'd left behind there seemed so foreign and very far away.

Randy and I agreed to rendezvous for the solar-panel meeting four days hence at Petroecuador's downtown headquarters. Having shut down an oil rig just three weeks before with spears and shotguns, *achiote* paint across his face, it was time once again to meet his adversaries head to head—and it showed. Standing there waving good-bye from his apartment door, standing in this Western milieu of faxes and cars and urban conferences, where the Cofan and their forest's fate would probably be decided someday once and for all the way some people's lives are decided in hospitals—far from home, coldly, clinically—Randy looked agitated, distracted.

Or maybe he just wasn't good at saying good-bye, at letting go, no matter what the circumstances.

▼▼▼

To get to the top of Petroecuador's fanciest and most important office building in downtown Quito, you have to hit the "PH" button on the shiny new American-made elevator. That's what the receptionist at the high-security front desk told me. I took the elevator, ascending the eight flights as the letters "PH" finally registered in my mind. The door opened and I saw the marble steps and ficus plants and chromelike handrails so burnished you could part your hair in them. Some very important people wanted to talk to Randy that day. His meeting had been arranged to take place in the finest possible setting—the company penthouse.

I was running late, and things were already under way by the time I reached the conference site, a small room on the penthouse's south side. Not wanting to interrupt, I took a seat outside an open door where I could hear and glimpse most of what was going on without entering. Randy and Belizario, representing the Cofan, were seated across from two company men in slacks and dress shirts. The men wore their ties slightly loosened as if arduous work were already in progress, hardball very much under way, at this 10 A.M. hour. And so it was. The two sides were presently reviewing with great concentration the basic points of the Paujil accord signed earlier that month.

For his part, and there's no other way to put this, Randy looked thoroughly preposterous that morning. It wasn't that his clothes were ill-fitting. They looked almost custom-tailored, hugging perfectly the sinews of that trim and fit body. Odd, though, the extent to which taste is a matter of what you're used to. After so much time with Randy, my mind simply balked at the sight of those expensive dress jeans coupled with the beige silky shirt. Then there was the shirt's collar—big and wide open—pulled over the lapel of a beige nylon suit jacket, a playboy V of chest hair left exposed in the process. It was all a sort of '70s leisure look made even more retro by the zip-up-the-side black ankle boots. But the style wasn't the real problem. Not at all. It was this: Culture had triumphed over race. I realized at that moment that I knew Randy as an Indian. Despite his Caucasian stock, in the category of dress clothes at least, he would always look more—and perhaps only—genuine to me in beads and face paint, tunic down to his knees. Belizario, sitting next to him, looked just as awkward in his own dressy clothes. They both had the out-of-place and somehow heartbreaking look of nineteenth-century Plains Indians dipped in suits and cravats and top hats and shuttled to Washington for treaty talks.

Rodrigo Cerón, the mustachioed environmental negotiator for Petroecuador, faced Randy from across the table. Point by point, he reaffirmed the company's commitments, made in the jungle under the Paujil accord, to communicate fully with the Cofan concerning any company operations on their land. Drilling activity would always be preceded by a review list of chemicals and machinery intended for use, as well as detailed cleanup plans for potential spills. This was all immaterial, of course, since the Paujil well had been unilaterally and permanently closed down by Petroecuador, and the Zábalo well, the one the Cofan had set on fire, was tied up in court. There was, in sum, no immediate threat of drilling anywhere in the lower Cuyabeno.

Or so Randy thought.

When the review phase of talks ended, the Cofan chief conferred briefly with Belizario while opening his briefcase. The staccato thrusts and tonal shifts of their Indian language took on an extra twist of exotica against the backdrop of high-rise windows overlooking Quito's urban sprawl, where eight floors down on the street a new Fruti Hamburger fast-food shop was celebrating its grand opening and billboard artists atop bamboo scaffolding were painting a rent-a-car ad. Belizario's usually assertive, talkative manner was clearly subdued in the face of this great deluge of foreignness. He let his cousin-in-law Randy do all the talking to the oilmen while he looked on quietly with his swarthy good looks, his hair riding over the back of his dress-shirt collar.

Randy shut his briefcase and handed Cerón a sheet of paper. For the past three days, the chief had been contacting solar-panel manufacturers in the United States by fax for bids. In Cerón's hand now was a bid from Sunnyside Solar, Inc., of Brattleboro, Vermont, offering enough solar panels to power a couple of 50-watt bulbs in every Zábalo hut for a total price of $21,875. The cost was almost $2,000 more than Randy had expected, but not the slightest quiver showed on Cerón's hand. He placed the document atop a small pile of other papers on the table. As soon as the remaining two or three outstanding bids came in, Petroecuador would select one and transport the panels to the Cofan within a month, Cerón said.

You could almost feel the penthouse walls slacken and sigh with the enormous look of relief that came over Randy's face. There would be no last-minute complications on this point. No reneging. The Cofan would soon be holding fluorescent proof of their power to negotiate and fight for their rights. Light had come to the jungle.

But then everything changed, just as quickly. The confident sense of accomplishment on the Cofan side of the table was all but extinguished when Cerón leaned over and pulled something out of *his* briefcase. It was a photograph. He held it up for Randy and Belizario to see. He asked them to take a good look.

"Recognize this?" he said. "Huh? Do you? This is the oil-drilling platform we built near the Zábalo River."

He pointed to a wide, wooden structure in a clearing of jungle trees.

"Or should I say this is what the platform looked like before you guys set it on fire."

Cerón looked directly at Randy now.

"It *was* you guys who set it on fire, wasn't it?"

Randy said nothing. The Cofan had never taken direct responsibility for the burning of the platform in the national press, and Petroecuador had never forced the matter, never tried to ascribe public blame. Both sides had been content to keep the little message between themselves without the potentially mutual damage of sensationalized media publicity.

"It *was* you guys who set it on fire, wasn't it?" Cerón asked again.

Randy was caught wholly unprepared for this. He wasn't sure what Cerón's intention was, but he sensed danger, so he decided to play it safe, to keep up appearances. He grinned mightily, elevated an eyebrow, and peered right back at Cerón.

"Us?" he said with a riff of sardonic laughter. "*Us?* Why, we don't know the first thing about what happened at that platform. Not *us*. Not a thing."

He laughed some more, now backed up by Belizario, who was doing the same. The only thing missing was a wink and a nudging foot against Cerón's leg under the table.

Cerón maintained his serious air for another moment before yielding to the strategy, going along, laughing a little feigned laughter himself. So that's the way it was going to be. He tossed the photograph onto the table.

"Okay, okay," he said. "I just wanted to hear what you'd say if I asked. Now I've heard it."

When he spoke next, his tone couldn't have been more serious. He stopped pretending even to smile.

"Are you aware, Randy, of just how much money your community has been costing my company?"

Again Randy remained silent.

"Not a little bit of money," Cerón said. "Not this little solar-panel money. I'm talking about hundreds of thousands of dollars. Each time your men detain and expel our seismic surveyors from the forest it costs us a lot of money. And now we've had to suspend operations at the Zábalo well due to fire damage and the court matter. That suspension alone is costing us several thousand dollars per day. Do you realize that? Counting everything, we've lost $200,000 already because of you. It's all adding up. This whole situation is becoming very, very expensive for us."

Cerón seemed to catch himself just then, modulating the rising tone of rebuke in his voice before it could get too strong and slip out of hand and tip this previously cordial scene into one of awkward ugliness.

"But never mind all that," he said. "Never mind. The point I really wanted to make, Randy, is to tell you that we still have every reason to believe there's oil at the Zábalo site—and we still have every reason to want to exploit it."

The look of ease and control that had been on Randy's face was draining away now. He leaned back in his chair. His shoulders dropped slightly.

"Of course we want to do a good job of protecting the forest when we exploit it," Cerón continued, folding his arms tightly across his loosened tie. "Which is why I want to let you know right now that we've scheduled an environmental impact study for the Zábalo site. During our temporary lull in work activity there we want to make a careful examination of the surrounding land so we can be sensitive to it when we resume operations."

The announcement, loaded down with bushels of negative implications, was made even worse by the timing: The study would begin in just *two weeks*. Petroecuador was in a hurry.

Cerón went on to give details on the size of the study team and what, in broad terms, it would do. But Randy scarcely seemed to hear. He was numb with dismay. Like Paujil, he had hoped the company would ultimately forsake the Zábalo site completely. A successful well there would, like a magnet, draw ax-wielding mobs of settlers along future pipeline roads from the heavily colonized Napo River. The *colonos* would move right into the heart of Cofan land. It would be Dureno all over again. And there wasn't much the Indians could do about it. Not right now, anyway. They couldn't exactly refuse the impact study. That was out of the question. Their official position, again, was not one of being anti-oil. It was oil exploitation with forest preservation—which is what Cerón had just said was the company's goal too, and which everyone knew was impossible. The Cofan's bluff, in a sense, had been called. They were being squeezed.

Of course, an impact study was better than nothing at all, better than the old company way of barreling in à la Texaco without any care whatsoever. The study might buy the Cofan some time, providing them with more openings for bureaucratic and legal challenges and delays. But just as easily it could mutate to a bad-guy-turned-good PR screen for Petroecuador, behind which the usual sloppy work and destructive roads could eventually proceed.

The main point, however, putting all unknowns aside, was clear: By going to all the trouble of an impact study, Petroecuador was serving notice that it was still very serious about oil along the Zábalo River. And if the company were that serious, it would probably, eventually, almost inevitably get what it wanted. The whole tide of momentum that had been with the Cofan the last few weeks, the optimism, the sense that they were winning the fight for the Cuyabeno, had been instantly changed by Cerón's surprise revelation in the penthouse that morning. The future was bearing down on the Cofan with a dark and frightening scowl—again.

Randy was coldly formal in accepting the details of the impact study from Cerón. He made clear his expectation that the study team consist of respected independent scientists, and he welcomed the team to visit the Cofan at the Zábalo village.

Moments later, the meeting over, I watched as Randy and Belizario walked out of the conference room. On Randy's face lay a patchwork of multiple emotions held together by an overriding look I recognized to be pride. It burned across his face, that pride, and it seemed justified, for several reasons, despite the conference's last-minute setback. An incident in the elevator immediately after the meeting seemed to prove the point.

We had just passed through the gleaming chrome-and-marble hallway to the elevator and were gliding down from the "PH" floor when a stop on the fifth floor brought in a balding, suit-and-tie oil-company executive. The executive stared at Randy for a moment, then said, "Excuse me, but aren't you Randy Borman?"

Randy nodded, and the man shook his hand with the enthusiasm of an autograph seeker.

"You had a meeting with us this morning, didn't you?" he said. "How did it go? Did you get everything you needed?" The reference was clearly to the solar panels.

Randy nodded again, and the man emphasized how much he hoped it was true, that the Indians were satisfied after making their long trip to the capital. With great deference, he then ushered us through the lobby, waving good-bye, saying what a pleasure it was to have met the chief of the Cofan.

"Did you see that?" Randy said to me as we entered the sunlit sidewalk full of pedestrians outside. "I don't even know that guy, but he knows me. Everyone in that building knows the Cofan. That's good. Politically, I think that means a lot. We still have their attention."

Facing the clamor and exhaust fumes of midday traffic, Randy began hailing a cab, his blue eyes searching the stream of cars while his beckoning arm reached out from the curb. He still looked grossly peculiar in his dress jacket and boots, like an impostor, like he'd awakened in someone else's clothes and couldn't wait to shed the encumbering mask.

Briefcase in hand, on the curb, he continued, "No matter what happens, you can tell Petroecuador takes us seriously. I think they fear us, if you want to know the truth. We're in a position to spear these guys nationally and internationally with more bad publicity, and we're ready to do it, and they know it, and they don't want it."

"Spear" them? I thought. Surely, given explosive tensions between these two parties just weeks before, there was a more delicate way of putting things than "spear" them. Besides, we were in the city now. Spears weren't part of the vocabulary here. I was half tempted to mention as much to Randy. *The city. We're in the city.*

A cab stopped and we piled in, Randy and I in back, Belizario up front. "Plaza de la Independencia," Randy told the driver, the two locking eyes in the rearview mirror. Across the street, in the courtyard of an old Catholic school, students in dark uniforms were making giant piñatalike figures of bullfighters from brightly colored crepe paper.

The taxi pulled away and Randy glanced anxiously at his watch. Then he grimaced. The same chief who from time to time held conferences in the jungle to determine what day of the week it was now was fretting over the status of the narrow minute hand on his wrist. He was thirty minutes late, it turned out, for a second scheduled meeting that morning, this one to discuss "Cofan survival" with a government commission on Indian affairs. Thirty minutes late—and the meeting was on the other side of town. Randy, it seemed, handled the Western sense of time about as well as he did the clothes. Back in the forest, he and the Cofan could be part of time, floating unencumbered inside its ponderous day-to-day current, and so be free from time. But in Quito it was different. Here one was pitted against time, set apart, in competition with it, and so destined always to be its servant.

Randy glanced again at his watch. Again he frowned. The taxi continued its slow weave through traffic. The fare meter, clicking loudly, again and again, kept close track of our account.

With nothing to be done, Randy leaned back in his seat and, with brow creased, closed his eyes for a second as if trying to blink back a bad memory. Which he was.

"Talk about coming out of nowhere," he groaned, leaning forward now, eyes again open. He was referring to Cerón's surprise revelation back in the penthouse, of course. "I mean *nowhere*," he said. "I was really starting to think we were on better ground with the Zábalo site." Then, unexpectedly, a slight tone of hope rose in his voice. "I guess we'll just have to wait and see how the study goes. But right now I can already see problems. That's an extremely delicate area ecologically, and there's no way they can do a valid study as fast as they seem to think they can."

Cerón had said the team would spend only five days at the site. There might be an opening for the Cofan in that, a potential challenge, and Randy was wasting no time making mental notes.

The soiled concrete and angular steel of Quito's modern business sector passed our windows as Randy continued. Airline offices and embassies went by, shopping centers and banks. Soon we began climbing into old colonial Quito with its crowded cobblestone streets and narrow alleyways. Along sidewalks, Otavaleño Indians in fedoras and long, braided ponytails sold brilliantly woven Andean rugs. A mufflerless motorcycle rode past spewing black smoke and deafening noise.

"But no matter what," Randy continued, raising his voice above the noise while the earlier luster of pride stayed on his face, "that meeting with Cerón today was historic. I don't care what happens. For the first time an oil company is officially admitting that the way it does business in the jungle causes problems, and those problems affect a specific group of indigenous people. That's what the solar panels say, period."

He took a long breath. Then another. Two nuns in black habits were standing outside a baroque cathedral collecting money for homeless street children. We were stalled in traffic. Randy went on. "But I guess, after this morning, I'm not so sure how big a difference our success today will make in the long run. Our bigger problem, when you stop to look at it, is not Petroecuador. It's the whole world economic attitude we're facing—the way most Westerners tend to think in terms of making money."

I asked him to elaborate, and as with his earlier reference to spears his mind floated back to the forest for an analogy. It's where he turned for his surest sense of justice and resolve.

"Let's say you live on a river with lots and lots of turtles," he began, "and you've decided on a way to harvest all of them at the same time, wiping them out forever, for a profit of ten dollars. But you have to weigh this against the alternative of leaving them where they are and having a few turtle eggs for breakfast every morning for the rest of your life. In the Western mentality, you always go for the ten dollars. It's that simple. You rarely consider the future when there's a little cash to be made today. It's a very, very basic mentality that makes no sense whatsoever. And it's going to wipe out the world unless the few people who see disaster written on the wall do something."

I recalled again how the "harvest" of oil in the lower Cuyabeno would effectively wipe out that entire forest—and the Cofan with it—for enough crude to meet U.S. needs for about ten days.

I also recalled the fresh image of Randy sitting just moments before in that corporate penthouse facing representatives of the very mentality he'd just condemned. I wondered: If Randy had such a sharp notion of what these men were about, what did they think of him? How did these "Westerners," as he called them, these tie-wearing executives stuck in the trappings and mind-set of the opposition culture, make sense of fair-skinned Chief Borman? Was he a crackpot to them? A meddler? An outsider just pretending to be an Indian? What?

"I'm not sure how they approach me, to be honest," Randy said. "I think I'm confusing to them. They're not sure what to make of me. But I do know they accept me as an Ecuadorian. Whatever else they may think of me, they know this is my home.

"Beyond that, I think in some ways I'm a relief to them. They prefer working with me over many indigenous leaders. I'm dependable and consistent in talks. I'll do what I say I'll do, so they know where they stand with me. I understand the thinking of their culture that way. The average indigenous negotiator from the forest doesn't. He has so many cultural differences that things bog down and everyone gets frustrated and any trust is lost. I can discuss oil-company methods and technologies many indigenous leaders simply can't.

"At the same time, I'm a bit scary to the company—and the reason's simple: They can't pull the wool over my eyes the way they can many indigenous leaders. If they slip up and renege on me, I'm going to respond the same way they would if someone slipped up and reneged on them: Protest, go to court, go to the media. And they know it."

Randy was at that moment describing a threat without actually sounding threatening, just persuasive. It was part of what I recognized as an innate flare for the nip-and-tuck art of negotiation on his part. Randy understood power. He knew how to identify it, how to organize to get it, how to seize it if need be, and how to use it once obtained. He seemed good enough at negotiating in general, in fact, that I wondered if he actually enjoyed it.

"Not really," he said. "I do this because I have to do it, not because I like it or want to do it. Right at this moment, I'd rather be fishing on the Zábalo River. Just quietly checking my nets in the forest. I always feel this way in Quito, no matter how I may seem to (the Petroecuador officials). I miss the forest. I just want to be in it. I can never wait to get back to it.

"Sometimes," he pointed out, "it actually seems kind of strange to me. I think, why are we doing all this protesting and negotiating? To save the forest. Why are we saving the forest? So we can live in it, so we can be in it as we choose. But instead, here I am right now doing this. I'm in Quito, not in the forest. But I have to be here doing this if there's ever going to be any forest for us to live in in the future."

Worse, it seemed to me, the morning's developments virtually guaranteed more of the same for a long time to come. Here was a man who had just spent two days canoeing and driving to Quito, followed by several days faxing back and forth to U.S. solar-panel manufacturers, followed by the morning-long meeting with Petroecuador just completed, followed successively by the Indian affairs meeting he was off to now. Then there was the return home, where he could immediately expect to meet with environmental-impact specialists and resume the nearly constant process of monitoring and policing Cofan land, bracing for more well-site openings and potential court cases and vigilante raids. "Etcetera" might as well have been a Cofan word. On and on it would go. And none of this left much time for fishing and hunting and weaving baskets, for being a Cofan. The bureaucratic trees of survival, in short, were threatening to block Randy's view of the forest—perhaps forever.

"Turn left here," Randy told the taxi driver just then, again checking his watch with agitation.

If there was one paradox capable of eclipsing all others in Randy's strange life, perhaps this was it. So odd that in the end it might be his Western side, the side making him such an able negotiator for Indian rights and tough oil-company adversary, that could finally bring about his undoing as an Indian as surely as deforestation ever could, chewing up all his time at conference tables, preventing him from living in any meaningful way the life of a Cofan in the forest he had chosen as his home.

"I hope it's just temporary," he said when I mentioned this. "I'm hoping it won't keep going on like this forever, this heavy involvement."

But Petroecuador had just made it perfectly clear it wasn't giving up on the Cuyabeno, I reminded him.

Randy turned and silently stared out at the sights of Quito passing by.

"So it probably won't be temporary," I said. "It sort of looks like it's going to go on and on, doesn't it?"

Randy kept peering out the window. He never answered the question. A long moment passed and I decided not to ask again.

6

Felipe, four years old, was fifteen feet above the ground, up in a custard apple tree, when it happened. He was sidling out onto a branch, about to grab a ripe piece of fruit, when he misstepped and suddenly there was no branch to meet his foot. Just air. Head over heels, in a free-fall tumble, Randy's eldest son plunged to the ground.

News of what happened failed to reach me somehow on the other side of the village that evening. I went looking for Randy the very next morning, only to find Belizario sitting on the chief's porch, eyes bruised black from worried exhaustion. "The accident was very, very bad," Belizario said. "There was a hole across Felipe's head. There was too much blood. Randy left during the night. They've gone back to Quito, to a hospital."

Remarkably, by separate routes, we had all just *arrived* from Quito the same afternoon the accident happened, finishing the long return trip following the Petroecuador meeting. It had taken two full days of traveling to get home, and now Randy and family had turned right back around, barely in Zábalo an hour, a badly injured child in their arms. They were retracing their steps into the Andes. Their boat was gone. Their house was empty.

Belizario stood and showed me the nearby tree where the fall had happened. "He landed here," he said. "His head hit this." He pointed to a gnarled tree root thrusting up from the ground with pointy, rock-hard nubs all along its length. "The sharp parts of the wood, they stabbed here and here." He pointed to two spots on the side of his own skull.

Randy, I learned later, had heard the fall from inside the house and rushed out to find Felipe lying on his back in a daze. Through the blood already saturating the child's hair, he began probing with his fingertips for skull fractures.

It wasn't Randy's habit to panic in such situations. He didn't think first of dashing off to some distant Quito hospital when an ugly fall or occasional hunting mishap drew a little blood. One hundred miles from the nearest airstrip, seventy miles from the nearest road, you learned to use your own needle and thread in such scenarios, stitching up cuts yourself. You augmented the handiwork with your own cache of Western antibiotics or a blend of herbal poultices—or some combination thereof. The same held for other ailments—blisters, bites, stomach aches, skin punctures, fevers, rheumatism. Randy, like the rest of the Cofan, treated the problem first, usually successfully, right where he was.

More serious injuries, from time to time, got the village-based remedy as well. When a grotesque gasoline fire a few years back left Lorenzo's son covered with second- and third-degree burns across half his body, Randy went to work, treating the young man on the spot, at home, rather than making the hard journey to the nearest infection-ridden rural hospital. For months Randy tended to his patient, applying fresh bandages, consulting with local healers, reading every word of a Western medical manual on burns, plying teas and antibiotics until full convalescence was achieved. The size and severity of the boy's burns would have easily challenged specialists at even the best of Western hospitals.

And when his own sons came into the world, it was Randy who was there to deliver them, arms scrubbed and outstretched inside a jungle house, coaching his screaming, sweat-laden Indian wife to push, push harder. It simply didn't cross his mind to surrender responsibility to a university-trained obstetrician or even a village midwife. These were his sons. It was his wife. He would perform the task. "Amelia does all the work anyway," he told me later.

Now the same hands that had brought Felipe into the world were again covered with blood, touching the boy's scalp. It took but a few seconds hunkered there in a crouch below the custard apple tree to assess the situation. The look and feel of the wound, the ominous shape of the exposed root that had caused it, all announced definite cracks in the brain's shield, the bone literally splintered, punctured. That, in turn, meant the immediate peril of unstoppable internal bleeding, a hematoma of ghastly consequences, blood literally flooding the brain. Possible coma is what it meant. Possible death. It was all beyond Randy's ability to treat. Herbs and stitching thread were of no use to him now.

Felipe was still conscious, crying with pain, as Randy heaved him from the ground. "We have to get to a hospital as fast as we can," Randy said, urgently turning to Amelia. "Get some things together and let's get Felipe into the boat."

They departed a little before sunset, fleeing upriver hoping to reach the airstrip at Tarapoa or Lago Agrio the next day in time to catch a flight to Quito on the Hercules.

That's all Belizario could tell me that morning after it happened. The Bormans were gone, date of return unknown. Randy had pledged to radio the village from Quito as soon as he had news. But for now, all everyone could do was wait, on tenterhooks, hoping they'd see young Felipe alive again, remembering only the sound of Randy's outboard engine, roaring upriver in the waning light, fading away slowly, to nothingness.

▼▼▼

I remember a different sound as I turned away from Randy's house that morning, having just heard the grave news. It was a terrible, unsettling sound, coming from some place far away. It was a sound like that of a great approaching storm, with great destructive winds, with all the whistle and howl one imagines swirling around a Siberian cabin during a January blizzard. What I was hearing in truth, however, were not storm winds at all but the breath of a single howler monkey, that creature embodying, surely, the greatest incongruity between sound and sound-maker in the entire animal world. How a two-and-a-half-foot-tall male primate could generate such blaring, weird, windlike roars—even in the cause of impressing a mate—was beyond me. So loud was the sound that it could easily carry a full two miles through the jungle, three miles over open water. It was a sound that puts chills in your heart.

But it wasn't alone that morning in the village air. There were other, more subtle and soothing sounds offering their scattered voices amid the thatched huts, sounds that I very much wanted to enjoy after the wilderness of oil and concrete upriver: The thump of moored canoes knocking gently against one another along the shore, the sigh of cicadas in the lavish canopy overhead, the hiss of cane grass ruffling in a shoreside breeze while macaws screeched their version of happy return overhead.

But it was the not-of-this-world sound of the howler monkey that dominated that morning after Felipe's fall—like a distant wailing off stage, the Greek chorus crying out as tragedy makes its black descent. The monkey eventually hushed, receding into the forest, but not before I reached the midway point of the village and the strange sight of Bolívar and Elías working intently on the frame of Bolívar's expanding house-in-progress. The men were putting in more ceiling and wall braces as if actually preparing for the mirage hurricane of terrible winds, battening down hatches. Their silent and furrowed faces were no mirage. The men exuded a brooding air as they measured, lifted, and tied supporting poles into place. In the two weeks I'd been away they had made considerable progress—window sections were set in place, walls prepared for wood planking—so the frowns would have been out of turn if not for the fate of their chief's son the day before.

Bolívar waved for me to join him and his father atop the still skeletal second-floor ceiling. This I achieved by clumsily shimmying and swinging my way up the house's various support beams. There was no ladder of any kind to assist in this matter, an apparent superfluity for people who casually scale tree trunks for forest edibles and jog headlong across the narrowest of log bridges in hunt of quarry. I was breathing hard and was a little nicked up by the time I executed a final awkward chin up to the second-floor ceiling.

"I'm not a Cofan," I said to my friends, finding a steady perch to catch my breath. Their faces puckered with mild laughter as they welcomed me back to Zábalo. "He's not a Cofan," they said to each other, mustering more chuckles despite their dreary moods.

Serious faces returned as we talked of Felipe. Randy's strategy, Bolívar said, had been to reach Transturi's luxury riverboat upstream where an on-board Western doctor was permanently stationed. The fact that Randy hadn't returned yet meant the doctor had confirmed the diagnosis of a fractured skull and the acute threat of hematoma—echoing the need for immediate hospitalization.

"But Felipe's a strong child," Bolívar said, straining to put a rosier closure on the matter. He wiped sweat from below the jet-black bangs of his own young face. "We have hope Felipe will be okay. We have hope like the Aguarico, never stopping."

With the Bormans gone, the family's pet woolly monkey had wandered over to Bolívar's house and was making a mess of a bundle of vines meant for lashing wall posts together. The monkey tossed the vines into the air, then wrapped them around its waist. The loss was minimal, given that Bolívar and Elías had progressed to another phase of construction. They pulled out a pouch of three-inch steel nails purchased upriver in Lago Agrio. Bolívar used the nails to reinforce the house's structure at critical junctures all along the frame, driving them in with a hammer he'd borrowed from Randy. A series of swift *thwacks* sent one in now—followed by a stream of others. Bolívar was breathing permanence into this comparatively spacious two-story structure, each bang of the hammer offering a sort of rough and reassuring synonym for "home."

The ten dollars Bolívar had spent on the nails, it turned out, came from a stash he had carefully saved from his part-time job guiding the American backpackers who came down to Zábalo for jungle treks. The backpackers arrived in groups of a dozen or so, sanctioned by Randy and shipped down ten times a year by Wilderness Travel, a Berkeley, California–based adventure trekking outfit. Besides wanting to finish his house before the January delivery of solar panels, Bolívar was keen to beat the next group of tourists due to arrive later the same month for a four-day trek into the jungle, something the Berkeley outfit marketed as the "Emerald Forest" tour. Along with Randy and the other Cofan workers, Bolívar did a little bit of everything on these treks. He served by turns as trail guide, canoe *motorista*, and stevedore; he cooked big pots of American-style spaghetti over jungle fires for the often homesick gringo palates.

Bolívar was about to drive in another nail when I asked him if he enjoyed his job working with tourists. Did he find it interesting? I wondered. Fun? He lowered the hammer to his side.

"Yes," he said. "It is good work. It helps us in Zábalo."

"But do you enjoy it?" I said.

"*Si,*" he replied, shrugging his shoulders now. "*¿Como no?* Why not? *Si.*"

His words again lacked enthusiasm, exuding instead a tone of timid perplexity. I wasn't sure he understood my question, frankly. The traditional Cofan emphasis on community well-being was getting in the way. I had noticed in several prior conversations with Bolívar his difficulty distinguishing between his own likes and dislikes on the one hand and what he saw as best for the community as a whole on the other. It came through in his way of using "we" over "I" much of the time. If Zábalo was happy, he was happy. What more was there? Whether it was personally "fun" having backpackers pass through the community—that was an issue he had never stopped to contemplate. Not really. There was no survival advantage in personal fun.

But what of boredom? I couldn't help wondering whether the exotic beauty of the surrounding forest—so exceptional by world standards— wasn't a thing of utter routine with Bolívar, a sort of ambient background noise so relentlessly daily in its manifestations that it turned the role of guide into something frightfully ho-hum. I pictured myself escorting groups of wide-eyed Indians with cameras and binoculars on four-day treks through my suburban Washington, D.C., neighborhood ten times a year. "Okay everyone, please stay on the sidewalk. Nobody wander. What? Where? Oh, those. Squirrels. Eastern grays, I think. Juveniles. They're hunting for nuts or trash or something, I can't tell what, below the street lights over there. The lights? They're programmed to come on, if you're interested, every evening precisely at sunset. Never fails. And now, around this next corner—*voilà*, there it is, where we get *our* food. A grocery store. G-R-O-C-E-R-Y. Fruit, canned tuna, microwave popcorn, hemorrhoid ointment—everything we need we get right here." Yawn, yawn, yawn. Again yawn.

But looking at matters this way was still more or less beside the point. That morning in Zábalo, high atop Bolívar's grand home-to-be, I could see Norma, Bolívar's big-boned wife with the liquid black eyes, sitting next door in the warm sun. She was hard at work using a knife to meticulously clean and polish the shells of a dozen *shasha* seeds she'd just gathered in the forest. Shiny brown and gently tapered, the seeds would later be cut in half to form bell shapes, then strung together to make beautiful necklaces and bracelets patterned on traditional Cofan themes. These would then go on offer to the visiting tourists—another source of income. Whatever the Cofan thought of all this side work in tourism, I suppose, the central fact remained: A whole barge of peccaries couldn't bring in the boat motors and fishing line and shotgun shells and books for the community schoolhouse the way an annual docket of organized tours could. Certainly in a country as poor as Ecuador you could do worse for your pay than stir fat pots of jungle pasta while pointing out the equivalent of front-yard squirrels to ever-earnest visiting foreigners. So Bolívar was being more pragmatic than stoical, I think, when he told me he hoped to train his own brood of sons to be forest guides after him, passing on this newest Cofan tradition.

It wasn't to be cruel that I changed subjects just then, bringing up the environmental impact study, the one Petroecuador was planning to begin at the Zábalo well site in just two days now. I figured Randy had mentioned the study to Bolívar before his quick exit the night before with Felipe. I was wrong. Bolívar winced as I relayed the news, as if one of the three-inch nails he gripped in his hand had just pricked his skin somehow.

Sitting there on the elevated roost of the house frame, we were high enough up to see a liquid poetry of morning light stretching lazily across the Aguarico. We were high enough up to catch a breeze off the water that made the palms around us move with the happy sway of drunken sailors. It was a day far too beautiful, I decided, for so much foul news. In the big blue Amazonian sky, a giant dolphin was riding a chariot made of pearls through the air, the chariot drawn by a regal train of enormous butterflies. That, at least, was what the cottony billow of clouds told my eyes. The sound of the howler monkey, roaring in the distance, had entirely ebbed away by now, giving way to a gentler song: Bolívar's sons laughing and leaping and chasing each other around the house. They were trying to put parrot feathers in each other's hair.

"The *petroleros* are coming back to Zábalo?" Bolívar asked me. "Even after we burned down the well?"

I nodded. "They say they want to study the area carefully so they won't do any harm when they start working on the well again."

The wince that was before on Bolívar's face now turned to a look of knowing, cynical revulsion. He needed no explanation of how absurd and fraught with deception such an approach might turn out, how

Petroecuador might try to hide behind a faulty environmental impact statement if the Cofan weren't extremely careful.

"*Muy, muy mal,*" he said. "*Muy peligroso.*"

He lifted his hammer, driving in another nail with fierce, pounding blows. Then he stopped, looking as if some great hand of realization had just slapped him hard in the face. "And they're all going to be here at the same time!" he said. "All the people. So many people!"

I was confused. "'All the people'? What do you mean? What people?"

"Where are we going to put them all?" he gasped. "Where?"

"Bolívar, what are you talking about?"

"The environmental study people *plus* all the students," he said finally. "The whole class of students! Everyone's going to be here at the same time!"

Energetically he explained how the very next day Indians from four different tribes across the upper and lower Cuyabeno reserves would be converging on Zábalo for a four-day seminar on plant identification and use. I quickly recalled Randy mentioning something about this to me in Quito. It was part of a month-long course sponsored by the Ecuadorian park service to promote the sharing of forest knowledge among indigenous groups, while training and certifying the Indians to be park guides. The framework for the course had been Randy's idea from the start, his brainchild, part of his quest to recognize, preserve, and reward with tourist dollars the skills of the Indian people who actually lived in the forest, who know it best. The Cofan chief had himself been slated to teach half the seminar classes in Zábalo, ranging from the medicinal uses of ginger roots to the role of deforestation in global warming. But he'd miss all that now. He'd miss the union of his Cofan with the Quichua Indians from down in Zancudo, the Siona from the Cuyabeno Lakes region, the Secoya from the upper Aguarico. He'd miss, too, the environmental-impact team passing through Zábalo simultaneously like strange uninvited houseguests, going about their business of surveying land targeted for a potential oil well no one in the vicinity had asked for or wanted now.

A feeling almost of dizziness came over me as I contemplated all these disparate goings on here in Zábalo, the onrushing convergence in one spot not just of people but of ideas, basic assumptions about what constituted a resource and how to use it. I gripped the frame of Bolívar's roof with increased firmness, glad the whole thing was reinforced with nails, built to last. Everything that was happening here seemed part of an elaborate and prolonged game of chicken now, all the pieces set in place, right in line, proceeding apace—the guides course, Bolívar's defiant house building, the backpackers arriving in January, the environmental-study team organized by an oil company hot to get on with its business. The two basic sides in this long-festering oil-versus-forest confrontation both seemed to advance on the faith that things would eventually, somehow, break their way, everyone ignoring with greater and greater concentration the growing mass and momentum of circumstances that, unless something *did* change, unless someone *did* back down, would just make for that much bigger a final collision when it came.

"*Tantos viajeros,*" Bolívar said again. "So many visitors." He clucked his tongue softly as a sudden corollary realization dawned on him. "And just think," he said, "of how much they'll *eat!* So much food!" He feigned a great shudder of horror, wiggling his arms, lightening this otherwise heavy moment in typical Cofan fashion—with humor. It was one more form of denial, perhaps, but I had to laugh, too. "I must go hunting, hunting, hunting," Bolívar said. "Oh, yes, right away. We'll need maybe ten peccaries just to feed all the visitors. Oh, yes! So much hunting to do!"

He had far too many worries on his hands to invite along his hapless foreign companion, of course, and my memories of our last outing were too fresh for me to accept even if he had.

The next thing I heard on that roof was the sound of Bolívar yelling down in sharp Cofan to his two sons below. The boys were squatting together in the crotch of a legume tree next to the house, ten feet off the ground. You didn't have to know the language to hear the presence of young Felipe, injured and on his way to Quito, hanging on every syllable Bolívar uttered. The boys got down the instant their father finished speaking. I asked Bolívar what he had said.

He put a fistful of nails in his pouch and stared out at the tree.

"I told them, 'When you go up high like that, the distance is too big that you can fall.'"

▼▼▼

The village was starved for information. Two days passed, and still there was no word from Randy in Quito. Nothing. Perhaps Belizario, who'd been deputized monitor of the cranky two-way radio inside Randy's house, had missed the chief's attempts to call. Whatever the case, the situation was the same: No one knew the status of young Felipe's injury.

Just as mysteriously, Petroecuador's environmental-impact study team had failed to show. On December 5th, the scheduled arrival date, we waited from dawn to dusk with climbing anticipation, eyes scanning the western sky, ears cocked for the booming chop-chop-chop of modernity's tribal drumbeat, distant and growing louder, the rhythmic blades of helicopter steel slicing paths above the thick matting of trees. But darkness descended and the drumbeat never came. Where was the study team? Had there been a change of plans? Had the helicopters gotten lost? Had the study been called off? What? No one knew.

I was tempted to go to the Zábalo oil-well site myself, making a second attempt to photograph the burned remains there before the EIS team arrived. But two factors held me in check. First, not enough rain had fallen in past weeks to raise the level of the Zábalo River, and any attempt at seesawing up and over exposed logs in a canoe, chopping others with an ax, was well beyond my endurance.

Second, the indigenous guides course, also set for December 5th, *did* come off as planned, and I decided to attend. In two leaky canoes patched with flattened plastic soda bottles and riverbank mud, more than twenty Indians arrived accompanied by two park wardens and a university botany professor from Quito. The crowd easily outstripped Zábalo's guesthouse capacity, leaving the overflow to pitch tents along the riverbank where I was already bivouacked, our makeshift city nearly touching the lapping waters of the Aguarico.

The seminar's maiden session was held in the Cofan community house, a thatched-roof, pavilionlike structure resting on stilts on the village's eastern edge. With Randy gone, all classroom duties fell to the visiting professor, who was himself of Indian blood. The professor's name was Dr. Jesús Inca, but his earnest indigenous students called him simply El Doctor. He wore Jordache jeans and a baseball cap, and stood before the pupils holding a metal pointer he never actually used except to fidget with intermittently with his fingers.

"Our rich Indian culture is fragmenting, changing, disappearing in this country," Dr. Inca began in Spanish, his soft falsetto voice competing from the start with the chatter of a nearby pygmy marmoset and the stubborn crowing of a village cockerel roaming directly below the classroom floor. "We must stop this loss of cultural knowledge," he continued, "or it will surely stop us." He pointed to the verdant wall of jungle just fifty feet away. "Right in there may be a plant that can cure people all over the world of AIDS. Someone in this room may already know that plant. But unless we preserve our knowledge, we'll lose our chance forever."

The rooster again crowed annoyingly while several students, ready to start taking notes, sharpened thick pencils by rubbing them across the rough-cut wood of the classroom benches.

It was definitely an uneven mix of students, this group. Lorenzo and Mauricio, typical of the half-dozen or so Cofan participants, exuded a quiet, formal air, their backs ramrod straight inside flowing cloth tunics, their handwoven headbands cutting a striking pastel green swath across the midnight black hair. The other Indians—from the Quichua to the Siona—were much more assimilated to Western ways, dressed in tight jeans and loose T-shirts and, here and there, broad-brimmed Panama hats. They were generally more casual and relaxed in manner. Some persisted in whispered conversations even as Dr. Inca spoke. The pygmy marmoset I'd heard earlier, meanwhile, turned out to be inside the classroom, a pet of a toothless Siona woman student who wore a "Budweiser Racing" T-shirt and whose long, stringy hair offered an unlikely nest to the clinging, clamorous, petulant primate. In a mocking effort to silence the creature, the woman kept tossing it clear out the classroom door, only to have it reenter within seconds by the exact same route, finding the woman and climbing back atop her hair, where it went on chattering like some strange organic hat.

Things grew marginally calmer once Dr. Inca reached the core focus of his lesson. The seminar's first two days were meant to acquaint the Indians with the scientific method of classifying plants in Latin by genus and species. The last two days would be an exchange of tribal plant knowledge among the Indian groups themselves.

Complicating the whole process, however, was language. Four different Indian tongues were represented under that thatched roof, so retreating to Spanish—everyone's second and much weaker language—was unavoidable. This created a challenge for Dr. Inca, compelling him repeatedly to shift course in midsentence.

"Bueno, clase," he said at one point. "We're now going to begin a discussion of the complexities of plant gender." He scanned the class for signs of understanding, of which there were none. He went on, "Or should I say, we'll examine the particular reproductive structures of . . . uh . . . I mean, let's see, we're going to discuss how to tell a man plant from a woman plant."

The class, swatting flies in the midmorning heat, smiled with dawning comprehension.

On a broad pad of yellowing paper, Dr. Inca proceeded to draw the sexual plumbing of the plant world—*"ovario, estigma, filamento . . ."* From there he listed major plant genuses in Latin, "rubiaceae, euphorbiaceae, cyperaceae, poaceae . . . "

I still wasn't sure how much of this these forest people were absorbing. I later asked Belizario what the course was about. "Leaves," he said. "We're studying leaves."

To alleviate class tedium, Luis, one of the two park wardens in khaki uniform and black rubber boots, unsheathed a huge bowie knife on his belt and slipped into the forest in search of a snack. He returned to disperse long pods of tasty guava seeds to all the students, then resumed his position at the back of the room, chair tilted back, languidly cleaning his fingernails with the same enormous bowie knife.

After a break for lunch, the entire troop of us entered the forest for a little hands-on shop work. As always, the move from open-air riverbank to jungle interior was like entering another galaxy: Darker, cooler, a sort of infinite outer space of wildlife, full not just of trees but of lianas, bushes, climbers, stranglers, mosses, lichens, fungi, herbs, flowering epiphytes— all of it packed densely and chaotically along the trail walls, greeting you, wanting to smother you, reducing you to something small and insignificant. I passed a clump of blooming frangipani and hibiscus plants huddled below a giant hardwood tree whose trunk was balanced atop a gnarl of fingery roots. A rivulet of leaf-cutter ants was descending the trunk while a pair of hummingbirds—each tinged red and blue—circled up like stripes on a barber's pole, spiraling higher.

But the unwieldy mass of our group didn't mesh well with the scenery, especially given the throng of twittering, curious village children now taking up the rear, themselves followed by the yelping population of village hounds led by Mauricio's brute, Jaguar.

Dr. Inca, standing at the head of this caravan, still holding his metal pointer, tried to make himself heard above the babble of different languages and the crunch of leaves under paw and foot. The afternoon's objective, he said, was to identify plants belonging to the different genuses we'd just learned in class.

I was standing near the front when he said this. To my left were Mauricio and Lorenzo, the thickly built Cofan elders whose calm, quick-to-laugh amiability always made for pleasant company. To my right was Luis, the young warden. Luis promptly reached across the trail and pointed to a dark green plant with long tapered leaves and a knobby stem. Turning our way as if to get us started in the exercise, he said, *"Poaceae. Este es poaceae."* He then shook the plant lightly for emphasis.

I'm not sure what Mauricio understood to be happening, for he immediately stripped the same plant of its leaves, then carefully tucked the leaves inside a string tied around his left wrist. He smiled then, as if to say, "We Cofan don't shake this plant while making strange chanting sounds. We use the leaves to make beautiful bracelets like this."

He held up the bracelet for Luis to get a better look.

"Si," Luis said. *"Es bella. Pero, el genus es poaceae."*

Knowing an invitation when he heard one, Mauricio harvested more of the same leaves and fashioned a similarly lovely bracelet on Luis' wrist—whereupon the warden gave up, thanking Mauricio for the gift, then turning and walking away, his face a flush of hopeless frustration.

Mauricio wasn't cut out for the full rigors of scientific inquiry, I suppose. Which wasn't to say he was anything less than obsessed with plants. Actually, so eager were he and Lorenzo to get at the forest's variegated offerings that they began gradually breaking away from the main group, pressing forward, passing Dr. Inca, edging into the forest on their own, farther and farther. I saw their move as a welcome chance to elude the annoying mob myself, and so tagged along.

We'd gone but a short distance when Lorenzo, halting his steady, measured stride, reached down to pick the intricate leaf of a small fern along the trail. "This," he said, holding the leaf to my face, "we use for headaches. We boil it and drink it. The pain goes away."

"And this we use for bee stings," said Mauricio, immediately putting a different long-stemmed leaf in my face. He crumpled part of the leaf in his palm and dabbed it on an imaginary bee sting on his arm. I nodded that I understood.

Rather abruptly, Lorenzo snatched what was left of the bee-sting leaf from Mauricio's hand. "This," he said, "we also use for stomachaches." He gripped the sides of his ample midsection and doubled over. "Stomach," he said.

"*Si, si,* that too," Mauricio added, looking slightly disconcerted, as if he'd been upstaged.

I began to sense, accurately I think, that some sort of amicable competition was forming here. The two men turned and grinned at each other, politely, with aging faces, like wise men at odds over some important issue.

The pace of our walk quickened slightly as my companions continued reaping all manner of plants, elucidating for me the use of leaf, root, or stem, then hanging on to everything they picked, discarding nothing, as if determined, each of them, to have the biggest, leafiest bouquet at the end of our freebooting stroll.

With each step, meanwhile, we drifted farther from the main group. I glanced rearward through the dense foliage and could make out only a flash of colored clothing here and there. The din of human voices and growling dogs was lessening as well, though the pygmy marmoset could still be heard, gibbering idiotically, clinging ludicrously just as we'd left it atop the Siona woman's hair.

More leaves were in my face.

"This one we use for cuts," Mauricio said.

"This one for blisters," Lorenzo added.

The trail forked, and Mauricio veered right. I asked if we shouldn't wait for the group. How would the others know which way we went? The two men shrugged and pressed on, picking and pulling more plants, their broad foreheads wrinkling with concentration below the short bangs of dark hair. The forest grew denser. The trail forked again. We'd lost the crowd entirely now. Only each other's voices and the distant cry of a white-throated toucan reached our ears. There was a feeling of playing hooky in all this, of finding better things to do in the greenery, free of mediating rules, while somewhere far behind us Dr. Inca was applying the ancient pronunciations of a textbook language to everything around him, doubtless employing by now the absurdly huge microscope he'd lugged into the jungle for even closer empirical study.

"This one makes your heart feel better," Mauricio said, holding up yet another plant.

"*Que?*" I said, not quite following.

He pressed his palm to his breast. "When your heart hurts, you take this and it feels better. Your heart feels better."

I still wasn't exactly sure what he was getting at. Had I pressed the matter, I'm sure clarification would have been forthcoming. But I left it alone. I sort of liked the original implication: Heartache medicine. The Cofan had a plant cure for broken hearts.

Next came herbs for diarrhea, dizziness, and fever, as well as another Lorenzo described as among the strongest medicines the Cofan used. He pointed to his mouth, then cupped his jaw with both hands, indicating a bad tooth. "Makes it feel better," he said.

We continued into the forest this way for at least an hour, the men showing me still more of their great organic pharmacy, plucking plants as if from endless shelves, intriguing even themselves somehow with each new find. Buttery afternoon light filtered down through cracks in the canopy, meanwhile. The light flowed in oblique softness onto the body of a towering kapok tree, enchanting maiden of the forest, whose trunk of flying buttresses, like a skirt, absorbed the light in pretty patterns of golden polka dots. In the distance, a lone piha bird sounded its three-note cry, sharp and solitary—*wee-WEE-o, wee-WEE-o.*

Finally, we decided to turn back, but not before Mauricio picked a very curious plant. He put down his now-teeming bundle of greenery and called me over. The leaf was again narrow and tapered. With his thumb and forefinger, he tore the leaf along its side and held it up to his nose, breathing deeply. Then he did the same for me, and a wonderful fragrance invaded my nostrils, fruity and thick, the smell of an exquisite perfume. I took a second lungful. Was it a lemon scent I smelled? Honeysuckle? Both?

Unlike all the prior plants, Mauricio had failed to tell me at the outset how this one was used. By the time I asked him, he was too busy calling Lorenzo over for a sniff. Lorenzo's eyes nearly rolled back in his head at the end of his long inhalation.

"Hmmmm," he grunted.

I repeated my question as now Mauricio took a second hit.

"Nothing," he finally said, exhaling, smiling. "We do nothing with it. *Nada.* It just smells good. We like the way it smells."

We were forming a small circle now, the three of us there in the forest, away from the others, beyond the forks in the trail, a fragrance being passed back and forth between us. It was my turn again. I took my dose. Another ethereal rush filled my nose.

"It just smells good," Mauricio uttered again.

"Hmmmm," I said. "Yes it does. Hmmmmmmmmmmmm."

▼▼▼

When Roberto told me it was a perfect time of month to see freshwater river dolphins, I didn't quite understand what he meant. Why was one time of month better than any other? All I knew with certainty was that three more days had passed and still no news had arrived about Felipe, nor had the environmental-impact team shown up at Zábalo—and I was getting weary of waiting.

"Forget them," Roberto said of the study team. "The oil companies, they never keep their word. Come on, get in."

I poured my gear into the canoe, glad to be in the company of young Roberto Cedeño again, the ebullient fireplug of a guide who had led Russell and me through this same forest two years before. I'd gotten word to him that I was in the reserve again and now he had found me, was rescuing me.

He hadn't changed much, Roberto, with his close-cropped beard and swarthy good looks, his khaki fisherman's vest and binoculars draped permanently around his deeply tanned neck as if he'd been born with them there. The only alteration was the baseball cap he wore. It was poised in the reverse style now, pointing backward, a slovenly hip habit that had rubbed off on him from Russell, I think.

Even before we had properly shaken hands, Roberto lifted his binoculars and began doing his renowned impersonation of a World War II gunner.

"Ten o'clock! Ten o'clock! A dusky-headed parakeet! Look! Ten o'clock!"

Headlong, I dove for my pack, ripping free my own binoculars, but I was too late.

"Fast," Roberto said, scolding me. "You have to be fast if you want to see the birds."

It was his cheering neurosis: He hated for anyone to miss even a fleeting cameo in this episodic theater otherwise known as a tropical rain forest. A *blanco* born and raised in the urban congestion of Quito, he had fallen in love with the jungle during his very first visit as a boy, and now it was his adopted home.

When finally we shook hands, Roberto surprised me with some very big news. He had resigned his position with Transturi Touring that very same week, electing to set out on his own as a freelance guide in the Cuyabeno forest, launching his own company. I would be his very first client, in fact. We decided on a three-day canoe trip up the Lagarto Cocha River, that blackwater stream along the Peruvian border whose meandering current rolled through vast stretches of flooded forests with densities of wildlife and a scarcity of human visitation unsurpassed in the lower Cuyabeno reserve. Neither Roberto nor anyone he knew had traveled as far up the river as he proposed we do now. We would be aiming for the farthermost reach of the reserve, the end of the line, terra incognita for all practical purposes.

We were on our way the very next morning, motoring two hours east of Zábalo, gliding across the placid surface of the Lagarto Cocha with a hired Quichua *motorista* at the stern. A deadbeat mist loitered from an unusually chilly dawn as we passed Imaya, the last permanent camp on the river, and Roberto turned to me. "That's it," he said. "I've never seen this area before. It's all new to me now."

Not that there was much time to dwell on the fact, given the technicolor exhibition of birds darting here and there.

"Two o'clock! Two o'clock!" Roberto cried. "A plum-throated cotinga. Look! It's beautiful."

A shock of aquamarine feathers, shining brilliantly, inundated my binoculars as I lifted them to the cotinga poised atop a spidery fig tree. The bird's small size made the eruption of color all the more arresting. A swatch of purple decorated the throat, surrounded by that hot turquoise blue that literally seemed to glow, like neon, exploding at you. To this day

I'd still be swearing it wasn't real if the bird, as if sensing my blasphemous doubt, had not suddenly taken wing, flaunting its gaudy beauty, negating all possibility of an illusion.

"Nine o'clock! Nine o'clock! An orange-cheeked parrot," Roberto cried.

I looked, catching the bird in flight, its face-first tease of orange coloring passing overhead.

Then came an Amazonian umbrellabird, a purple-throated fruit crow, and a boat-billed heron, the latter a species Roberto had seen only twice before. After the avian desert of Dureno, this experience was like treating your thirsty, parched palate to the gulping excess of a case of the very best champagne: It left you feeling drunk.

But the euphoria couldn't mask a creeping stiffness forming in my neck born of so much looking up, scanning treetops for fowl. I paused for a while, resting, not lifting my binoculars even as Roberto went right on saying three o'clock this and ten o'clock that.

I leaned against a gunwale and looked out across the dark, slow-moving water. Its surface was smooth, without a ripple, reflecting perfectly, like polished glass, the trees along the shore and the clouds sailing overhead. Islands of yellow justice flowers, their blooms in the delicate pose of buttercups, festooned the current, floating atop beds of rich green algae. In the distance, one of the flowery islands lay jostled by wavelets spawned by the curling rise and dive of an otter chasing a banquet of fish.

"Hey, you're missing some great birds," Roberto said, noticing that my attention had drifted. "Look, a red-capped cardinal. Top of the tree. One o'clock."

With my neck still stiff, I didn't even try looking up. I looked down instead, aiming my binoculars at the polished mirror of the river's surface. It worked. I stared into the water, past a few clouds and a couple of tree branches, until a red-capped cardinal filled my eyes. The image was sharp and exact, full of perfect color and detail. After a few seconds, the bird moved to another branch and I followed it, still peering down into the water though my subject was actually fifty feet above my head. I did this off and on for the rest of the day, gazing at precious Amazonian birds with the aid of a river so pure as to be a flawless mirror, so clear it actually seemed not an image but the deep and intricate soul of the forest itself, dulled not by a single drop of oil or a single dollop of polycyclic-whatever hydrocarbons or the muddy sludge of a dredging tractor hunting road-top-ping gravel. Human beings might as well have been a moon species, so foreign were they to this upstream Amazon tributary. It showed.

When I revealed my river-top method of bird watching to Roberto, he at first didn't believe it possible, then he didn't approve. It wasn't good form to play tricks with nature's tricks, he said. He admitted, nonetheless, that illusion was a strange and widespread part of the jungle universe.

"I was in a forest village of Quichua Indians recently," he said, "where I got involved in a really bad situation. A baby no more than a few months old had become lost. We heard it crying, screaming at the top of its lungs, but we couldn't find it. We turned the village upside-down—still nothing. Wherever it had fallen or crawled off to, it was suffering, because it kept crying, screaming like crazy. Some of the village women began crying too, ready to pull their hair out with worry. It was really odd. We couldn't find the baby. Where was it? Then someone looked up and spotted the parrot. Human baby cries were coming out of its mouth without stop. On and on they kept coming out until half the village was throwing sticks up there to shoo it away. It was one of the weirdest things I've ever seen. Perfect mimicry."

He continued, "That sort of stuff makes Indians jumpy, by the way. There's a bird called a laughing falcon that's not even an imitator, not really, but it has a whistle that in Spanish sounds like '¡Al hueco va! ¡Al hueco va!'—'To the grave you're going! To the grave you're going!' When they hear that, many of the village people along the Aguarico get so scared they do every-thing they can to kill it, to get it to stop the terrible sentence."

Sunset was now approaching, and the only ones going to their graves were the two of us, I decided, if we didn't get some dinner cooked. Up ahead, a high, flat bank proved perfect for our tents; and the river piranha we caught, pulling them into the canoe hand over hand on crude fishing line, fried up nicely over an open fire.

With nightfall came the sterling light of a rising, ripe moon illumi-nating the camp. We restoked the fire, staring into its core as jungle shadows and the murky undertone of insects floated all around us. I put on another log and watched Roberto's young, bearded face take on an orange Halloween luster as he began to talk, growing reflective in mood. He told me how, until a couple of months ago, he'd been sure the

Cuyabeno forest was itself on its way to its grave, another fatality of oil, joining the 2,200 acres of jungle destroyed in a multitude of different ways every day across the Amazon—*ial hueco va!* He had pretty much abandoned, in fact, his lifelong goal of starting his own business as a freelance jungle guide.

But then something big happened to change his mind, he said.

"What's that?" I asked.

"The Cofan," he answered. "They happened. If you had told me six months ago that a small bunch of Indians like the Cofan could stand up to Petroecuador with a few spears and guns and have the company back down, I would have called you insane. Now it's part of Ecuadorian history."

The success confirmed Roberto's long-held view that the Cofan had a better shot—perhaps the only shot—of saving the forest over all other concerned groups, domestic or international, government or private. Roberto's own future lay with the small Zábalo clan. They were the vanguard. "What's different is that they're not weekend environmentalists in love with the pretty forest or a tour company just looking to stay in business. They live here. Everyone can understand that. The forest is their bedroom, kitchen, and living room."

The Cofan also had, in the form of Randy Borman, an uncommonly powerful weapon, Roberto added. Indeed, the actual limits of the chief's power were so far unknown, this being a novel situation. One thing was clear, however: Without Randy's knowledge of both Indian and Western values and vulnerabilities, without his ability to match—to maximum advantage—his tribe's strengths against the invaders' various weaknesses, oil rigs would already be clamorously sucking crude out of the ground all along the lower Aguarico, Roberto believed.

All the same, not everyone saw Randy as a benign warrior-hero come to vanquish the enemies of the forest and save its people. A variety of other Indian groups along the Aguarico weren't at all comfortable with the success and high profile of Randy and the Cofan, Roberto said. They resented the front-page articles in Quito newspapers, the slickly orchestrated stream of Western backpackers exchanging prized dollars for guided tours. It was probably jealousy more than anything, Roberto said, but these Indians, the Quichua especially (who were ironically recent immigrants to the jungle), saw Randy as just another gringo doing exactly what gringos have always done: Taking and controlling Indian land. Randy was simply using the Cofan as a front to get what he wanted, tossing in the novel claim of environmental protection as part of his camouflage.

"Well?" I asked Roberto. "*Is* he just another gringo?"

He thought about the question for a long moment. He was still wearing his baseball cap with the bill pointing rearward. His brown curly hair peeked out just above his ears. "Randy's definitely the only gringo I know who speaks Spanish with an Indian accent," he said at last, chuckling. "But do I think he's stealing land? No. Randy wants to preserve this whole reserve so the Cofan can survive in their one little part of it. That's what I think."

"Is he a typical gringo in other ways?"

"That," he said, "is not so easy to answer. I think that if he leaves the forest and goes to Quito for a long stay, maybe a month or so, he starts thinking and acting as much like a gringo as you, Mike." He chortled again. "But out here, especially now that he has a Cofan wife and children, I see an Indian when I see him. I've gone hunting with him. He's one of the best hunters, Indian or not, I've ever seen. Never misses when he gets close to his prey. Always comes back with something. And what a trekker. He's been all over this reserve. He's probably the only person in Ecuador who's camped right here where we're camping now. It wouldn't surprise me. And he never gets lost, just like all the Cofan. I know the forest pretty well, but I still get lost on treks now and again. I was lost for most of a day a few months ago. I left a trail to follow a peccary and found myself alone in the middle of the jungle. I got scared. I got hungry. I had no idea which way to go. I climbed the tallest tree I could find and looked around and all I saw were the tops of other trees as far as I could see, in every direction. It was terrifying. It was just luck that I finally found my way to the river. But Randy's on that different level. In that sense he's really like an Indian: He never gets lost in the forest. He always knows where he is and where he's going."

A good quality to have, I thought, in the wilderness thickets of Cuyabeno ecology and politics, where a single misjudged path can make the prophesy of laughing falcons come true—for you, your community, the land below your feet.

I stood and stretched just then, taking overdue respite from the cross-legged fireside perch. As I did, I detected a noise in the near distance. It was coming from the direction of the river. A hissing sound, rising softly up from the still water. Roberto heard it, too. He stood, and we both peered through the gentle downpour of lunar light. And then, suddenly, there it was, a sight so delicate and wondrous I felt myself grow instantly motionless, frozen in place, with awe.

"This," Roberto said, almost whispering, "is why it's a good time of month to camp on this river."

Directly before us was a pair of freshwater river dolphins. They were moving upriver, cresting and blowing in the otherworldly luminescence of jungle moonlight. Watching them, wanting to extend my hand and touch them, they were so close, I realized I had never seen anything in the world so naturally resplendent.

The dolphins rose by turns in a ponderous upstream glide, appearing and disappearing. They were partners in motion. Each rise began with a gurgling bustle of parting water, then the upward slide of pale-gray flesh, wet and sparkling, shiny in the moonlight. Then came the hot breath streaming out, mammalian lungs letting go, a soft hiss and a light spray making room for another gulp of air. Then the submersion, the vanishing act, intelligent eyes dipping back into water, the moon's reflection bouncing and cartwheeling in the lingering wavelets of retreat.

Then came the next dolphin's perfect rise and dive. Then the other again. Back and forth they pushed on upriver, back and forth, moving steadily out of sight, out of earshot, getting to wherever they were going on that exquisitely lonely nighttime swim through a shower of falling moonlight.

▼▼▼

"They had to do surgery," Ron Borman told me, speaking of his nephew Felipe, Randy's son. "They had to remove a section of his skull four inches long and an inch wide. Things were a little scary for a while. But he's okay now. He's going to be fine."

Ron's relaxed smile reinforced the credibility of his words, creating news that was as welcome as the present surroundings were not. I'd been waiting twenty minutes to talk to Randy's brother. He'd been occupied all that time selling cans of sardines and bags of rice to a long queue of desolate-faced Cofan Indians outside his two-story wood-frame missionary house in Dureno. I was back in this oil-smothered upriver region, the historic homeland of all the Cofan, hoping to find answers to two unflagging questions. Ron had just answered one of them.

"We got back from Quito just last night," he said. "Drove the truck there and back. We wanted to check in on Felipe ourselves, in person."

He showed me a postop photograph of Felipe in manifestly good spirits, sipping a soft drink, his entire scalp mummified in a cap of white bandages. It turned out that Randy and Amelia's breathless trip by boat and plane into the Andean highlands had delivered the boy to Quito not a moment too soon. Indeed, Felipe's cheery disposition in the photograph belied just how narrowly the depressed skull fracture had missed killing him, how close to causing what doctors call an epidural hematoma, a flow of uncontrolled bleeding inside the skull that literally squeezes the brain like an iron hand until coma and death follow in short order. There would have been no way to help him, nothing to do during the long voyage out of the jungle but watch him go.

"He looks great, doesn't he?" Ron asked me as more Indians showed up to buy canned food. "The doctor wants to keep him in Quito three more days for observation. Then the whole family's heading back to Zábalo."

Ron admired the photo a moment longer before bending back to his original task. As a service to the Dureno village, the missionary sold discounted food and medicine from a side window of his house. His absence over the past few days, combined with the dearth of surrounding forest in which to hunt game, had left several of the Dureno families in a bind, short of food. They now gathered themselves into the purchasing line looking for all the world in their worn Western clothes, fists clenched around dirty, crinkled small bills, like men and women in a soup line.

I took my leave, deciding I'd rendezvous here with Randy three days hence on his way back from Quito. That left enough time to investigate the second question: Where to find the environmental impact team? Even after my three-day birding trip with Roberto, the team had failed to materialize in Zábalo. Perhaps Roberto was right: The company wasn't keeping its word. Perhaps the study had been canned. Plans for the well would simply proceed without it.

Whatever the case, I had decided to make the long trip back up the Aguarico to seek answers at the office of the game warden overseeing the entire Cuyabeno reserve. The office was located just inside the western-most border of the upper reserve along an oil road about thirty-five miles east of Dureno. Someone there was bound to know something about the study, I decided.

Leaving Ron Borman that morning, I set off for the *colono* shantytown on the other side of the river, opposite the Dureno Cofan village. There I took a seat at a doleful sidewalk eatery next to the filthy oil road. I was waiting for one of the converted cattle trucks that served as rural buses in these parts. But the buses were running late that morning and the Ecuadorian army was everywhere. Platoons of soldiers in full combat gear, faces in camouflage paint, were engaged in what appeared to be some sort of domestic harassment exercise. They roamed purposefully through the *colono* town, demanding identification papers of every adult they encountered. Producing my passport twice for overbearing eighteen-year-olds with polished black machine guns and olive-green foreheads was enough, I decided. I gathered up my pack and started walking, determined to flag down a bus outside of town wherever it found me.

I wound up traveling the road for more than three hours on foot, side-stepping as best I could the deeper puddles of sprayed-on oil and fleeing the road completely at the crud-slinging approach of oil tankers and other company work vehicles. The experience turned out to be instructive. If walking put me in closer touch with this great big oily mess, it also put me closer to the people who live with it daily, the immigrant peasants whose bleak hovels and cleared fields ran smack up against the oil road and its congruent pipeline. Everything I was about to see during this long day ahead of me was a very real sneak preview of life ten years from now all around Zábalo if real preventive measures were not taken.

One *colono* woman I met soon after beginning my walk told me how, six years before, she'd watched ten of her cows die slow, agonizing deaths after drinking from a creek contaminated by a Texaco oil spill. Another woman showed me grotesque skin rashes covering the bodies of all six of her children, rashes she claimed were the result of oil-polluted roads and bathing water. When I later came to a small roadside dispensary, one serving campesinos, I asked the nurse inside about the rashes I'd seen. "You mean rashes like these?" the nurse said, immodestly pulling up her own oil-flecked nurse's blouse to reveal a stomach riddled with scabrous lesions.

"And like these?" She lifted her skirt to her thighs, revealing more. "Of course they're from the oil," she said. "You can't keep it off your body here. I worked for ten years in other parts of the jungle—no problem. I'm here six months and I get this."

As it happened, widespread skin conditions such a these joined a host of birth defects, cancers, and respiratory illnesses to form part of the list of peasant grievances in the mammoth class-action lawsuit against Texaco now before a New York court. Benzene alone, one of many toxic compounds found in crude oil, was known to cause skin and nervous-system disorders in humans through prolonged exposure. It could damage bone marrow (leading to anemia and other blood disorders) and cause leukemia. It had the ability, moreover, to enter a woman's placenta, with potential gross deformities to developing fetuses. In large parts of Ecuador's jungle oil region, meanwhile, every man, woman, and child was in effect taking a benzene bath each day by simply drinking, washing, or walking anywhere in the vicinity.

By now, thanks to my own extended tromp along the oil road, I'd seen enough to grow wary of preceding any farther on foot. I tried my hand at hitchhiking to escape the surface mess, cursing all the while the still-nonexistent buses. A big blue Mitsubishi cargo truck eventually stopped. The driver said he was on his way to buy coffee beans from campesino farmers thirty miles away. I climbed aboard and immediately noticed the shotgun lying between the front seats.

"Bandits," the driver said, detecting my stare as we pulled away." They're everywhere. I have to carry the gun. Every poor bastard along this road knows I have enough cash on hand to buy five tons of coffee beans. My brother, yesterday, he got hit over the head by bandits and lost [two thousand dollars]. If any problems come up today, just let me handle it, okay?"

Nothing in his tone of voice implied exaggeration, leaving me to ponder whether riding in this truck was actually more hazardous than padding through the carcinogenic sludge along the road. I stayed where I was, unable to decide.

The next thirty minutes passed tensely for me, my eyes cocked for bandanaed hijackers. I looked for something else, too. According to the map I carried, we were now actually inside the upper Cuyabeno Wildlife

Reserve, having just crossed its westernmost border. There'd been no road-side sign indicating this, that I had seen.

"This is a park?" the truck driver said, utterly surprised when I mentioned the fact. "I didn't know this was a park. Are you sure?"

Yes, I was sure, but who could fault him for not knowing? The scenery had remained exactly the same—the same combination of stripped-down land and tumbledown farmhouses all strung together by the oil pipeline's black gravel avenue. The awful mixture never let up, streaming illegally and in utter chaos deep into the park, crossing its border, deep into this "model modern tropical reserve" as two rain-forest researchers wrote optimistically of the park just five years earlier.

The coffee-truck driver changed directions, turning north, leaving me to cover the last few miles to the warden's office on foot. The office, a diminutive concrete affair with flaking paint, turned out to be scarcely believable. It was hemmed in on one side by the coffee fields of illegal squatters and on the other side by an oil company parts supply depot. I thought I had the wrong place until Fausto, a young, friendly warden in a clean khaki uniform, came out to shake my hand. He was wearing sunglasses and something resembling a safari hat that was tilted to one side above a face smudged with a five-o'clock shadow.

"What are we supposed to do?" Fausto said in rapid Spanish when, after greetings, I asked about the coffee fields. "We can't shoot the colonos as they come into the reserve. We can't kill them. And there's no way to put all these people, thousands and thousands of them, all technically trespassers, in jail. Texaco made the roads, and we can't unmake them. The Ecuadorian government approved all of this, so we can't block the roads, either. So in the end we get this." He gestured back to the coffee plants abutting park headquarters.

I asked Fausto if he knew the whereabouts of the environmental-impact team Petroecuador was supposed to have organized for Zábalo the previous week.

"What team?" he said. "I've never heard of it. What team?"

I frowned. It wasn't a good sign. If such a study were actually in the works, Fausto, as a park warden, would surely have known about it. One thing, at least, was growing clear: Any fears Randy and the Cofan might have had of Petroecuador hiding behind a faulty EIS study were lessening by the moment—thanks to the fact that the study itself looked like it wasn't going to happen at all, a hoax from the very start.

Fausto suggested I inquire about the study at Petroecuador's field headquarters in Lago Agrio, fifty miles away. (I did, the very next day, also without success, which is when I finally gave up the hunt.)

But while I was still at the warden's office, Fausto announced he'd be happy to give me a tour of the surrounding park area, which meant, basically, looking at oil wells. Venturing out presented a slight problem, however: The headquarters office was completely out of gasoline. Its land cruiser, three motorized canoes, and two Yamaha 125 motorcycles—used by a tiny squad of eight wardens to patrol more than 1.5 *million* acres of reserve land—were all dry at the moment for lack of sufficient funds. Only after I had personally paid to procure three gallons of gas could Fausto and I set off on one of the Yamahas, riding double, taking an eastward course along another oil-sotted road. In short order we were passing petroleum tankers and sprawling shantytowns, dodging stray cattle and their splattered excreta—all inside the national park.

"Petroecuador," said Fausto, who was driving and shouting back to me, "claims all of this won't happen if they find oil in the lower reserve. They say they'll guard the roads. But my biggest question is, will *they* shoot the *colonos* who try to come anyway? Will they go that far? And what happens when the oil runs out? Will the company keep guarding the roads it's built forever, even when it no longer has operations in the jungle?"

We came to a long wetland lake running along the western side of the road. Fragments of remaining jungle dotted the landscape beyond.

"At the bottom of that lake," Fausto said, "there's spilled oil. It's all sunk to the bottom now—a company cleanup technique. They put in a special additive that just makes it sink. We used to see dozens of sand-colored nighthawks here. No more."

He continued: "It becomes virtually impossible to reverse. Virtually permanent contamination. Never again, perhaps, will it be safe to eat anything here."

We turned off into a "camp"—an organized network of oil wells—inherited by Petroecuador from Texaco. An armed guard posted at the camp entrance let us pass under the farcical premise that this was a national park and Fausto was one of its wardens. Inside, a series of side roads began splitting off from the main avenue at intervals of several hundred yards.

"Pick one," Fausto yelled back to me. He was still wearing his sunglasses and the safari hat pulled tightly over his head. "Pick a road you want to go down."

I did—the very next one—and Fausto turned. Within minutes we were parked and walking up to an unmanned fully operating well. It wasn't much bigger or more sophisticated in appearance than a very tall fire hydrant. It was painted red and was dotted with various valves and pressure gauges, and from its sides emerged two pipes that led away along the ground into the distance. We followed the pipes a few hundred feet to two large separation tanks accommodating several wells. The tanks themselves threw off three pipes which eventually led, in turn, to a sight difficult to describe. My mind at first was slow to comprehend. It took a moment to register the sheer scale of the contamination.

Spread before us over a quarter-acre area was a square pond made of crude earthen dikes. The pond was full to bursting with a stew of gray black liquid topped by constellations of iridescent foam. The three pipes we'd followed to this point were now vomiting their liquid contents into the pit. From one pipe the liquid emerged black. The other, green-gray. The other, clear. A nearly suffocating stench filled the air, meanwhile, a smell like hot tar mixed with sulfur.

"These are the by-products the company doesn't need," Fausto said of the stuff flowing from the effluent pipes. He went on to tick off a list of the wastes in this ghoulish brew: Arsenic, carbon dioxide, lead, hydrogen sulfide, mercury, acids, industrial solvents, lethal concentrations of chloride salt.

It was a dump, plain and simple, a toxic slurry, an oozing, unlined waste pit. If we'd been in an airplane or helicopter, looking down, we would have seen dozens of these pits spread across the camp in every direction.

A weirdly abrupt headache seized me as I stood there on the dike. My temples began to pulsate. I turned to ask Fausto if he was feeling the same, only to discover he had suddenly disappeared. The waste pit, it turned out, couldn't possibly hold all that was being expelled into it, forcing an overflow pipe to discharge the surplus waste into a concrete evacuation canal. Fausto had left to follow the canal for a short distance and now stood, his back to me, looking down a slight hill. As I approached, I saw that the hill overlooked what had once been a pristine Amazon swamp forest. Hearing my footsteps, but keeping his back to me, Fausto said, "Petroecuador is a good student. It does things just the way Texaco taught it."

Then I saw it. The gurgling run-off canal, brimming with the rushing, toxic brine of the pit, gave way here to a weird and elaborate concrete waterfall. Down a long series of uniform steps, twenty-five steps in all, twenty feet in width, the poisonous liquid tumbled and rolled before sliding directly into the forest swamp. Most of the trees beyond, as far as our eyes could see, had long since succumbed to the discharge, mutating to an ugly graveyard of still-standing trunks, leafless and contorted.

For a moment, everything was backward, all roles reversed. The forest stood before us as an object of great ugliness while the oily liquid waste had been transformed somehow to a thing of odd beauty. We watched the liquid surge toward the waterfall, then pass over the first step, gliding and roiling, pregnant with rich chemical pollutants that sent iridescent drops splashing into the air, glinting magnificently in the afternoon sun. Then came the next step and the next. With each tumbling fall, a coordinated line of new drops rose up like rough airborne diamonds lighting the way, marking the progress down, down, down. Then came the final step and the consummating surge into the dark swamp. A shiny band of surface bubbles crowned the arriving toxins, riding the graceful ripples of perturbed water, then dissolving as the ripples stretched into wider arcs—into shimmering, swelling, fatal rainbows that spread farther and farther into the swamp, farther and farther to the nearest stand of dead and dying trees.

7

Randy described the plan—and a hell of a plan it was—as we sat side by side in his small flat-bottomed johnboat, racing down the Aguarico toward Zábalo. The Borman family was back, at long last, heading home, and Felipe was just fine, his head shaved and neatly stitched up beneath a baseball cap. When we met that afternoon in Dureno, Randy seemed nearly drunk with pride at the way his son had pulled through it all, surviving the frightful surgery and two weeks of recuperation in Quito. Now, on the river, the rest of the family was happily drunk with the simple prospect of reaching Zábalo before sunset. Almost home.

And there was the plan. The plan. Randy seemed a little inebriated over that, too. Indeed, between the clamor of the outboard engine and the slap of waves, I wasn't sure I had understood the last part of what Randy had just told me. "Decommission the trucks?" I said. "You mean sabotage?"

"Yeah," he answered. "That's right. We'll cut some wires, loosen some bolts—whatever it takes to knock 'em out." He said this matter-of-factly, as if the issue of secretly wrecking sanitation vehicles in the city of Lago Agrio were no more difficult or significant than flicking a piece of lint off his *ondiccuje* tunic.

Randy wasn't wasting a second diving back into the straits of environmental activism. His mind had worked overtime while he'd been away, producing new ideas and strategies. The sabotage scheme, he said, would culminate a three-step process designed to fight pollution along the upper Aguarico River. The whole affair would begin with a piece of paper, a petition. Randy would draw up the petition, then travel up and down the Aguarico River collecting signatures. He would rap on the door of every last split-cane hut inside every last shoreside tribe—the Siona, Secoya, Shuar, Quichua. The petition would condemn the Lago Agrio city government and nearby oil companies for their routine and ruinous acts of dumping solid waste directly into the Aguarico River. The tons of filth—trash, human excreta, junked appliances—were already taking an ecological toll on the river's upper stretches, and the problem would only worsen as the boomtown expanded. Signatures gathered, Randy would present the petition in person to authorities at the Lago Agrio city hall.

If that didn't thwart the practice—and it probably wouldn't—phase two of the plan would take effect. Randy and a band of other Cofan would go to Lago Agrio, surreptitiously hijack as many of the city's sanitation trucks as possible, then dump the putrid cargo of garbage directly outside the front steps of city hall as further protest.

And if triumph were still beyond their grasp after that, the third and final phase of the plan would kick in, this one involving the direct "decommissioning" of the sanitation trucks themselves.

"Then we'll do it again," Randy added. "Each time they repair a truck, we'll sneak back in and cut more wires until our point gets across."

I was by now used to hearing Randy talk of taking important matters into his own hands, plunging into direct action. But there was something distinctly different about his tone this time. His outrage over the dumping came through loudly enough, something my own upriver travels helped me understand with sympathetic clarity. But the Cofan chief on this particular occasion sounded anything but sure that the response he had in mind was the right one. The vigilantism seemed a little showy this time, a little too high profile, gimmicky. Randy appeared to be forcing things. Missing from his voice was the impassioned, righteous resonance of immediate self-defense normally there.

"I had a lot of time to think while I was in Quito," he added, describing again how the plan had taken form. "A lot of time to think." To me, the announcement made it all the more odd that, above all, the entire garbage truck idea sounded so, well, *reckless*.

Randy had done all that thinking at Felipe's bedside, of course, holding the boy's hand, shepherding him through the critical medical treatment and recovery. The fact of the child's injury, more than anything else, may have accounted for Randy's big, loose talk of garbage trucks during the return trip home. Felipe himself was just ahead of us in a separate canoe with Amelia, looking like a miniature Buddhist monk with his loose-fitting clothes and nearly bald head. The incision across his scalp was already healing steadily toward a fading pink scar. Below that scar, Randy confirmed, a one-by-four-inch section of Felipe's damaged skull had been surgically removed, literally cut away. It had taken a Quito surgeon an hour and a half to perform the task, but the bone area would gradually return, replacing itself, thanks to the boy's young age.

No one lives forever, of course, and perhaps it's true that nothing brings the point home more forcibly than seeing the world's life-threatening hazards unleashed on one's children. All that time in Quito seemed to have left Randy, himself the recent lightning victim, retreating a bit from that side of himself given over to gentle, shrugging fatalism. For the time being at least, he was turning more squarely toward that other side of who he was, the side where the militant impulses lay, the take-charge anger. He wanted suddenly and impatiently to heal all wounds along his beloved Aguarico River while he still could, in the shortest time possible, while there still *was* time, getting around even to those obnoxious garbage trucks way up in Lago Agrio. No date had been set for the campaign, but the level of detail in Randy's plan left little doubt that, one way or another, it was going to happen.

During the ride down to Zábalo I managed to squeeze in a quick debriefing of my own adventures upriver. I told Randy how I had wandered the squalid oil roads trying unsuccessfully to determine the status of the Zábalo EIS team. The Cofan chief was equally baffled by it all. He'd had no contact with Petroecuador concerning the study while he was in Quito, but he clung to the assumption that the team would show up at some future point if, in fact, the company was going forward with its exploratory drilling plans as officially declared.

We were still a good five hours west of Zábalo, tracing the endless snaking crawl of the Aguarico, when, rounding a bend, we came suddenly upon a pair of very peculiar flying objects. The sight interrupted our conversation, throwing us into momentary silence. The objects sat motionless along the left shore, vaguely birdlike in appearance save for the metal pontoons descending from their bellies. On impulse, Randy slowed the boat and began heading directly toward them. As we grew closer, I realized that what we were looking at were ultralights, those aptly named miniature aircraft whose featherweight Dacron wings, mounted atop aluminum frames the size of go-carts, produced what were in effect motorized hang gliders. Each rear-propeller, two-cylinder engine was capable of keeping two passengers aloft for long distances with minimal use of fuel. These particular two, it turned out, belonged to a quartet of naturalists—three Ecuadorians and a Briton—taking a break from their long journey into the rain forest for fieldwork. The men sat in relaxed positions, helmets off, along the wide, sandy bank.

Randy landed us on shore, determined to get the closest look possible. He was the first person out of the boat, pacing down the beach to stare in awe, like the gee-gosh Indian he in part was, at these nouveaux Western gismos come to the jungle. He stood barefoot amid the crowd of other Indians and campesinos drawn in from every direction for the same reason, bewitched by these machines whose appearance, despite the scaled-down design, looked fantastically complex and out of place in the primordial forest.

Each ultralight eventually taxied back out into the current, pointed itself downriver, then cast off the momentary bonds of gravity for the resumed magic of flight, shrinking to a faint humming dot in the blue distance.

"I want one of those," Randy announced unexpectedly as he scrambled back into the boat. He restarted the outboard. "I want one of those. It's exactly what we need in Zábalo."

We pulled away from shore, our waterbound movements seeming so clumsy now after the lithe getaway of the ultralights.

"I've been thinking about this for a while," Randy continued. "I've read about these. If we had an ultralight, we could patrol all our land from the air. We'd see any oil-well clearings from the moment they started, *before* it was too late. It would even the odds against all the oil-company helicopters. We'd have the transportation to do something in a hurry, to get to Quito to protest, with photos we could take from the air. It's what we need."

Knowing each of these craft had to cost between $10,000 and $20,000, I asked him the obvious question. "How would you pay for it?"

"That I haven't figured out yet," he said. "Maybe an environmental grant of some kind, a donation here or there. Or we'll find a way to pay for it ourselves through tourism."

Randy gave his opinion that the ultralight, despite its small size, was surely safe to pilot with the right lessons. He then speculated on how he could use the craft to help catch poachers in the park and aid scientists on field trips.

But what I heard beneath the details was a much bigger message. Randy, I believe, saw this refined modern flying machine as his ticket to retaining more of his simple Indian life, resolving the dilemma that had loomed so large and seemingly insoluble during our long taxi conversation back in Quito. The constant monitoring of the forest for oil incursions, the trips upriver for talks, even the emergency journeys out of the jungle for health reasons—all could be cut to a thin fraction of their current time by an ultralight, bearing the dividends of a fuller, steadier, more consistent daily village life. It was his way out of the "trap," in other words, his magic bullet with wings that would keep him from getting overly bogged down in the taxing procedures of saving the land. Hell, I mused, he could even resolve the Lago Agrio garbage problem with dispatch, bombing city hall with big, stinky bags of refuse from the air, then making clean getaways.

But at what cost all this? I wondered. What risk? When the subject of buying an ultralight first came up, Jonathan Kandell, a visiting freelance writer from New York, told Randy emphatically what a wretched idea he thought it was. Kandell was riding in the boat with us that afternoon, making a one-day visit to the Zábalo settlement as part of a magazine profile he was doing of Randy. He took pains to stress how truly dangerous ultralights in fact were, how sales in the States had dropped significantly because of all the accidents, most involving the effects of wind gusts on the feathery, kitelike craft.

An equal source of danger, obvious to anyone who saw it, was the tricky process of taking off on water, the untamed jungle's only airstrip. Having just witnessed the procedure twice, I noted that the 65-horsepower engine had to be started by rip cord from the rear, behind the pilot and passenger seats, meaning whoever fulfilled the task had to leap carefully afterward to shore from a pontoon, an awkward, bouncing, unwieldy business when a quarter-inch-thick, four-foot-long propeller is rotating at 2,500 revolutions per minute just a few feet away.

I refrained from expressing my own reservations on the issue for one simple reason: I had watched Randy as *he* watched the ultralights take off, and I knew without a doubt he had already made up his mind. In some fashion or other, he was going to get one of these high-flying featherweights. That look of complete, single-minded determination was on his face, the same one he wore whenever he talked of oil. The chief of the Cofan wanted to save his corner of the forest from destruction. He wanted to save his people from oil. It wasn't part of his personality to back down and give up, at least not easily, without a big fight. He would have never made it this far with the Cofan—relocating the clan to the greater safety of Zábalo, taking a Cofan wife, beating back Petroecuador's probing incursions—if "no" was a word he cottoned to well. And now, it so happened, the Cofan chief wanted an ultralight. He wanted one very, very much. The idea had seeped deeply into his imagination, and it wasn't going to leave. That's all there was to it.

Yet this was an issue still belonging somewhere to the future, beyond immediate touch. For those of us presently in the Borman johnboat, gliding down the Aguarico, ambitions were of a much simpler sort: We just wanted to get back to Zábalo—fast. A hot, clear sky was scalding the river with blasts of tropical heat, its intensity making war on our bodies despite the alleviating headwinds of our forward motion. The usual pot of *chicha* made the rounds as a tonic, everyone downing with avid swallows the faintly sweet liquid. Randy kept the outboard at near full throttle, meanwhile, pushing his boat on, the motion at one point snatching Kandell's baseball cap off his head and pitching it into the current, forcing a quick circling back to retrieve it.

It was late afternoon by the time we reached Zábalo, where much of the village turned out to celebrate the felicitous homecoming of chief and family. Felipe, smiling self-consciously, was the subject of much staring and amazement among the welcoming Indians, as if by surviving his accident he had become some sort of walking dream come true. Even the family woolly monkey got into the act, clapping its hands in a serviceable version of applause, chattering wild hellos. Randy and Amelia walked up from the river in an affectionate style, arm in arm, greeting all well-wishers.

There was a round of *chicha* on the Borman porch, then a spell of socializing before everyone drifted back to their huts or to the nearby shore for the late-afternoon ritual of cooling riverine ablutions. I did the latter, slowly and contentedly washing away the soil and fatigue of the day's travel, then swimming in the smooth-flowing water. On the high bank above the shore, I noticed, Randy's father-in-law, Aniseto, was making steadfast progress in his quest for a new canoe, chipping and carving away at the long cedar trunk he'd felled and propped up on wooden blocks. Out in the river current, meanwhile, Bolívar tooled by in his own canoe, weighed down by a bountiful afternoon catch of catfish and fat peacock bass. He waved to the wet, naked children playing along the shore, who returned the gesture by cannonballing themselves back into the river with high splashes and high-pitched giggles.

Randy remained in the best of moods that evening, all smiles, clearly relishing the return to this his element—village man in the forest, Indian chief proudly come home—after so long in Quito. And who wouldn't be glad? As Randy had said that same afternoon, his voice firm with the tone of complete conviction, the Cofan had achieved in Zábalo most of the theoretical charms and promises of modern middle-class Western life: Independence, choice, leisure, freedom from want. It was a life of luxury, Randy claimed, in the best sense of the phrase. It was also a claim difficult to deny. It took but a brief visit to Zábalo to see the abundance of food produced by a work schedule of mostly half days. Families hunted, fished, and cultivated small plots with relative ease according to their needs in a generous forest. This, combined with the supplement of medicines and labor-saving tools brought in by the cash of limited tourism, made for what Randy called "a very, very, very nice life." Perhaps the best measure of this claim was the utter nonexistence of youth flight from Zábalo, that bane of rural villages across the developing world. The flow actually went the other way here, with young people in Dureno increasingly traveling down to the wilderness sticks of Zábalo, wanting to settle permanently.

For me, on those late evenings bathing in the river, the sunsets alone seemed enough to keep one here forever—phantasmally orange fireballs

rolling off sheets of purple sky, dropping into the horizon hands of waiting forest trees, with boisterous parrots winging in pursuit as if chasing
some feverish, unreachable dream. "Living here," Randy once said of the
ruthless daily beauty of the place, standing beside a magically huge and
flowering mimosa tree, "is like living in a painting." It was as good a way
of putting it as any.

And how fitting, then, that weaving right through the heart of that
painting was a river whose very name echoed poetic visions, translating to
"rich water"—*agua rico*. For centuries the myth had endured of limitless gold
fortune lying in wait across hidden pockets of this Amazon jungle. It was
as much a part of the forest as the lianas and jaguars, this myth, casting its
trance five hundred years before on those haggard, hubristic conquistadores from Spain. Drunk with greed and spent morals, they stumbled
through mountains and dark forests, dragging bloody swords behind them
in a search for all they could carry. The hunt, above all, was for El Dorado,
that fantastic shining city where even the mythic emperor's skin shone with
gold dust. And for a while the trail to paradise was said to follow a certain
Ecuadorian river to the north, one rumored by natives to be thick with the
precious stones so prized by the foreigners. "Rich water," the river was said
to be—very, very rich. The name stuck even after the trail, like all others,
turned cold, after there was no gushing fountain of gold metal, no El
Dorado gleaming at river's end, sprawled across faraway shores.

Centuries later what did lie at that spot near the river's end was a
Cofan community steeped in its own version of great wealth. The community wasn't patterned after the celebrated El Dorado, there being no
such model to emulate anyway. The place never existed. Still, while
impoverished campesinos withered away upriver in a comprehensive version of toxic hell on earth, the Zábalo Cofan had put together what was
surely one of the world's better versions of a sustainable, near-utopian society. The ingredients really were all there, nothing invented, open to all
members: Independence, choice, leisure, freedom from want.

I couldn't help wondering, though, having seen the place up close,
how much *more* utopian Zábalo could become, as it were, without unrav-
eling completely. Putting aside for a moment the threat of oil from
without, what was the level of threat from within? What would be the full
effect of the solar-generated electricity Randy had brokered for the com-

munity? Were value-altering, mind-warping televisions and boom boxes sure to hitchhike along that path? And what dislocating effect—commercial, social, or otherwise—would routine air travel in the form of an ultralight have on the community?

When, a few days later, I asked Randy about the possible corollary effects of maintaining an ultralight at Zábalo, his response came as a great surprise to me. He could have pulled the words right out of his sleeves had he been wearing any.

"My goal," he said, "is to save a people. In achieving that goal, the culture may have to change. That's something we have to accept. The people have to survive first."

I did the equivalent of a mental double take at this. The response was different, a nearly wholesale departure in fact, from the earlier, almost reverential way Randy spoke of preserving Cofan traditions and mores, of "operating an indigenous community." Now the goal was simply to save a people? What exactly did that mean? Protect them from literal death? The ghettoized Dureno Cofan weren't dying—not literally, at least not in an immediate sense. Their problem was that their traditional ways had changed, withered away.

A realization that had been coming to me slowly for weeks was now reaching full force in my mind. I could see at last that Randy's job, his role as chief, was in no way set in stone. It wasn't even *loosely* defined in any meaningful way. It was, instead, pretty much whatever he said it was at any given moment. Period. In this community of choice, freedom, and abundance, Randy had chosen that much for himself. He had staked out a sort of ultimate personal independence. He answered to no missionary board like his brother, no assembly of shareholders like the oil companies, no government agency like the park wardens, no university faculty like the wildlife researchers. He answered to approximately one hundred forest Indians who, in the end, couldn't realistically replace him as chief even if they wanted to. There was no one else among them who could serve as head oil-company antagonist. No one had the skills to fill Randy's footprints. That fact offered the chief the option of pursuing his own instincts almost exclusively, following virtually no one but himself. There were risks and drawbacks to such a situation, to be sure, but perhaps it was the only way the forest had any real chance of surviving here. Vigorous, vociferous democracies, with their full complement of strong-willed competing leaders, tend sometimes to be messy things in periods of crisis, lacking the sharp, hardened edge needed for survival. Or so one might argue. What wasn't arguable was the fact that Zábalo *was* ringed in crisis. And with no interior faction or individual in the way uttering Randy's least favorite word—no—forcing him for whatever reasons to abandon his central conservation agenda, he would never have to give up the fight. The tools employed along the way might in fact bring cultural change to Zábalo. But if I understood Randy correctly, the point was simple: So be it. This much at least would hold firm: The one way the community *wasn't* going to change was on account of the forest disappearing all around it. It wasn't going to change à la Dureno. The Zábalo Cofan would have some say in the matter, shaping the process and final destination, with all the trees still standing when everything was said and done.

Some of these thoughts were still going through my mind as I crossed the "rich" water of the Aguarico the very next day in a wobbly two-man canoe. It was late afternoon and every ounce of precious gold the conquistadores had failed to plunder from this dense jungle lay hoarded in the shimmering, sinking sun, leaving the water and sky burning like different sides of the same gilded coin. I had spent most of the day in repose, catching up on my notes, devouring a lunch of peccary soup with Bolívar's family before winding up at Randy's house for bowls of *chicha* and conversation. On the porch that afternoon sat a handsome pair of pottery vases, modestly adorned with the paint strokes of a traditional Cofan design. Amelia, who was seated next to Randy on a smoothly carved bench, stationed snugly under his arm as was her custom, said she hoped to sell the vases to the next cluster of visiting backpackers. Noting my interest in the painting style, Randy mentioned that on the other side of the river, just below his small banana field, lay an imposing cache of painted pottery shards dating back at least six hundred years to a community of Siona Indians whose descendents were now based farther upriver. Amelia's brother Carlos, fourteen years old, standing on the porch, spontaneously waved for me to follow him when my face lit up with unconcealed enchantment at the thought of visiting such a site.

In just minutes we were on our way, Carlos and I, streaming across the Aguarico, gliding through the sunshine. That recurring feeling of unreality, of living in a painting, was pulsing through me as we moved, synchronized to the gentle purl of our paddle strokes. Carlos did most of the work. He was a strong and rather tall kid for his age, but shy. He kept his lips pursed in a serious way as he paddled. We reached the far shore, then paddled upstream until we arrived at a formation of thin, jagged rocks set in a long horizontal band across the exposed wall of riverbank clay.

"There they are," Carlos said, pointing to the rocks until, looking closer, I saw they weren't rocks at all but thousands and thousands of pieces of broken pre-Columbian pottery, a rich stratum of artifacts in ruin.

With limber teenage arms, Carlos tethered the canoe to shore, then reached for his machete. "Here's a good one," he said, his eyes smiling with success. He pried a triangular shard loose from the clay with the tip of his machete. He dipped the piece into the water, cleaning its muddy surface, revealing across one side a crude design of painted lines and dots that had not been exposed to daylight for centuries. I took the piece in my hand, turning it different directions, gazing in awe at the work of this long-ago artisan.

I used my fingers to dislodge a handful of other shards. None of the pieces was bigger than my palm, all downsized by the press of time. There was a subtle variance in concavity from piece to piece, suggesting a mix of utensils—bowls, vases, plates.

My first assumption—that this was some sort of ancient dumping site for discarded pottery—was later corrected by Randy. The thick stratum of shards simply represented the point at which the jungle's softer upper soil gave way to a deeper hard-clay underpinning. There had been a Siona village here for at least several centuries, making and using pottery. These shards had simply drifted down separately and randomly over time to the same subterranean level. Randy told of his own experience losing a Matchbox car as a child in the jungle, discovering it many years later buried under a foot of earth next to his parents' missionary home, side by side with an obviously ancient Indian vase.

Most of the earth-tone pottery remnants Carlos and I plucked from the riverbank were ornamented in some way with red or black paint, involving various patterns of circles, dots, lines, and zigzags. We decided, as a momentary goal, to hunt through the shards for some sort of recognizable depiction of an animal or human being.

It was a long, muddy, engrossing search, involving scores of shards taken from a supply huge beyond measure, seemingly inexhaustible. The more we probed the clay wall, the more the pieces revealed themselves, virtually gushing out of the earth. We dipped each fragment into the river, rinsing the mud coating, then scrutinizing it for the features we sought. There was a niggling measure of guilt accompanying the process. A type of red paint on some of the shards—perhaps the same berry-extract *achiote* the contemporary Cofan used—had grown frail and soluble with age. This meant we'd wash the piece of its dirt coating only to watch the delicate underlying paint strokes, applied perhaps when the Black Plague was assailing Europe, vanish as well. All those years under all that dirt, awaiting a capricious thumb-and-water erasure on a random, sunny afternoon late in the twentieth century. A prickling chill jogged down my neck each time I thought about it.

Alas, we found nothing in the fragments of art resembling a person or animal, though the various patterns of nonrepresentational design were pleasing and engaging nonetheless. There was more to the exercise than aesthetics, too. An untutored reading of the artifacts showed an apparent preponderance of zigzags and circles as themes toward the top of the stratum, with lines and dots dominating toward the bottom. The creative skills and sensitivity of these Siona people, in other words, had shifted over time. One vision had supplanted another. It was a small piece of evidence, perhaps, and not all that surprising, but worth noting nonetheless: The people here had not remained static. Cultural change had come to this forest spot through the centuries, surely lots more than these small shards revealed, more than just ways of making pottery, while the forest itself stayed the same, going on in nurturing changelessness, providing the basic life raft for societal continuity. It may not have involved an ultralight, but proof of a general precedent was right here, along the river, just below Randy's tiny shoreside banana field.

I took a break from our excavation work, sitting on the canoe bow while Carlos pushed on, rinsing more pieces, showing me more designs, then casually tossing them into the river behind him. As I watched the shards disappear, each making a small *plunk* and splash, a mischievous urge came over me.

"Have you ever thrown one of these this way?" I said. I reached for a perfect shard, square in shape and almost completely flat. I positioned

172

myself at water's edge, dropped my right shoulder for a sidearm toss, and let it rip. The shard sailed across the smooth river surface in low, flat staccato skips that came faster and more bunched together the farther it traveled. Then it vanished.

Carlos' eyes grew wide. He dispensed with Spanish for a moment, saying something in rapid Cofan which, judging by the excited tone, translated roughly to, "Hey! Wow! How the heck did you do that?"

I skipped another one, showing him. After several tries, he had the full hang of it himself.

I'm sure any strong thunderstorm sweeping over this jungle bend would have dislodged and dumped into the river as much pottery as we did that afternoon. Our efforts, besides, were puny compared to the enormity of the remaining stash. But to the patron deities of archeology, wherever they may be, it was surely an outrage of monumental proportion the way we kept it up, now using those ancient shards in a quest for the record of most skips.

Carlos quickly outpaced his mentor, lengthening his throws with every try. He was precocious, unstoppable—twenty-one, twenty-two, twenty-three . . . the skips came in such quick profusion they were difficult to count. I gave up on my own feeble throwing and just sat down to watch Carlos let them fly. With each skip, he made the river's surface speak in a soft, snapping voice, kicking up a drop or two of golden, gleaming water along the way. He applied all his might to the throws while somehow maintaining a relaxed manner, leaning gracefully into each delivery with his young bronze body.

One throw carried nearly halfway across the river, its course bending slightly downstream from the pull of the river's current. When finally it disappeared, my eyes kept going, carried on by momentum, gazing farther out, glimpsing the thatch huts of the Zábalo community on the opposite shore, in the distance, looking centuries old from this point of view.

▼▼▼

I was dozing the next day in the shade of a guava tree, blanket unrolled, sparring my way through a hot, still, windless afternoon, when I heard the noise. It was coming from downriver, getting closer. It appeared to be a canoe of some type, with an overly large, overly deep-pitched outboard motor. Louder and louder the motor grew until I finally gave up on sleep and went to investigate, discovering in short order that there was no canoe anywhere in sight. The noise was coming from the sky. An ultralight aircraft was sloping down toward the water, about to land at Zábalo.

The craft touched down with a jaunty bounce upon its pontoons and then began taxiing toward shore. I joined the swelling crowd of Cofan waiting to greet the two helmeted men on board. Randy was present, too, both of us recognizing this craft as belonging to the pair we'd seen two days earlier way upriver near Dureno.

The men stepped ashore, introducing themselves as Jorge and Romulo, naturalist photographers from Quito working on a book of rain-forest landscape shots. They were in their thirties, with dark boyish faces and hardened builds and longish hair, looking every inch the brash and comely adventurers. But they weren't here to shoot pictures or to swap jungle yarns over bowls of *chicha*. Jorge and Romulo had a very big problem on their hands.

Randy invited the men to his house where they explained, their faces growing taut with seriousness. Jorge kept running his hand through his hair as he spoke. A young friend of theirs, a biology student from Quito, was lost somewhere in the jungle downriver, he announced. The man had left the base camp at Zancudo, on the Aguarico, almost twenty-four hours before and had not been seen or heard from since. He had set off alone, on foot, into the jungle to do research on caimans at a smaller camp on Iripari Lake. But for some reason the young man, barely twenty years old, never reached Iripari. He never confirmed his arrival via camp radio. Somewhere along the winding, well-marked trail he had disappeared.

A search crew had been combing the jungle since dawn that day, involving about two dozen soldiers from the Zancudo military garrison as well as guides and workers from Transturi Touring. The two ultralights had happened to be in the area as well and had spent the day dividing up sections of the jungle for aerial survey, with Jorge piloting one craft and Dennis, the Briton, the other. They were soon joined in this process by a Petroecuador helicopter radioed in from an oil rig along the Napo River. It was an all-out, all-points-bulletin hunt.

But nothing had come of the efforts, and it was now late afternoon, and someone downriver had suggested contacting the Cofan, enlisting their renowned tracking skills in the matter. Jorge restated his grave concern for the student's fate before turning directly to Randy and asking that the chief come at once, bringing with him some of his men. Randy agreed without hesitation. He put together a group of a half-dozen volunteers that included myself, and then, quickly, the final logistics were settled: Randy would fly with Jorge to Zancudo in the ultralight to get a head start on developing a search strategy. The rest of us, including Romulo, who gave up his seat on the ultralight, and Bolívar, who would serve as river navigator downstream, would set off at the same time for the ninety-minute trip in Randy's johnboat, arriving well behind the more expeditious ultralight.

We gathered the items we'd need for the trip—machetes, water jugs, day packs—while Randy and Jorge buckled themselves into the ultralight, snapping helmets on tight. With great practiced strength, Romulo pulled fiercely on the engine's rip cord, then carefully stepped off the bouncing pontoon as the spinning propeller climbed toward 2,500 revolutions per minute.

If Randy was nervous about this unscheduled maiden voyage on the ultralight, dream craft of his future world, he didn't show it. Chance was handing him a sudden test ride, and the moment for second guessing had well passed. He stared straight ahead, leaning back in the open cockpit, arms braced for takeoff, as Jorge taxied to the middle of the river. The rest of the Cofan, watching from the shore, looked decidedly less sanguine about what was happening. Amelia and others had told Randy to be careful, and now Amelia stood with the couple's young sons in front of her, her arms draped around their shoulders, her posture rigid and serious. Bolívar, next to her, had that expression on his face he'd worn when I'd hefted a tremendous pig onto my back, the face that said he hoped no injury would come of this.

But the takeoff was pure perfection, a smooth, steady rise out of the water, then up and beyond the steep canyon walls of riverside trees. In seconds only clouds and blue sky offered a backdrop to the shrinking passengers. A few seconds more and they disappeared completely, firmly stowed away on that minimalist flying machine of aluminum tubing, sailcloth wings, and open-air saddles.

Trailing in the johnboat, Bolívar did his very best to get the rest of us to Zancudo as fast as possible. The distressing context of our journey discouraged excessive conversation. A mood both reflective and anxious seized everyone on board—with the exception of fourteen-year-old Carlos, of pottery-skipping fame, who dozed much of the way in youthful innocence. I wondered what lay ahead for us. Would we find the missing student? If so, in what condition would he be? One thing was certain: We'd be staying in Zancudo that night. How many nights after that was anybody's guess.

Halfway to our destination the johnboat smashed into an unseen sandbar skulking just below the river's surface. The impact gave everyone a real start, jerking us forward and nearly bogging down the motor before Bolívar could maneuver us free. He quickly resumed the high speed, but with heightened caution now, intently scouring the water for hints of more booby traps lying in wait before us.

When we rounded the last bend before Zancudo, the day was in full wane. A gossamer softness of late-afternoon light drenched the river. In the distance we could see a small floating dock jutting out from the shore. Above the dock, on a broad, grassy bluff, were the scattered huts of the Zancudo military camp, as well as a thatched-roof mess hall belonging to Transturi. A large number of human figures, bunched together in an odd way, stood a few feet behind the dock. They were surrounded by a hive of other people running here and there, like angry bees, waving their arms, shouting. Some sort of purposeful activity was under way, though it was impossible from our distance to tell just what. The figures took on an increasingly strange then disturbing aspect as we got closer. Then the picture became clear: A half-dozen uniformed soldiers, like pallbearers, were carrying a bedsheet obviously filled with the weight of a human being. Other men were shouting directions and giving orders. The lost student had obviously been found, but something was wrong. Terribly wrong. If he wasn't dead, it was clear he'd been badly injured somehow.

We stepped ashore and into the maelstrom of men pointing and shouting all around. I queried the first soldier I came to for information. His face was harried and fearful. "No, no," he said. "It's not the student in the sheet. It's the gringo. Someone else. There's been an accident—with the plane."

The soldier dashed off as my heart catapulted to my throat. I searched frantically through the maze of moving bodies for Randy. I couldn't find him. But there, halfway up the hill, was Jorge. Someone had a consoling arm around his shoulders. There was blood streaked across his shirt. I immediately turned back to the shore. Both ultralights were there, tethered to the dock, floating on their pontoons, showing no discernible damage whatsoever. My confusion doubled.

Then, at last, I saw Randy. He was two hundred feet away, walking, talking, following the men with the sheet. Bolívar and the other Cofan had seen him too, and had already bolted off in a sprint toward him, crowding close to him now, flanking him, following him—their chief. I trailed in their footsteps, calling anxiously after Randy. "What happened?!" I yelled. "What happened?!"

He stopped very briefly to explain, looking as though the breath had been sucked out of him. I saw in his ordinarily cool, self-assured eyes a look I'd never seen before—an uncomprehending blankness, an unsteadiness. It had all happened so quickly, he said. One thing after the other. About thirty minutes earlier, while the rest of us were still heading downriver by boat, the missing student had suddenly appeared, staggering out of the forest—exhausted, dehydrated, scratched up, but basically okay. Somehow he had wandered off the Iripari trail the day before and then panicked, pushing himself on through the night, roaming blindly until he was deep in the jungle. It was the next day before he found a small, winding creek leading him back to the Aguarico and, finally, this camp.

"But then, who's in the bedsheet?" I said, gesturing to the pallbearers who were now halfway up the hill, heading toward a clearing used for helicopter landings.

Randy seemed close to becoming physically unwell by this point. "It's the other ultralight pilot," he said. "You don't want to see the way he looks."

With a mix of pain and adrenaline, Randy described what had happened: He and Jorge had barely arrived from Zábalo when the missing student miraculously shambled out of the forest. Seeing that all was suddenly okay, Jorge decided to fly Randy back up the Aguarico to meet the rest of us coming down in the johnboat. The two men buckled themselves into the craft while the pilot of the other ultralight, the Englishman named Dennis, the man we'd seen from a distance two days before near Dureno, a conservationist and highly experienced pilot, pulled the rip cord. The propeller began whirring toward top speed. Then, somehow, in a split second of lapsed judgment and lost orientation, trying to get off the pontoon and onto the riverbank dock, Dennis walked directly into the ultra-light propeller. Headfirst. It was over before anyone could stop him. The blades literally sliced up half his face and head while Randy and Jorge looked on from just three feet away.

I felt my throat grow dry with instant revulsion when Randy said this. I couldn't say a word. I looked back at the sheet still being born up the hill. "It's bad," Randy said. "I mean really bad. He's alive, but I don't see how he'll make it."

By now, we had resumed following the sheet carriers in their steady climb. They reached the hill's summit, then gently lowered their charge to the level ground. Against Randy's earlier admonition, I stepped forward, picking my way through to the center of the crowded circle. I looked down. Most of the left side of the injured man's face was gone. Simply gone. Cheek and cheekbone were cut away, leaving a pulpy red depression. The left eye, ripped from an obliterated skull socket, lay spread in pulverized strands across what remained of the man's forehead. Higher up, the propeller had literally sliced his skull wide open, creating a long, two-inch-wide window into his head, where the brain itself was plainly visible through a mess of blood.

My stomach fell as if through a trap door. Most horrifying, perhaps, was the remarkable fact that the man was still conscious. His remaining eye on the intact side of his face was open and blinking, staring up at the sky and, in a dazed way, at the people around him. He lay on his back with his knees raised, knocking them together rhythmically as an obvious response to the pain. His friends and companions—Jorge, Romulo, others—many of them in clothes smeared with his blood, their expressions ones of cannon-blasted shock around terrible, teary eyes, were now hovering nearest to him, holding his hands to comfort him and to prevent his several groggy attempts to reach up and touch his wrecked face and head.

"This can't be true," Bolívar said as we both turned away from the tragic sight, having looked on side by side long enough. "No es verdad."

We made our way through the onlooking soldiers, and Bolívar added, gesturing to the ultralights on the riverbank below, "A plane like that is dangerous, I think. It's too dangerous."

Without doubt, the butchered man's fate would have been one of certain doom, his hours numbered in this faraway jungle remove, except for one fact: A rescue helicopter was already on the way. It was just minutes from landing, in fact. Called in that morning from the upper Napo to assist in the missing-student hunt, the oil-company craft had only moments before left Zancudo for return to its base, the search having ended. A frantic radio message now had the surprised pilot making an abrupt U-turn, dutifully honoring the new request for emergency medical transport to Quito.

For those of us visiting from Zábalo, there was no longer any reason to stay around.

"Come on," Randy said to me. "If he gets to a hospital in time, I guess he *might* live. In what shape, who knows? Probably very bad. But we can't do anything to help out now."

In near silence we made our way down the grassy hill to the johnboat, where just feet away the knifelike ultralight propeller lay motionless beside a balsa-wood dock smeared with drying blood.

I learned months later that the injured man *did* live, and in precisely that dramatically reduced mental state one would expect of someone who, among the other severe injuries, had lost whole portions of the frontal lobes of his brain.

But few of us could contemplate matters so far ahead as we left Zancudo that late afternoon. The act of pulling away in the johnboat did little to help us jettison the horrific scene from our minds. Randy spent part of the return trip relating a few additional details of the grim accident. Bolívar responded with another expression of fear concerning the ultralight, commenting to Randy that perhaps the Zábalo Cofan should think very, very hard before getting one.

Oddly enough, Randy, the only one among us who had actually witnessed the accident firsthand, seemed to pull himself away from the feelings of revulsion and shock faster than anyone in the boat. In but a short while, he was strangely matter-of-fact about the whole thing, no longer visibly shaken, distancing himself emotionally, it seemed, from what had occurred. "Accidents happen all the time when you're not careful," he said glibly at one point. And when Bolívar expressed his reservations about getting an ultralight, Randy brushed them aside with little comment.

It became clear to me soon enough why this was the case. Randy, again, had already made up his mind to acquire an ultralight, one precisely like those we'd just left behind, and he wasn't going to let an unlucky event tell him no, just as he wouldn't let a person of contrary opinion do the same. But while he could more or less ignore a person, a factual event required the spin of interpretation. Accidents happen all the time, he had said, not quite finished with the issue.

I let quite a while pass in the johnboat before I raised my own questions. We were more than halfway home to Zábalo, and the sun was setting on the river, and the terrific gore of the Zancudo scene was still flooding my eyes as if I were still there, still looking directly at it.

I turned to Randy. "I guess that really *wasn't* a very good way to have your first ultralight ride turn out, huh?"

He let a few seconds pass himself before answering, and then replied only in the form of a shrug. His eyes carefully and calmly scanned the water ahead of us for obstacles in the disappearing light.

I went on, a bit amazed at his bland nonresponse. "Honestly," I said, "nothing about what happened makes you rethink your decision to . . ."

"That same type of accident," he said abruptly, "that very same type of accident, could happen with a boat propeller. Same type of thing."

Silence followed his remark. I waited for an elaboration, some sort of description as to how such a parallel held, but none was forthcoming, leaving the blunt implausibility of his statement to sink in. There were a million reasons why the accident potential of an ultralight and a motorized canoe were stacked heavily in favor of the former, and not just in the realm of propeller mishaps. But that wasn't the point. Randy, I realized, intended his comment to be taken seriously in that cold, Bormanesque way of saying: "Case closed, leave me alone, don't bother me with hard questions anymore." I took the cue and fell into obedience.

But my mind, as did Bolívar's, I presume, kept seeing Randy or some other Cofan winding up like the Englishman we had just left behind. Or trapped in a torrent of storm winds of the sort Jonathan Kandell had warned about. Or dashed against the trunk of a kapok tree from sudden engine failure or some other of the many ways one could decimate one of these craft.

It was two days later, in a conversation between Randy and myself, that Bolívar's negative opinion of acquiring an ultralight came up again, and the chief took time to point out that Bolívar was by temperament a very cautious person—*too* cautious being the clear implication. Bolívar, for example, had wanted to back down during the Paujil confrontation, the oil-well dispute in which by sticking it out, by not accepting a bullying bribe of cash money to leave, the Cofan had secured a large batch of solar panels as well as new and significant environmental assurances.

But instead of deepening my view of Bolívar, Randy's comments served in effect to expand the portrait of the chief himself. It was at that moment, in fact, that I realized I couldn't even begin to imagine Randy living in Zábalo and being anything other than chief of these people. This for the simple reason that I couldn't imagine him being a mere brave to someone else as chief, regularly taking directives from above, not always getting his way on critical matters when "no" wasn't something he responded to well. Again, there might have been something troubling about such a situation and Randy's role in it had it not been for the fact that everything kept coming back to the same central point: His was probably the most quali-fied personality to lead at that moment, pitting an absolute refusal to be denied what he wanted most in the world against the enormous antiforest pressures allied to do just that.

The bottom line was Randy felt he needed a motorized hang glider to help him save the forest. There was little question, at least, that aerial mobility would do what he claimed—drastically reduce or eliminate the great advantage helicopter travel conferred to Petroecuador. And who knew? That sort of mobility might in the end prove to be the difference in rescuing the jungle.

Whatever it took to get the job done—that was Randy's unspoken motto. Boldly raiding oil wells with guns and spears. Sabotaging garbage trucks that sabotage the river. Piloting a skeletal flying machine that helps maximize land security. It was a great big, ambitious strategy and he was the great big man for it.

It was too bad, then, that mixed into this often inspired and inspiring approach was that great big unfortunate kink. It was the one Randy never talked about, nor did anyone else in Zábalo, at least not openly, directly. But it was always there just below the surface of things, conspicuous for its silence—the knowledge that getting the job done might very well mean finishing off more than just what was ailing the forest.

8

It was Sunday morning, time for church, and Randy Borman was standing outside his house looking for *achiote* berries. He soon found one of the spiny seed pods hanging from a nearby bush, full of the red berries he needed. He tore it open, dipped in his finger, crushed a few berries, and began painting. He painted a long vertical line from the middle of his forehead down to the top his nose. He painted a second, shorter, horizontal line bisecting the first a quarter of the way down from its top. He painted, carefully and delicately, a Holy Cross.

As was the case on most Sundays when he was in the village, Randy would be leading the church service that morning. It was a special responsibility, and he was far from finished decorating himself in preparation. By the time he arrived at the village community house where most of the Cofan were already gathered clutching a few well-thumbed Bibles and hymnals, the chief had added to the cross on his forehead a series of lines across his cheeks, radiating out from his nose, representing the whiskers of a jaguar, that most powerful and revered of forest beasts. Over his torso, meanwhile, hung an immaculate blue tunic adorned at the shoulders with every imaginable version of Cofan jewelry. There was a necklace of ivory-white peccary tusks, a bright red neckerchief knotted and draped across his chest, a series of strings holding bell-shaped *shasha* seeds, and a shiny layer of multicolored bead necklaces measuring several inches thick. Across his hair, finally, was a special headband made from finely cut wood, and from bands on his upper arms hung long, slender palm-leaf strands grouped together in bunches as big and thick as horse tails.

Randy Borman, chief of the Cofan, was dressed and ready to praise God.

He stepped up to the floor of the community house with a purposeful air, drenched in all his finery, followed by Amelia, Federico, and Felipe. I'd never seen a Cofan child in face paint until Felipe that morning. Completing the boy's matching tunic was his own set of catlike whiskers, long and red, three on each cheek—son of jaguar. He, too, had a cross painted on his forehead and a neckerchief tied around his throat, and he looked as stiff and self-conscious with the colorful costume as any over-dressed Sunday-school boy anywhere.

On a bench facing the center of the room, the Bormans took their place among the village congregation. Luis, a man in his twenties with a deep, beefy voice, was already leading the worshipers in a hymn. The lyrics were in Cofan, accompanied by Luis' frightful-sounding guitar. The guitar was badly out of tune courtesy of an appalling split down its front side, a consequence of his dog's tripping over it the week before and knocking it down a set of steps.

After the hymn's sour, off-key finish, Randy opened the service with a short prayer, bowing his head. Everyone followed suit—the women in their brightly patterned skirts and blouses, emphasis on primary colors; the men in their blue tunics. As I surveyed the scene from my back-room seat, peeking up from the prayer, I became sharply aware of just how different Randy looked from everyone around him. It was much more than just the melanin-impaired skin in a sea of lustrous brown bodies or the blond-gray hair bowed alone amid row after row of jet-black heads. What set Randy apart, simply, was his getup. From head to toe, he had no peers that morning, his dress as elaborate and ambitious as it seemed he could make it. No other Cofan adult came adorned in face paint and shiny beads that Sunday. No one wore fierce-looking peccary tusks strewn by the dozens across his upper body. Even the older men like Mauricio and Lorenzo, more traditional in their habits, were embellished with simple hand-woven headbands atop their hair, nothing more. Randy, it seemed, was more Cofan than the Cofan that morning.

The prayer ended, and Randy opened his eyes and raised his head. He lifted from his lap the small blue Bible he had brought with him. His layers of beads and peccary tusks clicked and jingled with the motion. He opened the Bible and began reading, and suddenly he wasn't the only Caucasian leading the church service that morning. It was as if sixty-six-year-old Bub Borman, Randy's father, were there as well, riding Randy's voice, visiting far-off Zábalo through the holy book he had translated for the Indians he so adored. Randy kept reading, and a lifetime of mission-ary work filled the air, Cofan sounds wedded to the Old and New Testaments, meticulously and permanently stored in those tightly bound pages. Bolívar told me later that Randy was reading the story of King Solomon's judgment, in which a disputed child was ordered cut in half until the rightful parents revealed themselves by surrendering all claim to the child so long as no harm was done to him. From ancient Hebrew, to ancient Greek, to Latin, to the language of King James, to Cofan, the story was now arriving in that community house by the Aguarico, where chick-ens crowed underneath the plank floor and a cleansing Sunday-morning breeze blew in from the river right through the pavilion's open walls.

A cue went to Luis to begin strumming his crippled guitar for another song. The hymnals scattered about the crowd, thin and use-worn, con-tained both local and traditional Christian melodies coupled with Cofan words. The hymns had been collected, years before, by Randy's mother, Bobbie. There were only nine booklets in this crowd of about fifty, but many of the village worshippers knew the lyrics by heart. Their solidarity of voices produced a buoyant sense of connectedness and well-being in the air. It was a feeling disturbed by one lone individual. In the back of the room, looking calmly aloof, a visiting Quichua Indian named Eduardo didn't sing at all. He sat by himself, separated from the others, seemingly waiting for something or someone.

Slowly, row by row, a collection plate made the rounds. It was noth-ing but the plastic shell of a first-aid kit with the top torn off. After going through two-thirds of the crowded room, it reached me with less than two dollars in it. I tossed in the equivalent of fifty cents.

There was another prayer, followed by a lingering pause when no one said a word, everyone seemingly waiting for something to happen. The pause dragged on. Then the avalanche came. A rollicking discussion broke out in a huge wave, all of it in Cofan, involving nearly everyone in the room. Unknown to me at the time, the church service had ended after a scant twenty minutes, and talk had now zeroed in on something nearly as religious: Stalking sumptuous jungle animals. Zábalo's end-of-the-year Christmas feast was scheduled for the very next weekend, and preparations were very much needed. Faces that before had born the vaguely nonchalant expressions of routine were now ablaze with great enthusiasm as, one by one, the long list of banquet foods was reviewed to guide everyone's hunting goals for the upcoming week. Numerous peccaries were needed, of course; and a few monkeys would be nice, plus a curassow or two, some guans and other fowl, and a wide range of fish of various types and sizes. The goal was for each person to bring at least one forest animal or fish different from that of everyone else, a not-so-difficult task in this munificent world of speciation riot. Arrangements lingered on as a debate rose over just how many peccaries would be needed to feed the whole clan, and Randy put in a laughing request that piranha be kindly left off the menu, his least favorite eating fish.

This easy melding in one place of Christianity and the more earthbound concerns of forest living was not, of course, unusual for the Cofan, and certainly not for Randy, man of many worlds, man on both sides of every divide. "Ours is a very tolerant culture," he had once told me in an attempt to explain the Cofan's wide-ranging and smoothly compartmentalized grand view of life. The Indians saw worldly matters as segregated into several major sets of existence that did not necessarily contradict one another. In one realm, over here, you had the natural forest in all its knowable, day-to-day, life-giving beauty and complexity. In another realm, over here, you had the other forest, the spiritual forest, with all its special powers, its shamans and hallucinogenic *ayahuasca* vines and magical jaguars, its spirits and ancient mysteries. In a third realm, over here, separate from the first two but not in opposition to them, you had God and the Christian view of the world and all *its* spirituality. One could view all three realms as true and real, and in almost Hindu fashion revere all three in daily life—as well as accept as valid wholly different views held by other people in entirely different cultures. That morning Randy, with his jaguar whiskers and forehead cross, certainly embodied the tribe's enduring tradition of multiple worldviews, encompassing in his look all the ancient verities.

But this had not always been the case. Not for Randy, at least. There was a time, in his younger days, when he would have painted on the face whiskers but gladly left off the cross, unable to fully accept its validity. As he described it to me later, it was a period when "I tried to walk away from my faith." There were actually two periods of doubt, but the second and final episode, occurring in his twenties, was more complicated and significant. It happened to come at a particularly bleak time for the Cofan people, those years when Dureno was being decimated and Zábalo had yet to be fully established. Randy's sense of extended family, of home and of belonging, were being decimated apace during this period, giving way to an emotional confusion in which all the received answers were being turned on their heads.

But Randy's crisis of religious faith was connected less to these emotional reactions than to basic and persistent intellectual misgivings. His Western side saw a discomfiting lack of logic in many aspects of Christianity. Why would God, for example, allow genocide to happen? What purpose did it serve? Why, moreover, allow genocide in one place and not another? And why all the other inconsistencies, the conflicting interpretations of Christian doctrine, within different cultures and across different time periods, in which, for example, it was okay to have multiple wives in one millennium but not another? Did these inconsistencies—rooted mostly in the exigencies and subjectivity of human societies—logically rule out the existence of a Supreme Being? After a self-fashioned search involving experiences with prayer, shamanism, and a determined study of human history and cultures, Randy deduced that they did not. Two realizations were key. One, the act of denying God's existence required as much faith as did its opposite. And two, if it was true that all things would happen if given sufficient time to happen, then one of the things that would happen, by definition, was God.

From these deductions, Randy's thoughts and impulses eventually led him back to the fold. His attempt to walk away from the religion of his parents didn't work. He couldn't do it. It was like trying not to breathe. The same careful, reasoned thinking that had led him astray had led him back again. There was a renewed visceral appreciation of things as well. The enormous complexity of the forest alone, still intact in all its glory a short distance downriver from Dureno, was enough to remind anyone, but especially those who knew it best, especially a Cofan, of the fact that "there's someone upstairs obviously running the show," as Randy put it. In short, having grown up part of a missionary family where "Christ-like" was the prescribed model upon which to fashion a life, Randy finally found himself as an adult no better able to deny his Christian heritage than he was able to deny his Cofan heritage. It was something he had come back to, though now in a steady, clear, and simple version he laid out by quoting a simple verse: "Love the Lord God with all your heart, with all your strength, and with all your mind. And love your neighbor as yourself."

But to anyone looking in, of course, there was the easy temptation to suspect it was more than that. "So you're a freelance missionary of some sort—is that it?" I remember asking Randy two years earlier upon first meeting him. No, he wasn't, he had said. That label and any other of similar stripe simply didn't fit his vision of who he was, and he preferred there be no confusion in the matter. He may have retained their faith, in other words, but he still wasn't his parents.

Now, two years later, as I sat through the Cofan Christian service, that protest came back to me in full force, giving sudden logic to Randy's appearance at church that Sunday morning. What better way to allay all confusion, to make the point that he was simply a Cofan who also happened to be a Christian, than to lay on the native threads as thick as absolutely possible during church service each week. From headband down to bare feet, any visiting onlooker would have been very hard pressed to lay eyes on the Zábalo chief that Sunday and think Christian shepherd of souls.

The community feast had at last been settled in all its detail. Randy, necklaces jingling, closed the matter with a nod of his head. This allowed everyone to turn attention to the next item of business rising to the floor: River turtles. A pair of university biologists from Quito had arrived in Zábalo the day before to make a direct appeal to the Cofan: Don't hunt any more turtles or gather their succulent, prized eggs. In a campaign sponsored by Ecuador's largest conservation group, Fundación Natura, the biologists—Ana Mária and Jorge (not the ultralight pilot)—were traveling up and down the Aguarico trying to solidify support for a voluntary ban on turtle catches among all the Indian tribes.

Randy invited Jorge and Anita to speak now, taking advantage of the Cofan gathering. A graceful man in his late fifties, Jorge possessed kind eyes and a full, bushy beard that reinforced the aura of thoughtful professor. Anita had the young, tanned, healthy looks that come from so much work outdoors.

"Not so many years ago, thousands and thousands and thousands of turtles lived all along this river," Anita began, standing before the audience, speaking in Spanish. "The village elders speak of turtles in abundance, turtles everywhere. But now those same turtles are in danger of disappearing completely. You have to look hard for them. Most of the young are wiped out before they even hatch, eaten as eggs by people up and down the river."

One conservation response under consideration by Fundación Natura, Jorge added, was to collect large numbers of eggs of the two most threatened species—the Yellow-spotted River Turtle (*Podocnemis expansa*) and the Giant South American River Turtle (*Podocnemis unifilis*)—incubate them, and release the turtles upon maturity. But he had questions for the Cofan. How many weeks after laying did it take for the turtle eggs to hatch? How long for the young to mature? And did the Indians think it was a good strategy to pursue at all?

Randy translated the questions for those Indians unversed in Spanish, setting off a small calamity of instant debate in the native tongue. The group broke into five or six clusters across the room, taking up the matter with great vivacious spirit. After a while, Randy returned with a report.

"There are several of us," he told Jorge, "who think it would be much better to catch the young turtles *after* they hatch, as they're leaving their nests along the river. Then put them in a shaded holding pool along the shore, feed them the grasses we know they eat, then release them after six-to-twelve months by the hundreds, as they get big."

Jorge looked astonished. "Really? You think you could do it that way?"

"Sure," Randy said.

"You can catch the turtles, at the right time, after they hatch? And you're sure you know what to feed them as they grow?"

"There's no problem," Randy said.

At that, Jorge pulled out a small pocket notebook and began writing furiously. "This," he said, looking up for a moment at the Indians who were exploding several of his scientific understandings, "changes everything. Incubation can be so expensive. Your method, if it works, would be much more attractive."

"It'll work," Randy said.

Jorge finished writing and turned back to the chief with a serious face. "Of course, before we can do any of this we have to stop the current hunting of turtles along the Aguarico. We have to stop the rate of decline before we can reverse it. Will the Cofan agree to a ban on turtles and eggs until the population stabilizes?"

Randy's face grew concomitantly serious. Streaked with the red jaguar whiskers, it verged on the intimidating now. "Yes," he said, "we will. But we can't do . . ."

Before Randy could say another word, Eduardo, the Quichua sitting in the rear of the room, began talking over him. Eduardo was on his way home to his village of Zancudo after a trip upriver to Lago Agrio. He had stopped over in Zábalo for the night. He was a thick-chested man dressed in Western clothes, with an obvious streak of mestizo blood and an Elvisesque haircut that left a thick black lock curling down in his face.

"You have to start with the military," Eduardo volunteered to Jorge from his back bench seat. "As long as the soldiers along the river kill turtles, so will all the people. Change the soldiers first." His tone of voice was somehow dismissive and provocative at the same time.

Randy reacted with obvious irritation to the comment. He turned to Professor Jorge, looking the biologist in the eye, but his words were clearly meant for Eduardo. "It's not a matter of who goes first," he said. "Everyone on the river has to agree to this or it won't work. The Cofan can't agree to a ban by themselves."

Jorge turned to Eduardo. "We do plan to talk to the military," he said. "But will the Quichua in Zancudo agree to a ban now?"

With a demurring shrug, Eduardo said he didn't know. "Some of us can try to enforce a ban downriver," he said, breaking into a smile, "but we get sleepy every day and sooner or later we have to do it, we have to sleep. And what happens then, who knows?" He winked at Jorge, and then, audaciously, at the whole room of Cofan faces turned toward him, his message clear: "You guys may be dim-witted enough to stop eating turtles, but we certainly aren't."

Randy seemed to be having trouble keeping his seat after Eduardo's performance. A great tension now packed the pavilion air with the sudden force of a high-impact crash. The leap had been made to confrontation, face to face, out in the open. It was a situation aggravated by the already standing list of grievances between the Zábalo Cofan and their Quichua neighbors, who numbered several hundred up and down the river. Both sides in recent years had accused the other of overly ambitious land claims within the reserve, voicing complaints to various park wardens. A lot of Quichua viewed Randy—unfairly, Roberto had contended—as just another gringo exploiter using the Cofan to do his bidding. One Quichua chief upriver had gone so far as to write the head park warden a letter saying the oil companies were nothing of a threat to the forest compared to Borman and the Cofan. That one really rankled Randy, given how many physical and legal risks the Cofan had taken defending the reserve. "Those back-stabbing Quichua," is how he referred to them more than once in my presence, his love-thy-neighbor edict put sorely to the test.

"How many more years," Randy was asking now, dispensing with the niceties of Jorge as an intermediary, glaring directly at Eduardo, ". . . how many more years do you think it will be before the turtles are all gone? Huh? At the rate they're going now, how many more years? And then what? *What?* We'll never have turtle eggs to eat again. Never. What do you think about that?" A sort of sassy ridicule saturated his voice.

Eduardo deflected the questions by blatantly ignoring them. "I told you, the first thing you have to do is stop the military."

Randy threw up his hands. "Maybe if *you* stop, the military will stop."

"It's the other way around," Eduardo insisted, his voice taking on an equally sharp tone. "The military is the government. The government has to stop before we do. Don't talk to us about your ban until they stop."

"*Bueno,*" Randy said, turning back to Jorge. "If all the people on the river don't agree to start protecting the turtles, it's crazy for the Cofan to. We'll just be raising the turtles till they're big, and sending them down the river for the Quichua to eat. Why would we want to do that?"

The absurdity of the idea drew a few chuckles from the crowd, but not the kind that could diminish the feel of antagonism in that room, so raw and direct it verged on the embarrassing now. Jorge was still staring at Randy, clearly hoping the chief would say something more to break the stalemate of this classic prisoner's dilemma. But Randy was finished for now. He sat there on the bench still gripping his copy of the Cofan Holy Bible, peccary tusks and brilliant beads around his neck. He happened to be wearing at that moment several of his many hats—Indian chief, self-styled naturalist, son of missionaries, Cuyabeno activist. It was a unique distillation of who he was, as well as an anecdotal showcase for the sort of complex problems he faced. How interesting that back in Quito Randy had used the rapacious harvest of river turtles as a metaphor for myopic Western greed, particularly in the form of free-for-all oil consumption that was threatening catastrophe for the Cofan's forest home. But while the Cofan, mostly through Randy, could raise a small voice to the outside world, appealing for the changes in values and consumption patterns necessary for their survival as a forest tribe, they faced nearly as great a challenge changing important aspects of life along the Aguarico itself. The campaign close to home, in fact, was in many ways *more* complicated. Just deciding which hat to wear on which day was for Randy difficult enough. How hard and how publicly, for example, should he campaign for change in his own backyard as a naturalist committed to maintaining natural forest balances? How hard as a chief whose people are adversely affected by the upset of those balances? How hard as a Caucasian viewed with some suspicion, no matter what he does, by the neighboring tribes with whom he must work to restore those balances? Randy often combined several of these disparate identities when approaching local problems, frequently leading to success, as with the INEFAN indigenous guides course he had helped organize. But nearly as often, he ran smack into muddled standoffs like the one happening now. The fact of the matter, hovering there in the community hut that Sunday morning, was clear: Randy was nearly as great an enigma to many of his jungle friends and neighbors as to any Western stranger popping in for a visit from several thousand miles away.

The Cofan chief took on the shine of a diplomat to finally extract himself from the unpleasant face-off with Eduardo. Randy may not have cared much for no as an answer, but there wasn't much he could do about it here, at least not presently. He told Jorge that, for now, the Cofan would limit to a bare minimum their harvest of turtle eggs while giving the biologist time to gather support for a collective ban up and down the river. He said he hoped none of the spirited comments passed back and forth that morning had upset any of the Zábalo guests, but that the dire condition of the river turtles tended to make everyone a bit emotional. Jorge followed by asking Eduardo to strongly encourage his own people to consider a ban while pressure was put on the military's river garrisons to do the same. Eduardo tossed his hair back in a sort of vague nod.

And so the matter ended, and with it the gathering. Randy rose with a look of piqued disappointment on his face, his brow wrinkled below the painted cross. He led his wife and sons back to their house on the other side of the village, crossing the narrow field along the river in all his clinking, jingling Cofan jewelry. The other Indians followed in turn, scattering back to their homes and daily routines in the breezy midday warmth, looking eminently less nourished and gratified, spiritually or otherwise, than when they first arrived to worship God.

By the time I caught up to Bolívar about an hour later, he was already back at work on his unfolding masterpiece, the home-in-progress, Zábalo's first two-story structure. Only a thin skeleton of a frame when I arrived six weeks ago, Bolívar's house was now nearing completion. The walls and floors were reinforced with a myriad of stout structural braces—some tied together, some nailed—all rising up to a pitched roof frame where Bolívar was applying the finishing touches, tying on long palm branches whose thick fronds would act as leafy shingles. He'd spent the past two weeks cutting and gathering the branches along the river, then placing them in ready-to-use piles around his house. Elías, his quiet-mannered father, had already hauled a quantity of branches up to the second floor and was handing them up to Bolívar one by one. When these ran out, I fed another batch up from the ground, the fronds rustling and swishing gently as they crossed the edge of the second-story floor. Looking around, I realized there were far more branches spread in piles across the ground than could possibly fit on the roof.

"It's because I use *two* layers, Mike," Bolívar said when I pointed out the apparent surfeit. He peered down at me, arms akimbo, from his elevated spot on the roof. "I put one layer of palm branches on top of another. It's more work that way, but I won't have to replace the roof for six whole years if I do it like this. It makes the house very strong. Two layers are good."

His thin mustache was dotted with sweat, as was the rest of his sturdy physique. I would have gone up for a closer look at the method, but there was still no ladder anywhere on the premises and I had no particular craving for chin-ups at the moment.

I asked Bolívar where he planned to place his solar panel, scheduled to arrive with all the others in just ten days now. He and Elías, it turned out, had spent quite a bit of time discussing this very matter, with Bolívar favoring the southwestern edge of the roof where afternoon sun came through least hindered by surrounding trees.

Bolívar fired down a question for me next. There'd been a steady rise in rainfall the past week and a half, lifting the level of the Zábalo River from its lowest point in November. He and his brother-in-law David were taking a canoe up the river to hunt guans and curassows the next day. Did I want to go with them and try again to reach the torched and abandoned oil-drilling platform we'd tried in vain to visit a month ago?

I smiled and promptly said yes. One purpose for my stopping by at Bolívar's house now had been to ask if just such an effort wasn't possible. I would be heading back to the States in just two days, I told him, and I very much prized the idea of a final chance at photographs.

At this, Bolívar swung and shimmied his way down from the roof. He called out in Cofan to Norma, who was next door placing termite nests in a tin pan for the evening slow burn against mosquitoes. She disappeared inside the couple's present house and returned with two large peccary tusks in hand.

"These are for you," Bolívar said as Norma placed the tusks atop my opened palm. "They are from our hunt together, from the same peccary you carried out of the forest. Take them home with you to your country. Come back some day and we will hunt again and you will get more teeth. With enough visits you will have thirty teeth, enough to make a necklace like the one a true and brave Cofan man wears."

The long, arching, almost clawlike tusks made a dull clinking sound as I placed them in my breast pocket, thanking Bolívar meanwhile for the souvenir. The moment seemed suddenly ripe for some kind of summing up, a few words on the value of new friendship forged on the anvil of intense and demanding experience.

But before I could speak, Bolívar snatched the special moment for himself.

"Five o'clock! First light. No complaints," he said. "Be at my canoe. We travel early, early, early tomorrow! Understand?" He turned and began scrambling back up his house walls for more roof work.

It wasn't quite what I had in mind, but I told him yes, I understood, first light. I lingered wordlessly for another moment, trophy tusks in my pocket, contemplating something more, still feeling the need to say something with a little poignant punch. "You know, Bolívar, I just want to tell you that . . ."

"No complaints," he bellowed again, halfway up to the roof now, his back to me. "I told you, first light."

I sighed and watched him climb farther up the walls before giving him a big, grinning salute he couldn't see, aimed at his back, quietly replete with all the many thanks he deserved. I then took my leave, hearing as I walked away the gentle, swishing whisper of more palm fronds finding their place atop Zábalo's loftiest roof.

I followed the path leading to Randy's house, running parallel to the river. I'd been invited by the chief to sample a special yucca bread he was making himself that day. And sure enough, when I arrived, Randy and sons were on the front porch, immersed in the opening stages of a cooking process that would span much of the rest of the afternoon.

"This is something I doubt you've ever seen before," Randy said as I walked up, urging me to take a seat. A relaxed manner had returned to him despite the testy turtle showdown, and he was now delightfully determined to treat me to a final lesson in Indian culture before my imminent departure. Leaving her own chores inside the house, Amelia came onto the porch several times to sit close to Randy, chuckling affectionately now and again as if secretly pleased to see her husband doing the cooking. Her dark hair was pulled back and tied with a piece of green yarn.

From the myriad of disparate objects hanging erratically along the porch edges—fish nets, machetes, an old guitar, macaw feathers, old blowguns, jerry cans, bundles of wire—Randy had pulled down a device designed to wring moisture from peeled yucca. Called a *fensindeccu*, it was made from strips of kapok tree bark woven into a shape resembling a miniature hammock, about three feet long. Randy placed handfuls of peeled and grated yucca into the center of the *fensindeccu* weave, then looped one end of the device over a hook on a porch post. He took the free end, pulled it taut, and began twisting in such a way that the weave enveloped the yucca in a squeeze of great force, expelling a stream of cloudy liquid that trickled down to a waiting basin below. The process was similar to twisting a wet beach towel from opposite ends. The remaining yucca, spent of moisture, was set aside for making bread.

"And what do you do with the liquid that's left over?" I asked Randy as more of it trickled down into the basin. He was being extremely careful not to let a single drop hit the dusty porch floor.

He looked at me as if I were certifiably daft. "It's for cooking!" he said. "You add hot peppers and meat and cook it just right, and you have the famed Amazonian 'pepper pot.'"

My mouth watered at the mere mention of this celebrated favorite of jungle visitors for hundreds of years. That a yucca-laced starter broth was key to the dish was something I had forgotten—and something that now teased me immeasurably as Randy broke the news that he was preparing this one for the upcoming community feast.

The Cofan chief, immersed in this domestic distraction, had unburdened himself of the headband and many decorative necklaces he'd worn across his chest at church that morning. He had washed his painted face as well, though the red *achiote* streaks had failed to disappear entirely, leaving the jaguar whiskers and the lines of the Holy Cross still plainly visible, though in a washed-out pastel pink that actually matched somewhat better the light blue tunic he still wore. Felipe, who was helping Randy load the *fensindeccu* with yucca, wore the same metamorphosed pink whiskers across his cheeks, ever the miniature of father jaguar.

The dressed-down look seemed to give Randy an air of greater ease in his role as Indian. Supplanting the lavish ceremonial beads and headband were now the no-nonsense tools of daily Zábalo life. I watched as he unhooked the *fensindeccu* from the wall at one point and proceeded with deft fingers to methodically rework its web of fibers into a tighter weave to better squeeze the yucca. He later pulled out a narrow palm-branch spatula and a square screen sifting device he'd made himself from Jessenia palm stems stripped and woven together. These he held in reserve next to the pile of dried yucca temporarily stored atop a spread of fresh banana leaves.

Putting aside Randy's ebullient, off-and-on talk of preserving Cofan ways, I had come to realize that the chief actually had a certain genius for skillfully using tools of almost every sort. He could gaze up and down the cultural spectrum between his dual Indian and Western heritage, pin-point a tool's usefulness wherever it fell on that spectrum, then apply it to a parallel point of need in his forest life without displaying—in prac-tice, at least—any rigid or uniform bias toward one direction or the other on the continuum. Palm-branch spatulas, strong ginger teas, termite nests torched to stave off mosquitoes—they all worked best for certain types of needs, just as shotguns, shortwave radios, and outboard motors worked best for others. Even the ultralight, as a tool, upset this genius only in terms of what made good safety sense, not as a wholesale departure from the old to the new, the simple to the complex—not as a repudiation of handmade vine backpacks as the best on-the-spot way to carry peccaries out of the forest.

Speaking of the ultralight, two days had passed since the awful, bloody accident, and its gloomy sadness had yet to relinquish a grip on my mind. Randy and I had not discussed the pilot's maiming since the day it happened, and to my knowledge there had been no mention of it in church that morning. But sitting on the porch now, I found myself telling Randy how just the night before, barely twenty-four hours after it hap-pened, I had incorporated the scene into a nightmare. In the dream, I was falling from the sky toward a propeller whirling and waiting for me atop a thatch roof. Randy nodded when I finished, saying in a more casual way that the accident had been on his mind, too.

"It was the suddenness of it all," he said, placing another load of yucca in the *fensindeccu*. "It's amazing how suddenly it happened." He began twist-ing the yucca, putting muscle into it, squeezing the shredded tubers, squeezing harder. "Just six months ago," he said, "the brother of one of my best friends in the States died suddenly like that. He was working on his car, had it propped up and was lying under it on his back, when it fell down on him. Horrible thing. Thirty-four years old. Two kids. Crushed by his car."

Water from the yucca dribbled into the catch basin with the patter of soft rain.

I told Randy how it struck me as rather astonishing that there weren't actually many *more* such random tragedies in everyday life, given the world's seemingly infinite range of hazards. I mentioned a few of my own wiggling escapes from mortality's hook. Closer to where we sat, of course, there was Felipe's recent fall and Randy's bear-hug embrace of a lightning bolt.

"There's someone bigger than us in this world looking over things," Randy said in response. "That's what explains it. I believe that as a matter of faith."

The chief was squatting on the porch floor now with Felipe and Federico by his side. All the yucca set out for cooking was now dried, resting on banana leaves, leaving only the task of sifting the whole quantity into the finer texture needed for making the tortillalike patties Randy had described as his goal at the start. He pulled out the sifter he'd made, and all three sets of Borman hands went to work—big, small, tiny—everyone massaging the yucca through the mesh screen, two-year-old Federico's clumsy digits doing the best they could. Softly, into a large wooden bowl below, the yucca settled like freshly grated cheese. This prompted swarthy grins from the Cofan boys as if they were playing a game.

Randy, meanwhile, nourished the seed he'd just sown into our talk. "Faith," he said, "is the key to everything. It's really too bad that so many nominal Christians back in the States don't have it, because, in the end, it's all there really is in the world, faith. There's nothing in life that can be proved absolutely to be true. Nothing."

"Are you sure about that?" I said. "You really believe that?" His comment tweaked my own philosophical sensibilities to a degree. I thought I detected, moreover, a sporting invitation to debate in the tone of his voice. In accepting that invitation, I was about to enter with Randy a headlong discussion of ideas nearly as abstract and wide-ranging as the bread making was immediate and concrete.

"Two plus two never equals five," I said to the chief as an opening salvo, trying to sneak a little Aristotelian certainty past him. "It always equals four. Always."

"Why, that's not true at all," he answered without a moment's hesitation. "That's simply not true. At their most basic level, numbers are just symbols that stand, ultimately, for human concepts that can't be proved. So you can't be really sure two plus two ever equals four. There's no certainty in it."

"But if I grasp two stones in one hand and two stones in the other, and then I put them all together in one hand, I'm grasping four *real* stones."

"That's only if you have *faith* that your senses of touch and vision are accurate."

Fair enough, I thought. Very well. There were several ways to approach this issue, and I'd just have to chart another course, that's all. Randy had paused, meanwhile, in the mounting midday heat to swab light beads of sweat gathering across his pinkish jaguar whiskers.

"I think, therefore I am," I said, quoting Descartes as Randy's hands roamed back to work on the yucca sifter. I quickly ran through the philosophical planks of Descartes' paradoxical argument, where radical doubt is harnessed in the pursuit of certainty. "I can doubt all my senses," I said, "but I can't doubt that I am doubting. Therefore I exist. I *really* exist." Randy knew the argument, and he was more sympathetic to it, but he still wasn't swayed.

"In the end, it doesn't get you anywhere, that approach. The last step still requires a leap of faith or else you're just stuck with yourself. You wind up coming back to the beginning: Everything in life is a matter of faith."

Federico was suddenly making a mess of the grating process, his clumsy, tiny fingers pushing yucca every which way but through the screen.

"No, no, no," Randy said, speaking English to his son with a stringent voice. "Rub it in. Don't try to push it in. Rub it."

He demonstrated, gently rubbing his hand atop the layer of yucca in a circular fashion, first clockwise then counterclockwise, working it into the screen so that it dropped through the other side with the look, again, of finely shredded cheese. When Federico seemed to have the hang of it, Randy pulled his hand away and looked back at me.

"Like I said," he continued, "all of life is about faith. All of it. What passes for truth and knowledge today will be out of fashion tomorrow. To give you just one example, I'm reading Einstein's book *Relativity* right now. It's powerful thinking. But it's just a theory, and it's being attacked left and right in the States every time you turn around."

He might as well have said he was reading the Rosetta stone, so removed from anything in this jungle did it seem. *"Einstein,"* I said. "You're reading *Einstein?* For pleasure? Where'd you get it?" The most committed bibliophiles I knew in the States, people with lives awash in technology, weren't apt to pore over a little Einstein for thrills. And here was Randy out in the exact center of nowhere curling up with the century's greatest theoretical physicist.

"Yeah, it's for pleasure," he said, "if by that you mean simple curiosity. It's a good intellectual workout, which I love. It's a copy someone sent down to me from the States. And it's fascinating. But how long will it hold up? And take Darwin as another example. How long will Darwin's theory last, which is pretty silly in a lot of ways. I mean look at bird wings, for example. They're absolutely useless until the thousands of years when the final product finishes evolving. Kind of seems implausible, doesn't it?"

"Then how did birds get wings?"

"Slower, slower," Randy said, responding not to me but to Federico, who was again having finesse problems sifting the last bit of yucca. "Take your time," the chief said. Gazing down with his arctic-blue eyes, he showed Federico the desired pace meant to complement the circular hand motions, passing on Cofan culture the way culture is passed on the world over, parent to child.

"How did birds get their wings?" I repeated when he had finished.

He pointed up. "God," he said. "It's that simple. I don't know about you, but it's hard for me to accept a God who cavalierly creates the world in six of our present twenty-four-hour days and then adds a few dinosaur bones just to confuse the innocent. Are you following me? So let's say Darwin was right—and a lot of his thinking is very plausible. Well, I think there was some help along the way. I believe fully that my God works through so-called 'natural laws.' In other words, he accomplishes his goals through ways that are fully understandable to us scientifically, biologically."

A canny way of looking at it, I thought. More of the thinking man's view of God. You could have your Supreme Being, but dress him up in the measurable units of a Western worldview or, for that matter, dress him down to the seeable and touchable simple beauty of a forest life. I rather liked the idea.

But before Randy could expound further on the notion, Felipe and Federico looked up at him with big, inquisitive eyes. The boys had now finished sifting all the yucca and were awaiting new instructions. What next? their faces asked.

Randy showed them. He scooped up the yucca and told us all to follow him. We trooped over to the kitchen, a small 15-by-15-foot hut connected to the main house by a plank walkway. A bed of coals lay already prepared inside, spread across an open hearth, sending wisps of faint smoke rising to the rafters of a soot-blackened thatch roof. A clucking hen sat nestled in a corner laying eggs below an array of cooking utensils. Randy reached for a large ceramic griddle, round and slightly concave, its surface glassy from the special silica-rich wood ash mixed into the clay before kilning.

Randy placed the griddle directly atop the coals, then swept its surface free of all debris using a long black turkey feather plucked from one of his own birds outside the house. He used a small gourd bowl next to pour a pile of grated yucca onto the center of the griddle. Using the bottom of the now-empty gourd, he spread the pile into a round tortilla shape, simultaneously pressing down to get the slivers of yucca to adhere. Finally, with a freshly cut banana-leaf stem, he solidified the tortilla edges, bumping the stem along the entire circumference. He did all of this with an unhurried grace that was nonetheless efficient and marked with the feel of routine.

"You look like a real expert at that," I said as he reached to turn the tortilla over, revealing a golden-brown hue reminiscent of perfectly cooked hash browns.

"You get it down when you do it enough times," he said.

A faint smell like that of toasted bread was now joining the heavy scent of woodsmoke in the hut. A moment later, Randy removed the tortilla using his short spatula stick cut from the bough of a palm tree. He laid the tortilla on a banana leaf to cool.

"That's a very Western notion, isn't it?" he commented, now guiding the philosophical thread of our conversation into a new direction. He swept the griddle with the turkey feather before pouring in another mound of yucca.

"What notion?" I said.

"Expertise. Being an expert at something. Everyone wants to excel in the West, to define themselves by being the best at something specific, and getting ahead at it. Part of me has the same instinct. I can relate to it."

"Does that mean," I asked, "that there's something specific you want to be the best at?"

He thought for a second, flattening the yucca with the gourd bowl, then firming up the tortilla edges with the banana-leaf stem.

"Yeah," he said. "Being a good leader to my people. That's all. That's something I think about often. You see how in the States so many people strive to be doctors or lawyers or some other professional position. But a lot of people can excel at that. It's a pretty set way to go. It's all been done before. You just decide to go with it. But I've got something, I think, no one else is trying to excel at—saving a forest and leading a group of indigenous people." He flipped the tortilla with an easy turn of the palm stick. "I'm trying to be the best at it I can possibly be, too. No one else with my background, that I know of, is doing what I do. No one. Do you know of anyone?"

"An American living in the jungle as the head of Amazon Indians? Not offhand," I said.

We both laughed.

"And are you excelling at it?" I asked. "At being Cofan leader?"

"I think so. Yeah, I'd say that's true. And I'll tell you the main reason why: I've put my neck on the line. Everything that's important to me is totally at stake here. That's a motivation."

He pointed to the piece of yucca bread cooling on the banana leaf. "That one's okay to eat now. Help yourself."

I folded the piece in half, then folded it again. A taste like that of a warm, soft saltine cracker filled my mouth as I took a bite, the yucca wonderfully toasted yet supple. I ate with relish.

Randy went on. "Truthfully, when I first decided to commit myself to the idea of Zábalo and this sort of Indian life, my first idea was that I would benefit. It's what I wanted. It would be good for me. But I knew it was going to be very hard work to make the community possible and to protect it once it got going. And I knew I wasn't going to fight my hardest for something if I didn't have a personal stake in it. No one does.

"You look at the Peace Corps volunteers who come to this country or the anthropologists or the missionaries, too. If the going gets rough, if shooting starts or some other hardship sets in, they can just leave, go home to the U.S. or England or wherever they're from. But for me, it's my own neck here. I've put myself in the position where I can't leave. My wife and kids are here, plus a tourism business—a whole way of life in the forest. I stand to lose *everything* if we fail. That's what makes me different. That's why I excel. I'm not a visitor here. I live here. I'm *from* here."

Randy swept the griddle clean with light strokes of the big turkey feather. Three more tortillas had come off the glassy clay surface, one of which was in the chief's hand, being devoured.

"What would I do if I didn't live here?" he said between bites, the jaguar whiskers quivering with his jaw movements. "What would I do? Maybe I could go on the lecture circuit in the States for a while, talking about forest destruction and the disappearing Cofan. But then what? Where would I live? Where would I take my family?"

He paused to shake his head as if the questions were literally unanswerable. "My life is here. It's wrapped up in what we're doing here. I'm totally committed to this community as a healthy, ongoing place to live. I *personally* want it."

"Does that mean you're hopeful?" I asked. "If you can't envision an alternative, does that mean in your mind you see this life being here always?"

"We've certainly had a good year this year," he said. "We won some big battles by standing up to some very scary opposition that runs all the way up to the president of the country. That's given us some political gain. And no one's gotten killed in the process. We've managed to get through everything in a peaceful manner. We're all still alive."

"But are you hopeful?"

His response came now with the air of a forced confession. He had clearly wished to sidestep a head-on collision with the question.

"Hopeful is too strong a word," he said. "Hopeful, no. If you want to know the truth, I am still basically pessimistic about our situation. Despite our gains, I haven't seen enough evidence yet, overall, to make me feel otherwise. There's still untapped oil underneath this reserve, and it's not going anywhere. On the other hand, at the same time, nothing can happen to stop me from *acting* as if I'm very optimistic. We have to keep doing that. I may not be truly 'hopeful,' in other words, but as long as there's an outside chance we can overcome this thing and survive, I can keep on hop*ing*. Does that make any sense to you?"

I said it did, nodding my head in the smoky light of the small hut as the last few tortillas came off the griddle. I grabbed one, still warm, and began chewing slowly, thoughtfully, sensing all the while, however, that something wasn't quite right. There was something more to what Randy had just told me, something deeper in his words, something I wasn't quite getting. It was just beyond my mind's reach and it bothered me until later, finally, I grasped the true sense of what he was saying that afternoon. It wasn't hope he was talking about. Not really. It was faith. He was talking about being faithful. It was that big commitment of spirit handed down in his missionary-family genes, though with a wholly different face this time. Randy was faithful to the idea of Zábalo—very much so—except this wasn't the same as being hopeful about anything. Faith is a matter of believing in something without evidence to prove it and often without evidence even to encourage you to believe it. Hope is different. Hope is believing something *might* be true or some outcome *might* happen. Faith involves a sense of inevitability, on the other hand, and a sense of self-invincibility to see the inevitable through, even against less-than-hopeful odds. Such were the dynamics that best applied to Randy and his world. In being faithful to Zábalo, he had faith that things would definitely, eventually work out and that he wasn't going to kill himself in the process of making them work out. I'm not sure he would have proceeded in any other case. All of life, he had said, was nothing but the stuff he was clinging to now—faith.

And with that faith came confession. Randy admitted that he had a deep personal interest in wanting Zábalo to survive. He wanted it for himself. And a wedding of fates made that fact serve the interests of everyone in the community. What I never sensed in all my visits with him were crude self-promotion and enrichment as goals at the root of his efforts. Everything he did was meant to keep all boats afloat, everything fashioned to fit the community as a whole. His faith required as much, by definition, if he was to have the world he personally wanted. Everything was brought full circle in this way, the ring made complete.

To be sure, there were aspects of Randy's actions along his chosen path that were worth second-guessing. Walking a perfect course in any complex endeavor is a difficult task. When there's no precedent whatsoever for what you're doing, no model to consult, no frame of reference of any kind—it's doubly so. Randy said he knew of no one else in the world doing what he was doing—which was both part of the reward and the danger. Every step of every day was that of a pioneer.

It was late afternoon now, and all the tortillas were finished, the cooking process at last complete. Randy stood up from the blackened kitchen floor where he had been on his knees for more than an hour, leaning over the bed of coals. The large wooden bowl of grated yucca was empty, and on the splayed banana leaves were more than two dozen tortillas in a stack. They had all turned out perfectly save for the one he slightly overcooked while turning his attention momentarily to a bowl of very sweet *chicha*.

By my own count, Randy had used at least ten different forest plants as ingredients or tools in this cooking process. That alone seemed sufficient evidence to support the viability of something the chief, weeks before, in a moment of daring, had said to me. His comment had stuck in my mind, refusing to leave, asserting itself over and over again. It surfaced again now as I sat in that small kitchen still cloudy with the smoke of pan-baked yucca. As if on wings, migrating, my thoughts traveled up through that smoke and back to the cloudy mist of that rainy morning several weeks before. Randy and I were sitting in front of his house that morning, on his porch, talking about Petroecuador and oil spills and environmental studies and negotiations to keep the Cofan land intact. The low, puffy gray sky seemed almost close enough to touch through the tree branches all around. I remember how Randy had stood up at one point, his face a sudden knot of tumult matching the rumbling clouds overhead. He reached for a machete lying nearby and turned the blade back and forth in his hand. There was, it turned out, one more option open to the Cofan in all this jungle complexity, and no matter how difficult that option was, just knowing it was there, I think, helped Randy believe—in himself, in the Cofan, in everything. It was his faith's dark fallback position.

"Sometimes," he said, still holding the machete, "I think all we need are these. Just machetes. Nothing more."

So began the only moment in all my time with Randy Borman that he seemed to make a clean and utter break with practical matters around him. He caught me off guard, in fact, that rainy morning on the porch. I didn't see it coming. His mind had switched subjects without notice.

"Machetes for what?" I said.

"To revert," he answered. "To revert totally."

For all the romantic allure of the forest, Randy wasn't too much of a dreamy thinker. Not really. He talked of living in a painting now and then, and some of his vigilante schemes exceeded his grasp a bit. But for the most part he was a nuts-and-bolts sort of thinker with an eye for the way the world actually turned. It was one of his strengths, I suppose. Only now came a flight of fancy, a flourish of reverielike thinking that carried nonetheless a force of deep feeling as true and intense as anything I'd heard him say before.

"With a batch of good machetes," he said, "we could forget the rest of the world. We could revert totally to the forest. I sometimes wish we could do that—just be left totally alone by everybody, friend and foe. We'd be deep in the forest and we'd be all by ourselves. All contact would stop with the outside world. Right now, we have enough machetes to last us through our lifetimes. That's all we'd really need. The machetes. Beyond that, the outside world could just disappear. We'd revert totally to the forest—on our own."

Randy heaved a wistful sigh. He seemed to want to say something more, but didn't. He kept staring down at the blade in his hand. In a simple way, he had brought up a simple strategy, one that might greatly uncomplicate the Cofan's lives, whatever the intervening hardship. It made the mind boil with possibilities. Could the Indians really do it? Could they cross the line? Could they slip into the vast jungles of Peru? Cross into Brazil? Go really deep? Get lost forever? Keep moving forever?

I've thought about the idea many times since, playing the sound of Randy's voice over and over again inside my head, wondering if in fact I heard not fantasy but the hint of a tale foretold.

9

Bolívar took a deep breath. Then another. He switched off the canoe motor and stood up. A savory pot of the richest stew could have been brewing somewhere in the far-off forest the way he inhaled deeply now, lips pressed together, taking in long, airy draughts through flared nostrils.

"Peccaries," he said at last, exhaling in a rush. "A whole herd of them, I think. Do you smell them?"

I breathed in till my lungs could hold no more. Then I let go. "I don't think so," I said. I detected the faint sweetness of blooming orchids along the shore and the oily dampness of a fish net rolled up at my feet. I detected the beginning scent of my own skin, moistening under a hot morning sun. But peccaries I did not smell.

Not that my olfactory response had any bearing on things. In the manner of a divining rod tipped suddenly to its treasure, Bolívar turned the canoe bow toward what his nose told him were pigs on shore. With David, his short and stalwart twenty-year-old brother-in-law, he scrambled ashore, shotgun in hand, both men sniffing all the while, sniffing like human bloodhounds, sniffing furiously, excitedly, comically.

I decided to stay behind, watching from the canoe as the men vanished into greenery. This interruption of our journey presented no serious setback.

We were making great time up the Zábalo River, blessed with much higher water and a canoe much smaller than the community-owned behemoth of our first trip. We'd been forced to seesaw up and over just two exposed trees so far, creating a pace that would lead us to the once-elusive trailhead with just thirty more minutes of travel. From there it would be a couple of hours on foot to the burned-out remains of the oil-drilling platform.

Reclined against a gunwale, I waited in the riverside shade, my legs dangling over the water. I had the urge to doze until, ever so slightly, a pair of tiny tree stumps rising from the water several yards to my right actually moved. I looked to see the marble eyes of a five-foot-long caiman staring back at me with what seemed a very distinct expression of hunger.

I snapped to an upright position, pulling my legs back into the boat in a noisy way that made the marble eyes disappear. Moments later, Bolívar and David returned empty-handed from the jungle. The pigs had eluded them completely, Bolívar said. He laid his shotgun across the canoe hull with a sigh of disgust. The failed outing was making his already foul mood that morning even worse. The night before a jaguar had attacked and tried to drag away one of his neighbor's dogs, the second such attack in the Zábalo area in recent months. Bolívar's increasing fear was not that one of his young sons would be the next target (humans were rarely attacked) but that one of his own dogs would be devoured by the forest cat, a humiliation of high order for a proud hunter such as himself. With all this in mind, he launched our canoe back upriver, muttering in dismay how jaguars were making sport of dogs all around his village, practically right outside his door, but he couldn't bag a single peccary from a virtual stampede so close he could smell them.

Our progress up the river continued smoothly, at least, leading us closer to our main objective. We etched graceful lines and curves into the polished black water where six weeks before there had been an insurmountable tangle of exposed trees. Well before 10:00 A.M. we reached the trailhead, setting off on foot. I'm not sure what about our course actually constituted a trail, for unmolested forest was all I could see. But Bolívar assured me this was the way, and I had made enough outings with the Cofan to trust utterly their forest orientation even when the alleged pathways were completely invisible to me. Bolívar reiterated his view that without too many detours for hunting, we'd be at the well site in about two hours.

But of course there were many detours. Bolívar and David had come dressed to kill that day, clad in long-sleeved military shirts of camouflage coloring. The shirts were castoffs from the Ecuadorian army, and provided excellent advantage against jungle prey. With their rudimentary shotguns and tall rubber boots and slashing machetes, the men roamed left and right, straying liberally from the "trail," leaving me to follow as best I could through the usual obstacles of fallen trees and swampy water and steep-sided creeks. Soon, a series of turkeylike guans and curassows began falling from middle- and upper-story branches, their heads shot almost completely off thanks to an aim of amazing exactness. Bolívar took each feathered carcass and wedged it into the elevated crotch of a nearby tree. This would inconvenience any passing jaguar until, somehow, on our return trip, we would come back to this exact spot to retrieve it.

The arduousness of the hike, peppered with the small thrill of each new kill, nearly conspired to steal away the focus of our journey until, up ahead, we saw the seismic-testing trail. It announced itself with that peculiar flood of rectilinear light so dramatically out of place in the verdant dimness of rambling forest. We entered the arrow-straight avenue, its width about fifteen feet, and I noticed that here, as on other such oil-company trails I'd seen, the Cofan had painted over Petroecuador's coded metal signs hammered intermittently to trailside trees. COMMUNIDAD COFAN were the words splashed across each sign. Whether by design or simple sloppiness, the blood-red paint they used dripped and ran in places like the gory lettering of a third-rate horror film's coming-attractions poster.

We crossed the seismic trail, then plunged back into the full-canopied darkness of the forest. For a quarter of an hour we walked until, in the distance, an even greater field of light came into view, marking another clearing. The closer we got, the more it became clear just how big this opening was. It had no discernible end, no rear boundary; on and on it seemed to go. We emerged finally from the last line of standing trees to find a sweeping, clear-cut field of destruction suffused with the sun-blasted look of a parking lot.

We had reached the well site at last. It lay stretched across an area of six acres, carpeted with the chain-sawed stumps and remains of more than two thousand trees. In his army-issue shirt of camouflage coloring, Bolívar

pointed to something visible in the distance, rising up from the center of
the clearing. It was the drilling platform, constructed on the spot from
forest timber. The platform had the vague look of a theater stage, one
upon which some calamitous drama had been acted out. At points across
its surface lay the charred remains of what clearly had been three enormous bonfires. The fires had burned great holes of destruction down
through the platform's top and into the network of support braces below,
gutting the foundation, wreaking havoc.

We headed toward the platform, with Bolívar leading the way,
explaining matters as he walked. He told me how, on that day four months
ago, the Cofan had arrived here as a group of twenty men, saboteurs ready
to do their work. The well was unmanned at the time, idled by the lawsuit that ran all the way to Ecuador's president and that was still going on.
As they entered the clearing, the Indians had discovered that no drilling
machinery had been flown in yet, though the wooden platform itself was
nearly complete. They promptly gathered up dozens of wood planks lying
about the clearing, some nearly the size of railroad ties, some ripped from
the platform itself, and piled them up on the platform surface in structures
resembling squat tepees, some as high as six feet tall. They then doused
the piles with gallons of oil and gasoline left behind in barrels for the company's many devouring chain saws. Someone lit a match and the blaze
began, with flames flaring skyward like fireworks for more than ten hours,
the smoke as thick and as black as night.

I watched as Bolívar stepped up to the remains of the drilling platform's surface. He gestured to the troika of charred craters around him left
by the bonfires. "Would you play games with people who do something
like this?" he asked me, smiling with satisfaction. He pressed his foot on a
damaged black beam. It snapped in two, collapsing noisily. "All the other
Indian people of Ecuador, they fear Petroecuador. But we burn the company's property because we're brave. The company looks at what we've
done here and they know we're brave. They can't scare us."

He stepped down from the platform, motioning for me to follow him
to a second wooden structure, this one a landing pad for company helicopters. It, too, had been badly burned by the Cofan, pocked with the
blackened sores of four bonfires. While we were approaching the edifice,
Bolívar paused over a certain tree stump, one of hundreds we were step-

ping over. He kicked the stump. "Such a waste," he said. "This was a cedar tree. Very good for making canoes. Such a waste."

We passed the ruined heliport, then came to eight smaller structures located on the periphery of the clearing. These had been the workers' quarters, crude wooden shelters now nothing more than mangled ash heaps.

"I helped with this part," Bolívar said, his eyes radiating pride. The look turned to revulsion, however, as he showed me nails on a tree where the Cofan had found hanging a jaguar pelt and the talons of a harpy eagle poached by the workers.

"It was a good idea to come here and burn this place down," Bolívar said, now using the edge of his machete to bend the offending nails into the tree. "It was a good thing for us to do. Very good."

We began heading back to the main drilling platform.

"Who's idea was it," I asked, "to do all this? Was there a vote in the community? Who made the decision?" /

"Randy made the decision," Bolívar said. "Randy thought we should do this. He decided it was the best action to take, and we agreed with his idea."

We reached the platform and all three of us stepped up to its remaining surface. I unsheathed my camera while Bolívar and David struck poses next to the violent black remains of a bonfire. On a protruding beam that was half-burned, Bolívar took a seat, shotgun across his lap. David stood next to him in the erect posture of a sentry at utmost attention, shotgun at his side.

I peered through the camera lens, taking in my subjects. My eye roamed down to the black boots the men were wearing, then up to the camouflage army shirts across their upper bodies, then down again to the crude weapons at their sides. There was no mistaking the image. They had the look, these young men, of being dangerously armed, not just with guns, but with moral bearing and strong will, all of it outside the official understanding and prescribed boundaries of government. They had the look, in other words, distinct and darkly impressive, of guerilla soldiers. And so they were, at least by degree, standing now atop a burned-out pedestal that bore mute witness to their part-time insurgency.

I snapped a couple of shots before the three of us shifted to another crater. The men struck the same soldierly poses, but this time they conspired among themselves to add severe frowns to their faces, almost scowls.

It was an effect that clinched the overall image as well as the message that seemed to go with it: Randy Borman was getting results. If the goal of the white chief had been to make these Cofan men, and all the others back in Zábalo, more aggressive in their habits, more militant in defending their rights, he appeared to be well on his way. His work was paying off.

I turned my lens on the rest of the clearing for a moment—the collapsing heliport, the incinerated workers shelters—then back to Bolívar and David. With each click of the shutter they held those terrible frowns in place, letting them harden across their faces as if the potent, acrid smoke of burning platform beams and floor planks and shelter walls were still detectable to them, still filling the air around them, blackening the forest

EPILOGUE

Since my last visit in the fall of 1993, something very strange has happened in the lower Cuyabeno Wildlife Reserve: Things have calmed down. Petroecuador has made no new effort to crash the park gates to resume oil exploration at the Paujil or Zábalo wells—or anywhere else in the reserve.

After the struggles of 1991–93, this unexpected quietude has put the word *milagro* on the lips of Randy and the rest of the Zábalo Cofan. And perhaps it *is* a miracle. After all, when the Cofan negotiated an end to their daring raid on the Paujil well in November 1993, they hadn't actually succeeded in shutting the well down for good. They had only gotten a pledge of improved environmental safeguards for the forest and a compensatory batch of solar panels for themselves. So when Petroecuador unilaterally halted all activity at the well a week later, dismantling the machinery at the site, there was quite a bit of speculation as to what had really happened. Was the company suspending operations temporarily to allow the tide of negative publicity to crest? Or did the Paujil well really turn out to be a bust, having failed to turn up commercial-quality oil?

The passage of time now suggests the latter to be the case, making talk of miracles a leading fashion among the Cofan. Had the Paujil well turned up usuable oil, company pressure to drill throughout the lower reserve would have gained enormous momentum by now. The Cofan, under such a scenario, would still be struggling mightily today—in court and on the ground—to stop new wells from starting up or, failing that, trying to uphold environmental safeguards for wells put into action. The odds, as always, would have been tough, with land degradation and a tide of incoming settlers virtually assured.

Again, happily, none of this has happened. After all this time, Petroecuador has yet to follow through on even the first step of an environmental impact study for the Zábalo well site. Everything, quite simply, has been put on hold, everything stopped, and it all goes back to the Paujil well. In a region of Ecuador where proven reserves of commercial-quality crude exist in almost every direction, the Paujil well somehow turned up nothing. The failure has cooled interest for exploration in other parts of the lower Cuyabeno reserve—at least for now.

The Cofan had hoped for exactly for this sort of outcome all along, of course. In a letter to me last spring, Randy revealed an interesting subtext to the story. In the months prior to their raid on the Paujil well, the Zábalo Indians had spent part of each Sunday morning studying a different Old Testament story during their weekly church service. On the Sunday just before the raid, the feature passage was the story of Gideon and his trumpet was, in order of sequence, the featured passage. Randy read the story aloud under the thatched roof of the community house. Afterwards, the whole community made a plea to God for help in their similar role as underdogs against overwhelming odds. "Then, just as Gideon's 300 charged the Midianites," Randy wrote me, "we charged the oil company—in faith." And just like Gideon, the Cofan eventually watched as the seemingly invincible camp of their enemy was brought tumbling down and swept away. "Whatever your theology, the fact that the well was dry is to me the real miracle of the whole story," Randy wrote.

But the story is far from over. Randy admits that Petroecuador has no intention of abandoning the lower Cuyabeno for good. As Ecuador's total oil reserves dwindle over the next five to ten years (they're expected to run out completely in just twenty years) pressure will rise to explore the Cuyabeno more throughly, testing beyond the initial unsuccessful site at Paujil. The dice, in other words, will roll again. Oil could still be found. The doomsday scenario could still be played out.

But before that day arrives, the Cofan, with help from Transturi Touring and free-lance guides like Roberto Cedeño, hope to prove something. They hope to increase eco-tourism in the reserve carefully, to the point that it offers a compelling sustainable alternative to oil as a source of income for the poor Ecuadorian economy. The goal, quite plainly, is to permanently destroy Petroecuador's "economic excuse" to destroy the forsest, says Randy.

Meanwhile, back in the Zábalo community itself, life goes on. The settlement's several dozen solar panels arrived in early 1994, giving each hut a blue-white fluorescent glow that for a few hours each night twinkles softly against the dark flow of the Aguarico River. As for other modern gadgetry, Randy has yet to procure an ultralight, but still has hopes of eventually getting some sort of light aircraft to patrol Cofan land and facilitate the transport of tourists into the jungle.

And with less time tied up fighting Petroecuador, the Cofan over the past two years have been able to focus more on other conservation projects, especially the business of rescuing the Aguarico's threatened river turtles. With input from a variety of experts, the village has gone forward with its self-styled experiment designed to capture tiny hatchlings along the river and place them in artificial, shoreside ponds. There the turtles are lovingly fed a size that better equips them to survive to adulthood on their own. Last year, the Indians successfully released the first of their 500 young turtles, representing the species *Pedocnemis expansa* and *Pedocnemis unifilis*. Half the turtles were released after six months at a size roughly that of a half dollar; the other half after twelve months, more than twice as large. The project, which Randy calls "very interesting, totally unique, and kind of fun," stands a good chance of compensating for the effects of continued overhunting in the area.

In the meantime, the Zábalo Cofan have added to their own numbers along the Aguarico's shores. Bolívar and Norma now have a fourth child, another son, crawling inside their first-of-its-kind, two-story hut. The boy answers to the name Elio. And just a few houses farther upstream, Amelia Borman now nurses young Joshua Aniseto, born last April 26, the Bormans' third child. There were complications with the pregnancy, requiring a rushed trip at night by canoe to a hospital in Lago Agrio, then on to Quito. But mother and child pulled through in good condition, and Joshua arrived weighing eight pounds, three ounces.

AUTHOR'S NOTE

I f you'd like to assist the Zábalo Cofan in their campaign to protect the Cuyabeno rain forest, you may contact the community by writing to:

Organizacion Indigena de la Nacionalidad Cofan del Ecuador
Attention: Randy Borman
Cassilla 17-11-06089
Quito, Ecuador

Financial contributions should be made out to: Communidad Cofan de Zábalo, c/o Randy Borman.

For tax-deductable contributions in the United States, send donations to:

CEHAB
c/o Dr. Frank E. Poirier
Department of Anthropology
Ohio State University
244 Lord Hall
124 West 17th Avenue
Columbus, OH 43210-1364

Letters supporting the Cofan cause may be sent directly to the president of Ecuador. Mail correspondence to:

Sixto Durán Ballén
Palacio Presidential
García Moreno
Quito, Ecuador

or fax letters to the following number: 011-5932-580-751